The Battle of Ap Bac, Vietnam

The Battle of Ap Bac, Vietnam

They Did Everything but Learn from It

David M. Toczek

FOREWORD BY
W. B. Rosson

NAVAL INSTITUTE PRESS
Annapolis, Maryland

Naval Institute Press
291 Wood Road
Annapolis, MD 21402

First printing in paperback, 2007

Library of Congress Cataloging-in-Publication Data

Toczek, David M., 1966–
  The Battle of Ap Bac, Vietnam : they did everything but learn from it / David M. Toczek ; foreword by W.B. Rosson.
     p. cm.
  Reprint. Originally published: Westport, Conn. : Greenwood Press, 2001.
  Includes bibliographical references and index.
  ISBN 978-1-59114-853-1 (alk. paper)
  1. Ap Bac, Battle of, Áp Bác, Vietnam, 1963. I. Title.
DS557.8.A53T63 2007
959.704'342—dc22

                                                                    2007014711

Printed in the United States of America on acid-free paper ∞

14 13 12 11 10 09 08 07   9 8 7 6 5 4 3 2
First printing

The author and publisher gratefully acknowledge permission for use of the following material: Extracts from letters, dated 26 and 28 August 1999, from Professor James R. Reckner to David M. Toczek, West Point, NY. Reprinted by permission.

To Carla

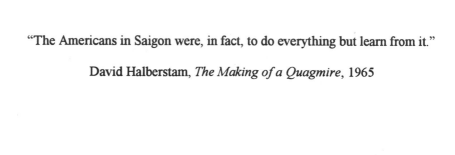

"The Americans in Saigon were, in fact, to do everything but learn from it."

David Halberstam, *The Making of a Quagmire*, 1965

Contents

Photo essay follows page 116.

Figures

Foreword

The provocative title of this book spawns several questions: What was the Battle of Ap Bac? When and where was it fought? Between whom? What lessons did the battle produce? By whom should they have been heeded?

In his quest for answers to these questions, David M. Toczek is unlikely to have encountered difficulty with the first three. In connection with the remaining two, however, he found himself face-to-face with a seemingly simple undertaking that proved, in the course of research, to possess vastly enlarged dimensions and ramifications. How he dealt with this challenge, and what he produced in the way of answers, find expression in an expertly sequenced, well-documented, and persuasive treatment of his subject.

In the course of framing his approach in the preface, Toczek underscores at the outset a policy adopted by Washington in 1962 that was to exert important influence on America's involvement in Vietnam throughout the period embraced by the book, 1950 into 1965—and beyond. Termed unofficially the "policy of optimism," it entailed an outward posture of confidence in our efforts and those of the South Vietnamese. On this basis, shortcomings in South Vietnamese military leadership, training, and operations came to be represented by U.S. authorities in as favorable a light as possible. Unsurprisingly, both the policy and the attitude it created at higher decision-making levels led not only to unrealistic estimates of progress in pursuing the war, but also to a blurring of need for hard analyses of the direction and adequacy of U.S. advisory, training, and support programs. It also brought into sharp focus a division between adherents of the policy and some who considered it misleading—a division exploited by the press.

The sequenced treatment begins with examination of what is called "The Background." This chapter serves to provide an essential backdrop for later analysis of the belligerents, the battle itself, and the battle's aftermath—all as a prelude to conclusions. Central to the backdrop is discussion of the assumption by the U.S. early in 1955 of responsibility from France for advising, training, and supporting the fledgling Army of the Republic of Vietnam (ARVN). This responsibility was later extended to include the republic's small navy and air force, as well as non-regular Civil Guard (CG) and Self-Defense Corps (SDC) units.

Unfortunately, despite intelligence indicating that the principal threat to South Vietnam was that of Maoist revolutionary warfare manifested in the early stages of insurgency—the creation of an infrastructure within the population, propaganda, and conduct of guerrilla warfare—American authorities elected to organize, train, and equip the ARVN and its sister services along conventional lines in the image of the U.S. armed forces. The rationale? To deal with possible invasion by People's Army of Vietnam (PAVN) divisions, which had defeated the French at Dien Bien Phu in 1954. Understandably, the U.S. stance was also influenced by the memory of the North Korean invasion of South Korea in 1950.

In this setting, the ARVN was set apart from the grass-roots, population-oriented side of counterinsurgency, whose U.S. advice and support were to be provided by the Central Intelligence Agency (CIA), the Agency for International Development (AID), and the United States Information Agency (USIA). This arrangement was to prove detrimental to prosecution of the kind of war being fought in Vietnam.

Adding to the value of the backdrop is a description of the evolution of the U.S. military advisory structure in South Vietnam and its modus operandi. Established as a small Military Assistance Advisory Group (MAAG) in Saigon in late 1950, the organization progressively expanded in size and functions to become the Military Assistance Command, Vietnam (MACV), in 1962. While this and other features of the evolution are instructive, one ends up facing the reality that the U.S. advisor in Vietnam was just that—an advisor. Without command authority, his effectiveness resided in his ability to function within a foreign culture, to provide a motivating example, to win the confidence of those he was advising, and to succeed through persuasion. The question arises: Should the U.S. have insisted on command of the South Vietnamese military as the price for its support?

Rounding out coverage of the "background" is a well-crafted treatment of the guerrilla foe from its origin in World War II. Although the guerrillas became a force to be reckoned with in North Vietnam during the First Indochina War, their capabilities were less-developed in South Vietnam. Even so, cadres and munitions caches in place in South Vietnam following the Geneva Accords of July 1954 permitted the guerrillas to grow to a strength of about 9,000 by 1959. Shortly thereafter, these formations acquired the title of People's Liberation Armed Forces (PLAF). During the three years preceding the 1963 Battle of Ap Bac, the PLAF, notably in the Mekong Delta area, became increasingly aggressive and effective in small-scale operations against the ARVN, CG, and SDC forces.

In a discerning look at the belligerents—the opponents at the Battle of Ap Bac—Toczek focuses first on the ARVN. His primary purpose in doing so is to underscore the fact that the U.S., influenced in part by its experience in working with the armed forces of South Korea, molded the ARVN in the U.S. Army's image. Moreover, influenced by a tradition of U.S. Army success through conventional warfare, the U.S.—again as it had done in Korea—supplied U.S.

Army doctrine, organization, tactics, and techniques to the ARVN. Although some consideration was given to training the ARVN to deal with the nonconventional aspects of the insurgency, labeled the "other war," it was without major emphasis during the 1950–1965 time frame. Rather, as indicated earlier, it was left to the CIA, AID, and USIA to provide American advice, training, and support for South Vietnamese efforts in that domain. This divided approach was to take its toll.

Within its conventional organization and orientation, the ARVN harbored serious shortcomings. Prominent among these was deficient leadership at senior- and middle-levels in particular. Loyalty to President Ngo Dinh Diem was the governing criterion for all senior- and middle-level posts, as opposed to professional competence and experience. Selected largely from the upper classes, officers tended to look down on the enlisted ranks. Corruption was commonplace among senior officers. Most senior- and many of the middle-level officers routinely "operated from the rear." Some sought to avoid direct confrontation with the enemy or to operate in such fashion as to alert him or afford him avenues of avoidance or escape. Desire to "save face" as a result of mistakes or poor performance gave rise to distorted reporting.

In the realm of tactics and techniques, the ARVN preferred daylight "sweeps," a legacy from the French, but one easily detected by the enemy. Conduct of night offensive operations was rare. The PLAF, in contrast, put the hours of darkness to full and frequent use for operational and logistic purposes. Although steeped by U.S. advisors in the need for fire and movement in the conduct of conventional operations, the ARVN manifested difficulty in using the two effectively in combination. Disturbingly, preparatory fires tended to be unnecessarily excessive and employed without concern for the negative consequences of noncombatant casualties caused by them.

Appropriate notice is taken of U.S. measures to improve ARVN mobility and firepower through the introduction late in 1961 of U.S. troop transport helicopter units and, early in 1962, of U.S. helicopter gunships. Added early in 1962 to the ARVN's line-up was the U.S. Model 113 armored personnel carrier (M113 APC), a light, versatile tracked vehicle mounting heavy and light machine guns. During the months preceding Ap Bac, both the helicopters and APCs had been employed by the ARVN with generally encouraging results, but not without adverse results here and there.

Before discussing the other belligerent, the PLAF, Toczek calls attention to two factors that affected operations requiring concerted action by the ARVN, CG, and SDC units. The first of these was the absence of a single chain of command. Instead, one found two chains. The first of these extended from President Diem through the Ministry of Defense to the ARVN headquarters, thence downward to corps, divisions, and units within divisions. The second, a "civil" chain, extended from President Diem through the Ministry of the Interior to corps (the corps commander wore a "second hat" as the senior civil authority for his region) and downward to province chiefs and district chiefs within the provinces. (Province and district chiefs usually were ARVN officers.) The "trouble spot" in the second chain resided in the province chief who, although independent of the first, or military chain, commanded the CG and SDC units within his province.

For the most part, ARVN divisions that were located within a several-province area were able to work compatibly with the province chiefs to achieve unity of effort among divisional, CG, and SDC units. At times, however, personality clashes, conflicting orders via the two chains, or differing interpretations of orders "fouled the works." An example awaits the reader in the chapter describing the Ap Bac battle.

The second factor, its roots in the psyche of President Diem, was a directive from the president—one customarily issued personally by him to corps commanders, division commanders, and province chiefs—to keep combat casualties to a minimum while inflicting maximum casualties on the enemy. Though arguably a laudable maxim under some circumstances, the directive served to inhibit many who received it. Here again, an example will be forthcoming in coverage of the battle.

In thinking back over the ARVN's shortcomings and related constraints, the reader may have entertained the question as to how many of them could be overcome by U.S. advice. If so, he or she joins many who asked it during the time frame embraced by the author.

In addressing the other belligerent, a strong case is made that the PLAF enjoyed the advantage of a powerfully motivating Maoist revolutionary war concept called *dau tranh* (struggle) whose objectives were to rid Vietnam of foreigners and to unite the entire country under Hanoi's rule. *Dau tranh* is shown to have consisted of two interlocking and mutually supporting components: Political struggle and armed struggle. These two were parts of a seamless whole of conventional and unconventional operations in contrast to the ARVN concentration on conventional operations alone.

In terms of organization, it is explained that the PLAF consisted of main force, regional, provincial, and local units that were all guerrilla in character. Units down to and including the company (roughly 100 in strength) were assigned a communist party commissar, or political officer, who was responsible for unit cohesion and morale as well as for correct political attitude, intellectual training, and thinking habits on the part of the unit members.

A single chain of command for political and military activity was in place. For operations, three tactics were preferred: Ambushes, raids, and armed propaganda (the latter carried out within the populace, mainly at village and hamlet levels). A basic operational pattern was to reconnoiter thoroughly, prepare methodically, execute rapidly, and disperse. ARVN "sweeps" (called "mopping-up operations" by the PLAF) were countered mainly by avoidance and ambushes. With the advent of helicopters on the opposing side, extensive training was devoted to antiaircraft fire employing mainly small arms normal to PLAF units.

With the backdrop now in place, Toczek follows with a masterfully thorough and interest-provoking account of the Battle of Ap Bac—one he entitles "The Fight." Assisted by an effective terrain analysis, several excellent map-diagrams, and an easily understood narrative, the account not only brings out the strengths and weaknesses of the two sides, but leaves little doubt as to the outcome.

The account in capsule explains that the ARVN 7th Division located in the Mekong Delta discovered a PLAF radio station operating in the vicinity of Ap Bac. It planned and mounted an operation codenamed *DUC THANG* 1 (VICTORY 1) to destroy the station and a PLAF protecting force nearby—a force composed of small regional, provincial, and local units totaling some 340 guerrillas whose training and combat experience varied widely.

The division's plan, simple in concept and uncomplicated in maneuver and use of firepower, entailed employment of divisional and provincial CG units, the latter under provincial command. Totaling about 1,200 in strength, the divisional/CG force had the further advantage of an M113 unit and U.S. helicopter support to enhance mobility and firepower.

The PLAF having been alerted by advance deployments on the part of the 7th Division, the dawn-to-dusk, one-day fight commenced on 2 January 1963. Although the divisional plan appeared initially to be progressing favorably, uncommon skill and tenacity on the part of the PLAF combined with a litany of problems for its opponent—mistakes, inept use of supporting firepower, dearth of senior leadership in the forward area, mounting personnel casualties, loss of five helicopters, refusal of orders, and general lack of aggressiveness—found the attacker short of all objectives at the day's end. And this despite sustained, at times valiant, effort on the part of the U.S. advisors to troubleshoot, urge their counterparts to press on, and otherwise keep the operation on track.

To crown what the senior U.S. advisor to the 7th Division later termed "[a] miserable damn performance," use of a reinforcing ARVN airborne battalion to seal off a PLAF escape route came to naught when the ARVN corps commander, apparently fearful of added casualties, intervened to drop the paratroopers in a "safe" location. The result? The PLAF used the ensuing hours of darkness to disengage and disappear via the escape route. On the morning of 3 January, the attackers walked onto the objectives unopposed.

The fight having received its due, the sequencing progresses to an analysis of its aftermath. Here, with the book's title in mind, one finds much to learn.

Of immediate importance was determination of the victor, with comparison of casualties on both sides providing a convenient starting point. Of several differing totals (among them an exaggerated PLAF report on ARVN and U.S. losses), the figures compiled by the senior U.S. advisor to the 7th Division provided a reasonable "feel": Three Americans killed in action (KIA), six wounded in action (WIA); 63 ARVN KIA, 109 ARVN WIA; and an estimated 100 PLAF KIA. Absence of an estimate of PLAF WIA is explained by the fact that the PLAF then and later made strong efforts to remove its dead, wounded, and weapons from the battlefield. It apparently succeeded in the case of its wounded at Ap Bac. Verdict? A possible edge to the PLAF.

In another realm, the PLAF, through its infrastructure, promptly laid claim to victory on the basis of its having held off the attack of a much larger force, destroyed five helicopters, inflicted heavy casualties on its foe, and retired from the field in good order. In this they were joined by the U.S. advisors who preferred to describe the outcome as an ARVN/CG defeat, a view shared and soon expressed in print by reporters on the scene. In sharp contrast, the senior U.S. commander in Saigon, faithful to the policy of optimism, declared the outcome to be an ARVN/CG victory. His reasoning: That the attackers had "taken" their objectives, that the PLAF had abandoned the field, and that the PLAF had sustained greater casualties. A new battle had been joined!

Going beyond determination of the victor, the author's aftermath analysis focuses on the problems exposed by the ARVN and CG at Ap Bac and what should have been done about them. Foremost among the problems: The efficacy of the ARVN, the structure and effectiveness of the American advisory system, and the validity of U.S. Vietnam policy. On the latter score, he intensifies his insistence that the U.S. should have changed from primary reliance on conventional military warfare to primary reliance on a combination of conventional and unconventional political and military warfare (à la the PLAF). This is, of course, what it did in the wake of Tet 1968, a period beyond the time frame of this book.

Also subjected to scrutiny is the strategic question of whether the U.S. should have considered withdrawal from Vietnam or the neutralization of Vietnam (as in the case of Laos in 1962); the question of whether the U.S. military chain of command from Washington to Saigon should continue to go through the Commander in Chief, Pacific, in Honolulu; and the question of whether the U.S. should insist on subordination of South Vietnamese military forces to U.S. command.

The other two major problems exposed by Ap Bac receive strong emphasis: South Vietnamese civilian and military leadership and the syndrome of optimism within U.S. officialdom. In both cases, analysis is strengthened by research that provides a wealth of supporting material. Significantly, it is made evident that much of the indigenous leadership problem lay in the nature of a culture whose traditions and values could not be forced into compatibility with American concepts and practices. With respect to the syndrome of optimism, it is also made evident that, once having taken root, it endured despite obvious signs that it was detrimental to realistic planning for, conduct of, and assessment of the American effort.

The aftermath analysis completed, Toczek presents his conclusions— conclusions punctuated with a number of uncompromisingly bold convictions. The book having begun with a preview of the policy of optimism, it is fitting to observe how that policy fares in the conclusions. In essence, the reader is reminded that, despite the warnings sounded by Ap Bac, U.S. officialdom from Saigon to the White House and points between largely accepted the view that the U.S. approach was sound and that the war was being won—indeed, that the South Vietnamese armed forces would mature in such fashion as to achieve domination of the enemy and an end to the war by the close of 1965. Moreover, that by that date, the U.S. advisory, training, and support apparatus, except for a small mission, would have withdrawn. In hindsight, unbelievable!

In other respects, the reader will have anticipated the following conclusions from the sequenced treatment and analysis that preceded them:

- The culture and values of a client state whose armed forces have been molded in the U.S. image will play a greater role in determining the effectiveness of those forces than will the training, indoctrination, advice, and example they receive from us. As a case in point, cultural and value differences denied success to the U.S. in its efforts to develop fully competent, professional leadership within the armed forces of South Vietnam.

- Military operations cannot be successful in supporting a strategic vision if the political goals and dimensions are unclear. Conversely, political success cannot be ensured unless a determination is made that the instruments of power are strong enough to achieve the desired ends.

- By failing early-on to emphasize counterinsurgency operations that integrated both military and political action, preferring instead to concentrate on conventional military and antiguerrilla capabilities, the U.S. and its protégé placed themselves at a marked disadvantage in prosecuting the kind of war being fought in Vietnam.

On the positive side, some of the lower-magnitude lessons of the battle were heeded: Armor shields to protect gunners atop M113s were installed; rules covering engagement by fire from helicopter gunships were sharpened; and procedures for going to the rescue of downed helicopters were improved. With respect to higher-magnitude lessons, however, most went unheeded. "They [the U.S. authorities] did everything but learn" from them.

This book—the definitive study and analysis of the Battle of Ap Bac— supplies a welcome opportunity to rethink, relearn, and, when appropriate, to act on the lessons of the battle.

> W. B. Rosson
> General, U.S. Army (Retired)
> Deputy Commander, U.S. Military Assistance
> Command, Vietnam (1969–1970)

Preface

I claim we got a hell of a beating. We got run out of Burma and it is humiliating as hell. I think we ought to find out what caused it, go back and retake it.[1]

Lieutenant General Joseph W. Stilwell
May 1942

Yes, I consider it [the Battle of Ap Bac] a victory. We took the objective.[2]

General Paul D. Harkins
January 1963

By the spring of 1942, the American war against Imperial Japan was off to an inauspicious start. America had lost a large part of its surface fleet at Pearl Harbor the previous December and had lost the Philippines to the Japanese by early May. At the same time, Allied forces fighting in Burma suffered a series of defeats at the hands of the Japanese Imperial Army, ultimately resulting in the loss of Burma and the isolation of China. Although the situation in Burma looked bleak to the Allies by early May, President Franklin D. Roosevelt's administration press releases promised that the Allies would soon defeat the Japanese and maintain an overland route into China.

This policy of optimism even appeared in directives to the headquarters of Lieutenant General Joseph W. Stilwell, commander of American forces in the China–Burma–India theater. General George C. Marshall, U.S. Army chief of staff, ordered Stilwell's headquarters to maintain an "attitude of calm optimism with respect to [the] Chinese future" and to ensure that plans and conversations did not "imply any thought of helplessness in [the] situation."[3] Despite this rather direct guidance, Stilwell emerged from the Burmese jungles at the end of May 1942 and openly admitted defeat to reporters with his famous quotation. Instead of blaming Stilwell for the defeat, the press lauded his honesty and willingness to address his army's shortcomings. A lead editorial in the *New York Times* observed that President Roosevelt, for all his inspiring rhetoric, "could learn something from General Stilwell," and lesser officials could emulate him "both as to diction and as to policy."[4] To the press, Stilwell's honest appraisal was refreshing and demonstrated his grasp of the realities of Chinese political and military weakness.

Although fighting a different enemy in a different theater and time, General Paul D. Harkins, the commander, U.S. Military Assistance Command, Vietnam (COMUSMACV), faced problems in 1962 similar to those of Stilwell. Both Stilwell and Harkins were responsible for advising foreign governments and leaders whose goals did not always match those of the U.S. Both men sought to develop and train host-nation armies that could fight effectively against a hardened foe. Both faced the difficulties of demonstrating quantifiable progress to their military and political superiors.

Yet these two military men chose to approach their problems from vastly different perspectives. Stilwell, cynical and painfully direct, rarely offered a rosy outlook to his superiors, who often intimated, or directed, that he should do otherwise. He was continually in the field, evaluating the situation, commanding, leading. When he suffered a setback, he admitted it. He continually squabbled with Chiang Kai-shek, generalissimo of China, who successfully engineered Stilwell's recall from China in late 1944. Despite the American general's straightforward manner and eventual relief, his efforts still paid dividends. By 1945, China had over 30 trained and equipped divisions. Playing an important role in the Allies' forcing of the Japanese from Burma, they were a tribute to Stilwell's focus and drive to accomplish his objective of a modern Chinese army.

Harkins, on the other hand, was not only a self-proclaimed optimist, but he also closely followed the guidance of General Maxwell D. Taylor, the chairman of the Joint Chiefs of Staff (CJCS) and Harkins's mentor, to frame the situation in Vietnam in the best possible light.[5] Of a staff officer mentality, COMUSMACV rarely visited units in the field. Suggesting at the Honolulu conference in July 1962 that the Government of Vietnam (GVN) would require only about one year to achieve victory once it began to apply pressure to the insurgents, Harkins consistently gave the impression that the GVN was prosecuting the war successfully against the People's Liberation Armed Forces (PLAF).[6] Even when the Army of the Republic of Vietnam (ARVN) suffered setbacks in the field, the Military Assistance Command, Vietnam (MACV), put the reverses in the best possible light and downplayed their importance.

One notable reverse occurred in January 1963 near Ap Bac, a village in Dinh Tuong Province, 40 miles southwest of Saigon. Although the American advisors who were present characterized the battle as a defeat, both Harkins and Admiral Harry D. Felt, the commander in chief, Pacific (CINCPAC), Harkins's immediate superior, proclaimed it an ARVN victory. A reflection of the belligerents and their doctrines, and influenced by the terrain and the personalities involved, Ap Bac clearly demonstrated the deficiencies of the GVN, the ARVN, and the advisory system.

Unfortunately, MACV refused to acknowledge that there remained serious problems in Vietnam. While Stilwell admitted to the Burma defeat and received laudatory commentary from the press, MACV's proclamation that Ap Bac was a victory only served to raise the ire of the reporters in Vietnam. Worse, instead of learning from the defeat at Ap Bac and recommending necessary changes to American policy, as Stilwell and his headquarters had done in Burma, Harkins and MACV predicted imminent GVN success, thus continuing on what would become a disastrous path for both Americans and Vietnamese in Southeast Asia. Following the lead of COMUSMACV and other senior Washington officials, the John F. Kennedy administration embraced their optimistic appraisals of the situation in South Vietnam and reinforced the image of sound American policy decisions in Southeast Asia.

From a historical perspective, the true significance of the Battle of Ap Bac remains subject to debate. Contemporary Western accounts highlighted the ARVN's shortcomings, and many called for a reassessment of American policies in Vietnam. Publications of the National Liberation Front (NLF), the political front organization of the PLAF, touted the victory as a signal of the growing strength of the insurgency and the hollowness of the GVN. Within two years, books appeared that cited Ap Bac as evidence that the GVN was already in serious trouble, even before the growing commitment of American combat forces in late 1965. This one-day fight had become the touchstone for those who opposed increased American involvement in Southeast Asia. By the late 1960s, however, the larger American battles and campaigns had come to overshadow Ap Bac, and it slipped into relative obscurity.

After the Second Indochina War's end in 1975, historians began to wrestle with writing textbooks that encompassed the entire conflict. These works focused mainly upon the American experience in Southeast Asia and gave short shrift to the First Indochina War and the American advisory period that followed. Mentioning Ap Bac in passing, few gave it more than a cursory examination. Of the works that attempted to describe the battle in any depth, few provided accurate narrative or maps. It took Neil Sheehan's *A Bright Shining Lie* (1988) to return Ap Bac to the historians' view.

Over the last ten years, Ap Bac has received increased attention. Some authors have characterized it as a decisive battle; others have attributed GVN President Ngo Dinh Diem's assassination directly to the outcome of that fateful day in early January 1963. Yet for all the recent scholarship, many questions still remain unclear: How could the PLAF, inferior both in numbers and technology, defeat the ARVN? What was the actual significance of Ap Bac? Was it truly a decisive battle? Why didn't the U.S. attempt to change its policy after such a serious defeat? In short, this study seeks to examine Ap Bac within the context of its antecedents and belligerents to determine what, if anything, changed in Vietnam and Washington, D.C., as a result of the battle on 2 January 1963.

This book, while gaining inspiration from *A Bright Shining Lie* and drawing from the Vann-Sheehan Vietnam War Collection, is not a restatement of Sheehan's argument and differs in many respects. While the chapter concerning the battle generally follows his narrative, it encompasses the entire operation, which did not end until a full two days after the battle proper, and provides maps to allow the reader to follow the units' movements. Although no study of this battle would be complete without discussing Lieutenant Colonel John Paul Vann and his actions at Ap Bac, this work seeks to place his role as a U.S. Army officer in South Vietnam into perspective. Although Vann was the senior American advisor in the area during the battle, his fame (or infamy) as one of the few advisors who knew the realities in South Vietnam is perhaps undeserved. He certainly was not the only advisor to voice his concerns, nor was he guilty of conducting a one-man mutiny to undermine American efforts in South Vietnam. He may have been concerned with how the ARVN was conducting its fight against the PLAF, but even he had not yet fully understood what a counterinsurgency required. Put simply, this work does not embrace the appealing, though overly simplistic, concept of John Paul Vann as the metaphor for American efforts in Southeast Asia. Instead, it seeks to explain why, despite a significant GVN defeat just outside of Saigon, the U.S. failed to reevaluate its overall policy in South Vietnam.

NOTES

1. Joseph Stilwell, *The Stilwell Papers*, ed. Theodore White (New York: William Sloane Associates, 1948), 106.

2. David Halberstam, *The Making of a Quagmire* (New York: Random House, 1965), 158.

3. Barbara Tuchman, *Stilwell and the American Experience in China, 1911–1945*, rev. ed. (New York: Bantam Books, 1985), 384.

4. Ibid., 385.

5. General William B. Rosson, Salem, VA, letter to author, Lubbock, TX, 16 September 1997, reflecting the record set forth in the *Pentagon Papers*.

6. Ibid.

Acknowledgments

As with any project, certain individuals merit thanks for their assistance and encouragement. First and foremost, I would like to extend my heartfelt appreciation to Dr. James Reckner, Texas Tech University and the Vietnam Center, whose guidance as my advisor, instructor, and mentor has proven to be practical, inspirational, and good-humored; General William B. Rosson, U.S. Army (Retired), whose patience and insightful comments provided me with direction and encouragement; Dr. Dennis Showalter, Colorado College, who not only suggested that the original work merited an audience and increased research, but also guided the revision process; Dr. John M. Carland, U.S. Army Center of Military History (CMH), who provided beneficial commentary on the manuscript; Majors David Shugart and M. Wade Markel, U.S. Army, who, despite their work loads, always listened to my ideas, pointed out their flaws, and offered constructive criticism; Steve Hardyman, CMH, and Ed Annable, National Infantry Museum, who assisted me in referencing and locating the majority of the included photographs; and Dr. Steve Waddell, U.S. Military Academy (USMA), and Dr. Heather Staines and Nancy Hellriegel, Greenwood Press, whose editorial expertise guided me through the publication process.

A special thanks must go to those who made my research trip to the Socialist Republic of Vietnam possible, particularly Dr. Reckner, who not only invited me to travel with the representatives of Texas Tech University, but also granted funding as well; Chancellor John Montford, Texas Tech University, who provided my transportation support; Colonels Robert Doughty and Cole Kingseed, USMA, who immediately recognized the trip's potential, encouraged my participation, and ensured that I was available to take part; Colonel Lee Wyatt, USMA, who obtained the bulk of the funding from the Office of the Dean; Dr. Jeffrey Clarke, CMH, who also contributed financial resources; and Melissa Mills, USMA, who put it all together. I must also specifically thank Khanh Cong Le, the Vietnam Center, for his help with all aspects of the trip, from securing my visa to coordinating my interviews. Without his assistance, the trip would not have been nearly as fruitful.

The greatest thanks of all must go to my wife, Carla Toczek, whose patience and good humor, though taxed, served me well throughout.

At the risk of seeming redundant, I believe it only just to acknowledge specific individuals who, through their written and verbal exchanges with me, influenced this piece. While I have not, in certain instances, cited individual conversations or correspondence in my endnotes, I would like to acknowledge the contributions of Dr. Ben Newcomb, Dr. Patricia Pelley, Professor Douglas Pike, and Dr. James Reckner, Texas Tech University; Dr. Dennis Showalter, Colorado College; and General William B. Rosson, U.S. Army (Retired). Despite the thoughtful assistance and guidance from others that I received throughout this process, any errors in interpretation or fact are mine alone.

The views expressed herein are those of the author and do not purport to reflect the official position of the USMA, the Department of the Army, or the Department of Defense.

Abbreviations

AAA	antiaircraft artillery
AAR	after action report
ABN	airborne
ACR	armored cavalry regiment
ACTIV	Army Concept Team in Vietnam
AGD	Adjutant General Division
AID	Agency for International Development
ALO	air liaison officer
AP	armor piercing ammunition
APC	armored personnel carrier
ARVN	Army of the Republic of Vietnam
AT	antitank ammunition
BAR	Browning Automatic Rifle
BG	brigadier general
C^2	command and control
CAS	close air support
CATO	Combat Arms Training and Organization Division
CG	Civil Guard
CHMAAG	Chief, Military Assistance Advisory Group
CHUSASEC	Chief, U.S. Army Section
CIA	Central Intelligence Agency
CINCPAC	Commander in Chief, Pacific Command
CINCUSARPAC	Commander in Chief, U.S. Army, Pacific
CJCS	Chairman, Joint Chiefs of Staff
CMH	U.S. Army Center of Military History
COMUSMACV	Commander, U.S. Military Assistance Command, Vietnam
CP	command post
CY	calendar year
CPSVN	Comprehensive Plan for South Vietnam
DPC	Douglas Pike Collection
DRV	Democratic Republic of Vietnam

FAC	forward air controller
FEC	French Expeditionary Corps
FM	field manual
FO	forward observer
FY	fiscal year
GEN	general
GVN	Government of Vietnam
HE	high explosive ammunition
HEAT	high explosive, antitank ammunition
HSAS	Headquarters, Support Activity, Saigon
ICC	International Control Commission
IN	infantry
INCEN	incendiary ammunition
JCS	Joint Chiefs of Staff
JFK	*The John F. Kennedy National Security Files*
JGS	Joint General Staff
KIA	killed in action
LCM	landing craft, mechanized
LCVP	landing craft, vehicle and personnel
LD	line of departure
LTG	lieutenant general
LZ	landing zone
MAAG	Military Assistance Advisory Group
MAAGI	Military Assistance Advisory Group, Indochina
MAAGV	Military Assistance Advisory Group, Vietnam
MACV	Military Assistance Command, Vietnam
MAP	Military Assistance Program
MATA	Military Assistance Training Advisor
MDAP	Mutual Defense Assistance Program
medevac	medical evacuation
MG	major general
NCO	noncommissioned officer
NLF	National Liberation Front
NSC	National Security Council
NVA	North Vietnamese Army
PACOM	Pacific Command
PAVN	People's Army of Vietnam
PLAF	People's Liberation Armed Forces
PZ	pickup zone
RAG	river assault group
RG	record group
ROE	rules of engagement
ROK	Republic of Korea
RVNAF	Republic of Vietnam Armed Forces
SDC	Self-Defense Corps
SOP	standing operating procedure

SP/4	specialist, fourth class
STCAN/FOM	*Services Technique des Constructions et Armes Navales/ France Outre Mer*
TDY	temporary duty
TERM	Temporary Equipment Recovery Mission
TF	task force
TOE	table of organization and equipment
TRCR	tracer ammunition
TRIM	Training Relations and Instructions Mission
USAMHI	U.S. Army Military History Institute
USAMHIDL	U.S. Army Military History Institute Digital Library
USARPAC	U.S. Army, Pacific
USASEC	U.S. Army Section
USFV	U.S. Forces, Vietnam
USIA	U.S. Information Agency
USMA	U.S. Military Academy
UTTHC	Utility Tactical Transport Helicopter Company
VC	Viet Cong
VNA	Vietnamese National Army
VSVWC	Vann-Sheehan Vietnam War Collection
WIA	wounded in action
WP	white phosphorus ammunition

1

The Background

[T]o assist and support the Government of Vietnam in its efforts to provide for its internal security, defeat communist insurgency, and resist overt aggression.[1]

MACV mission statement
February 1962

Although the armies that fought at Ap Bac were Vietnamese, they did not share a common heritage. One army traced its roots to a colonial power's attempt to maintain its influence in Indochina; the other, a Vietnamese attempt to oppose the French from remaining in control of Southeast Asia. One represented the desire to maintain the status quo in the region; the other, a desire for a unified Vietnam. Yet, despite their differences, each resembled the other in a fashion. Both received materiel and training assistance from other states. Both were also products of their past experiences. How each belligerent fought at Ap Bac was not only a representation of its state in January 1963, but also a reflection of its past. The histories of the opponents speak as much about the outcome at Ap Bac as do the reports about the battle itself.

ORIGINS OF THE ARMY OF THE REPUBLIC OF VIETNAM

The ARVN traced its roots to the Vietnamese National Army (VNA).[2] Concluding a military conference with the Bao Dai government in Dalat on 8 December 1950, the French authorized the foundation of the VNA. Answering to the emperor, who served as the commander in chief, the VNA wore Vietnamese instead of French uniforms. Most of the officers and noncommissioned officers (NCOs) were French, and those Vietnamese officers, NCOs, and soldiers serving in the French army were transferred to the VNA.[3]

The VNA got off to an inauspicious start. More concerned with their own efforts to defeat the Viet Minh, the insurgent army fighting against the French for its independence, the French did not make a concerted effort to establish a viable Vietnamese army. By May 1951, the VNA still numbered fewer than 40,000 soldiers. Of 34 projected battalions, only 24 existed, some of which were ad hoc units, and only seven possessed Vietnamese officers. By the following year, despite the VNA's growth to 40 battalions, it still did not have a general staff, a chief of staff, or even a full-time minister of defense. Worse, there were few senior Vietnamese officers to fill command and staff positions, let alone junior officers to fill company grade billets.[4] A National Security Council (NSC) paper issued in March 1952 asserted that the "lack of capable [Vietnamese] officers at all levels of command, French budgetary difficulties, shortages of equipment . . . [and] differences of opinion between the Vietnamese leaders and the French" prevented "maximum progress in the army's development."[5] From its birth, the VNA struggled to gain support from the French, because without it the Vietnamese army could not hope to play a role in defeating the Viet Minh.

The VNA's shortage of qualified officers continued through the following year. As of late 1953, there were only 2,600 Vietnamese officers, of whom "only a handful" held field grade rank, but there still remained close to 7,000 French officers serving in the VNA, now numbering some 150,000, a relatively significant percentage of the force's required officers.[6] The foundling Vietnamese army suffered not only from officer shortages, but also from a lack of enlisted soldiers. General J. Lawton Collins, acting as President Dwight D. Eisenhower's personal representative in Vietnam, reported in late 1954 that many battalions were severely understrength due to desertion and defection to the Viet Minh. All lacked sufficient combat support and combat service support units.[7] American observers were not the only ones to comment on the VNA's weaknesses. Dr. Phan Quang Dan, a leading Vietnamese political leader, offered his harsh appraisal of the army's situation, declaring that "[t]he Vietnamese Army is without responsible Vietnamese leaders, without ideology, without objective, without enthusiasm, without fighting spirit, and without popular backing."[8] In short, the VNA suffered from severe shortcomings in personnel, equipment, purpose, and popular support.

As the VNA grew in fits and starts, so did the American military presence in the region. The growing French commitment of resources to Indochina in the late 1940s, and not the invasion of Korea, sowed the seeds for an American military mission. Although the U.S. was no stranger to the region, it had managed to prevent itself from becoming directly involved in the postwar difficulties that resulted between Ho Chi Minh's victorious Viet Minh and the French. By early 1950, however, the American legation in Saigon cabled the State Department that "French troops [in] IC [Indochina are the] only military force of importance in [the] entire area. [The] French accordingly feel it is of interest to US and other western powers to assist France both militarily and politically."[9] Following the legation's suggestion, the NSC formally recognized the importance of Indochina in NSC Memorandum 64 (NSC 64), dated 27 February 1950, several months before the communist invasion of South Korea in June. The council declared that "Indochina is a key area of Southeast Asia and is under immediate threat. . . . Accordingly, the Departments of State and Defense should prepare as a matter of priority a program of all practicable measures designed to protect United States security interests in Indochina."[10] With NSC

64, the U.S. formally started down its post–World War II path of involvement in Indochina's future.

As part of this program to protect American interests in the region, the Joint Chiefs of Staff (JCS) recommended to the State Department in April the "immediate establishment of a small United States military aid group in Indochina." Its primary purpose was to facilitate coordination between the Vietnamese and French forces and supervise the allocation of military equipment. The State Department returned its concurrence to the proposal in May, but with one provision: "The Department of State assumes, of course, that such a Mission would be instructed to act in accordance with the advice of the Chief of the United States Diplomatic Mission to Saigon."[11] While the Military Assistance Advisory Group's (MAAG) role evolved throughout its existence, its subordination to the legation and, later, the embassy did not, a relationship that vexed each chief, MAAG (CHMAAG), to varying degrees.

Although the first members of the Military Assistance Advisory Group, Indochina (MAAGI), arrived in Saigon on 3 August 1950, the group was formally organized on 17 September. Brigadier General Francis Brink, a seasoned veteran of the World War II campaigns in Southeast Asia and the Chinese Civil War, assumed command on 10 October and formally assembled his headquarters on 20 November. In keeping with NSC 64 and the Mutual Defense Assistance Program (MDAP), a plan that provided thousands of tons of equipment to the French in Indochina, the MAAG was limited to providing technical assistance to maintain the MDAP equipment. Brink's guidance from the Defense Department precluded him from offering advice or training to the Vietnamese. As the MAAG was authorized only 128 officers and soldiers, training of the VNA was strictly a French affair.[12]

By the following spring, the State Department reported to the NSC that "[t]he Military Aid Program to Indochina enjoys the highest priority immediately after the military effort in Korea," emphasizing MAAGI's importance, given its relatively small size.[13] For the rest of 1951, the MAAG continued to support the French efforts in Indochina with its 128 authorized personnel. The State Department, however, believed that the MAAG needed strengthening. In its March 1952 draft of an NSC paper, the State Department recommended that "[s]teps should be taken to strengthen the MAAG Mission." This recommendation did not find favor with the JCS, who rebutted that the word "might" ought to replace "should," since they were "unaware of any cogent requirement for the strenghtening [sic] of the MAAG Mission," not a surprising retort given the ongoing fighting in Korea.[14] As would happen so many times throughout the 1950s, the State Department, and not Defense, desired an increased American presence in Indochina. Although they did not always triumph, the JCS won this round, and the MAAG did not increase in size through 1952.

This failure to increase its size did not preclude the MAAG from attempting to influence French training methods. Considering American efforts to train Republic of Korea (ROK) soldiers a success and an applicable approach to developing an effective VNA, both the CHMAAG, Major General Thomas

Trapnell, Brink's successor as of 1 August 1952, and Lieutenant General John O'Daniel, then the commander in chief, U.S. Army, Pacific (CINCUSARPAC), invited certain French officers to visit ROK army training centers on the Korean peninsula. The French, though impressed with the centers' efficiency, declared upon their return to Indochina that "US instructional methods cannot be effectively adopted in Indochina." The situation in Indochina, unlike that of Korea, had no stable front lines, nor was it "'classic' combat." Further, the ROK units followed U.S. doctrine in using the division as the basic combat unit and not the battalion as the French employed. Finally, and perhaps least believable, the French argued that "French and Vietnamese temperaments are not adaptable to specialization, regimentation and subordination since these methods do not consider the personality of the individual." Despite Trapnell's observation that the French offered "completely fallacious arguments" that possessed "no validity," the Americans failed to convince the French otherwise and remained on the sidelines of the training arena for the next year and a half.[15] This struggle to influence French training methods was one of the CHMAAG's primary concerns for the next three years.

Despite the MAAG's presence and the CHMAAG's desire to undertake a greater role in Indochina, the French retained the initiative in prosecuting the First Indochina War against the Viet Minh. More than willing to accept American financial and material aid in combating the Viet Minh, the French wanted no part of American instructors or training methods. In a discussion with Admiral Arthur Radford, CJCS, General Paul Ely, chief of staff of the French Joint Chiefs of Staff, stated that increasing the number of American advisors and their role in training the Vietnamese would have undesirable effects on French prestige and the French political situation. Ely's assessment of the political situation was astute; shortly after the general's departure from Washington, D.C., the American ambassador to France observed that the French Foreign Office "deplore[d] the constant recurrence of speculation on the matter [of an increased American role]. . . . [T]here is no question of any other American training mission being sent to Indochina."[16] Put simply, the French did not see an expanded role for the MAAG; for the time being, it remained a strictly technical advisory unit.[17]

The level of French influence over America's activities in Vietnam was not limited to determining the scope of the MAAG's influence but extended even to determining the rank of the MAAG's chief. Lieutenant General Henri Navarre, the French commander in Indochina, made his position clear concerning the pending appointment of Lieutenant General John O'Daniel as the next CHMAAG: "General Navarre hopes that General O'Daniel will arrive as a *major* general and have the *same* [rank] as his predecessor." Despite his regret that O'Daniel would temporarily lose "one star," Navarre "wanted it clearly understood from [the] start that his very willing acceptance of General O'Daniel was predicated on [the] understanding that [the] latter's functions were limited to military assistance."[18] In short, the American military effort in Indochina was limited to providing materiel and did not involve influencing the VNA or providing anything but technical assistance.

Despite Ely's clear opposition to increased American involvement in training the VNA during his visit to Washington, D.C., in March 1954, he quickly reversed his position upon assuming command in Indochina later that same year. Perhaps influenced by the catastrophic defeat at Dien Bien Phu in May, the reports of VNA units deserting en masse, and his predecessor's remarks that it "was impossible to train Vietnamese troops to combat fitness," Ely told O'Daniel, CHMAAG from 12 February 1954, "that a greatly enlarged MAAG training section should be established and that two large training camps would at once be turned over for American training of Vietnamese national troops." Ely then went on to stipulate that the camps would remain under French or Vietnamese command, and that any such transaction would require approval by the French government. Although limited in nature, this approach by Ely gave O'Daniel the opening he sought to increase the MAAG's role in Indochina.[19]

With the signing of the Geneva Accords in July, the situation in Vietnam changed drastically. Article 16 of the accords directed that no additional foreign troops enter Vietnam after 11 August 1954. By this time, the MAAG had grown to 342 (128 advisors and 214 U.S. Air Force technicians), but it was not large enough in O'Daniel's view to handle the possible training of the VNA. To that end, he asked that the JCS increase immediately the MAAG's personnel authorization approximately sevenfold to some 2,400 personnel before the 11 August deadline, a request that touched off a debate between the Defense and State Departments over how best to protect American interests in Indochina.[20]

The JCS refused the CHMAAG's personnel request because it felt that before the U.S. undertook the training mission, certain conditions in Indochina needed to be met. Of the four listed, the JCS's first condition declared it "absolutely essential that there be a reasonably strong, stable civil government in control." Writing a month later, the JCS wrote again that given the "unstable" political environment in Indochina, it was "not a propitious time to further indicate United States intentions with respect to the support and training of either the Vietnamese regular or police forces."[21] The argument that a strong civil government must precede a strong military found no sympathy in the State Department. Secretary of State John Foster Dulles espoused the exact opposite view. To him, a strong Vietnamese army would set the conditions for a strong civil government.[22] Once again, the service chiefs were loath to commit personnel resources to Indochina, despite the requests of a respected and rather senior major general and the secretary of state. The Defense and State Departments were at loggerheads.

The ongoing political maneuvering in South Vietnam exacerbated the differences between the Defense and State Departments. The VNA's chief of staff, General Nguyen Van Hinh, was an enemy of Ngo Dinh Diem, the prime minister of South Vietnam. A French officer and citizen who had married a French woman, Hinh originally received tacit French approval for his opposition to Diem. In August 1954, Hinh began planning to establish another government with the Cao Dai and Hoa Hao religious sects.[23] With Emperor Bao Dai in France, this move would have made Hinh the senior governmental official in South Vietnam. As tensions mounted, Diem attempted to relieve Hinh, who vigorously refused to give up his position. At the same time, the chief of staff responded with threats of removing the prime minister. Hinh did not disguise his desire to govern Vietnam, once displaying a cigarette lighter given him by Gamal Nasser, the Egyptian army officer who had come to power by way of a coup not long before, with the comment that Nasser "had the right idea."[24] Observing Hinh's play for position was American Ambassador Donald Heath, who wrote to Washington that the Vietnamese chief of staff received "quiet encouragement if not unofficial support" from French officials in Saigon and "the working level in Paris" to challenge Diem's position.[25] Concerned about the danger Hinh posed to the foundling GVN, the French and American governments pressured Bao Dai to call General Hinh to France for consultation in November 1954, effectively removing him from competition with Diem.[26]

Few observers at the time realized this type of political maneuvering would remain a constant factor throughout the Vietnamese army's existence. One official who did foresee this trend was Ambassador Heath. Somewhat prophetically, he suggested in late October that the "Army-Diem conflict may be stirred up again by Diem's intransigent dislike of burying the hatchet against anyone he feels is morally in the wrong and disloyal," a pattern that repeated itself throughout Diem's tenure.[27] Again and again, government officials and officers alike who seemed to go against the Ngo Dinh clan's wishes found themselves out of office, or worse.

The Defense/State Department debate concerning the level of American involvement in Vietnam came to a head at a NSC meeting in late October 1954. Admiral Radford, the CJCS, again emphasized the JCS's position concerning the training issue. Taken to task by Dulles over what was essentially a "hen-and-egg" issue, Radford conceded that if "political considerations were overriding in this matter, the JCS would do the best they could to achieve the desired objective." President Dwight D. Eisenhower, supporting Dulles's position, agreed to allow the MAAG to undertake the training mission and summarized his instructions by saying that what was needed "was a Vietnamese force which would support Diem. Therefore, let's get busy and get one." Instructions to the embassy in Vietnam followed that same afternoon, directing "the Ambassador and the Chief of MAAG [to] collaborate in setting in motion a crash program designed to bring about an improvement in the loyalty and effectiveness of the Free Vietnamese forces."[28] As with most other complex organizations, establishing the training mission was more easily directed than accomplished.

Negotiations between General Ely and General J. Lawton Collins, the president's personal representative in Vietnam, began almost immediately. On 13 December 1954, the two signed an agreement that provided for a MAAG training mission, the autonomy of the Vietnamese army, and a force structure for fiscal year 1956. Despite the agreement, Collins complained to Ely the following month about the French government's "deliberate foot dragging, in approving [the] Ely-Collins minute of understanding." After another round of modifications by the French government, Ely and Collins signed another agreement on 11 February. On the following day, the Franco-American Training

Relations and Instruction Mission (TRIM) officially received responsibility for training the Vietnamese army.[29]

The TRIM's mission was clearly outlined in a memorandum issued by the VNA's chief of staff on 10 April 1955. It directed the TRIM advisors "to assist and advise, on strictly technical aspects, the Vietnamese military authorities to whom they are assigned, to rapidly and effectively rebuild the Vietnamese Armed Forces on a new basis." This mission statement set the groundwork for the relationship between American advisors and Vietnamese commanders that spanned almost twenty years. With the expected French departure from Vietnam, the VNA's rebuilding "on a new basis" intimated the growing American influence in the training, equipping, and organizing of the fledgling Vietnamese army. American, and not French, doctrine was now the driving factor in Vietnam, at least in principle.[30]

Providing a list of authorized activities for advisors, the document allowed TRIM personnel to "[a]dvise, in the event of need, and assist, when requested by the Vietnamese officers to whom they are attached, in the preparation and execution of tasks." Advisors were also permitted to report on their units' status in written form to the TRIM chief and act as his representatives, visit and observe VNA units, and expect to "be kept informed of current regulations, orders and documents not strictly confidential or secret." While these provisions gave great latitude to the TRIM, they were not all encompassing. The Vietnamese were no longer willing to fight under the command of foreign powers as they had in the past: "TRIM advisers [sic] have no command or supervisory authority over the Vietnamese Armed Forces organizations or activities."[31] From the outset, the South Vietnamese officers wished to possess overall responsibility for their actions, a fact that many Americans lost sight of in their pursuit of a free South Vietnam.

By March 1955, 209 French and 68 American officers composed the TRIM. Throughout the remainder of 1955 and early 1956, the MAAG assigned 121 more American officers to the TRIM to replace the departing French. Although the training mission worked to improve the VNA's readiness, there were problems. Of all the Americans assigned as advisors, none was fluent in Vietnamese and less than ten spoke French fluently. Personnel shortfalls worked to delay training efforts. With such a large army to train, there were simply not enough officers and NCOs to fill the required number of advisory positions. Constrained by the accords and the JCS, the MAAG, Vietnam (renamed from MAAG, Indochina, on 1 November 1955), remained at 342 after the departure of the French in early 1956. With no one to replace the French, the CHMAAG chose to commit the majority of his personnel (217) to advisory capacities. As a result, the logistical effort in Vietnam suffered tremendously.[32]

While the Americans gradually extended their influence over the VNA, Prime Minister Diem still faced political opposition from other quarters. With Bao Dai still residing in France, Diem was the senior government official in South Vietnam, but he was not yet master in his own house. There remained the matter of how well the religious sects and crime organizations would cooperate with his government. No longer able to use Hinh as a front man because of his departure, the Cao Dai, the Hoa Hao, and the Binh Xuyen put aside their differences and formed the United Front of Nationalist Forces on 3 March 1955. Not happy with Diem's recent political decisions, particularly the ones that restricted their freedom of action, they issued an ultimatum demanding a new national government.[33] Each group had interests to protect from Diem's interference and stood to gain from his downfall. All wished to maintain their private armies as entities separate from the VNA while maintaining government subsidies to do so, and all wished to continue to rule their literal fiefdoms within South Vietnam. Even more troublesome was Emperor Bao Dai's earlier April 1954 decree giving the Binh Xuyen full control over the *Sureté*, or secret police, in exchange for a "staggering sum."[34] Yet Diem possessed an effective solution to these challenges to his authority: the Vietnamese army.

Diem reacted to this threat by directing the VNA to destroy his political rivals. Fighting against the crime syndicate broke out on 28 March 1955, when a VNA airborne company seized the Binh Xuyen headquarters that doubled as Saigon's main police station. The following night, the Binh Xuyen answered by mortaring the presidential palace and attempting unsuccessfully to regain their command post. By 31 March, the French had managed to negotiate a 48-hour cease-fire between the belligerents that lasted to the end of April. On 28 April Diem reported that the binh Xuyen had again mortared his residence. This time, the VNA pushed the crime syndicate into the Saigon suburb of Cholon, and by mid-May out into the Rung Sat swamp on the eastern edge of Saigon, effectively destroying overt Binh Xuyen influence in Vietnamese politics.[35]

With the Binh Xuyen out of the picture, Diem now turned to deal with the Cao Dai and Hoa Hao. Using bribes and other incentives, Diem incorporated portions of the Cao Dai into the VNA on 31 March and approximately 3,000 Hoa Hao troops on 1 June. The remainder of the religious sects that did not rally to Diem came under pressure from the VNA, and by August Diem had close to 20,000 VNA soldiers in the field against them.[36] Fighting continued through the winter of 1955–1956, and, by the following spring, Diem had effectively neutralized his political rivals. This battle with the sects was a seminal event in Diem's political development. While it is difficult to determine what his conclusions from this process of consolidating power were, he most likely learned the "political importance of the army, and the essentiality of personally loyal ranking officers," two critical factors that were never far from Diem's mind for the next seven years.[37] In the midst of struggling with the sects, South Vietnam had become a republic, and the VNA traded its name for the more-familiar Army of the Republic of Vietnam (ARVN). Whether called VNA or ARVN, it was truly a weapon that Diem was not afraid to control or wield.

As Diem strengthened his position, the MAAG struggled with how best to train and organize the ARVN. Between 1957 and 1959 alone, the MAAG developed over 200 different tables of organization and equipment (TOEs).[38] The U.S. military, however, was not the only agency concerned with the ARVN's training and organization. Throughout this period, the American ambassador and other State Department officials offered their solutions for how best to prepare the ARVN to defeat the growing insurgency. Although the

ARVN slowly improved in readiness, American civilian and military organizations in Vietnam could not agree upon what training and organization would best suit the ARVN.

The Americans did not restrict themselves to only training issues but sought to rectify the South Vietnamese logistical difficulties as well. The French had shown little interest in establishing a functional logistical system for the VNA. Suffering from little martial experience, the Vietnamese army possessed even less logistical knowledge. Reliant upon the French system, which was weak at best, the Vietnamese had little infrastructure with which to supply their new army. Depots were unorganized; requisitions went unfilled. As the French withdrew from Vietnam after the Geneva Accords, thousands of tons of American equipment littered the countryside because the French felt no obligation to consolidate it. Taking the best equipment with them, the French left the VNA with unserviceable and stripped military ordnance.[39]

As early as January 1955, members of Congress had expressed concern to the Department of the Army about the ultimate disposition of equipment provided to the French under the MDAP. With the withdrawal of French forces, the congressmen believed that if care was not taken, large quantities of American equipment could fall into the hands of the communists.[40] By November 1955, the U.S. Army dispatched a special mission to Vietnam under the leadership of its budget chief. His team found that the MAAG could not simultaneously support training and logistics. The ARVN, in his estimate, could not conduct sustained combat operations because of its tremendous logistical difficulties. Thousands of tons of equipment lay in heaps all over the Vietnamese countryside because the French had opened most of the crates on delivery, making it impossible to account for or locate specific shipments.[41] In short, lack of Vietnamese logistical expertise, French self-interest, and personnel constraints imposed by the Geneva Accords made it nearly impossible for the MAAG to support the ARVN effectively in both training and logistics.

The Department of State, in coordination with the Department of Defense, offered a solution to the MAAG in February 1956. Secretary of State Dulles, in a cable to O'Daniel's replacement, Lieutenant General Samuel T. Williams, described an "additional military logistical group . . . [that] would operate under, though not as formal part of, MAAG-Viet Nam." Formal authorization followed two months later from Dulles: "A Temporary Equipment Recovery Mission [TERM] of 350 American military personnel is created for the purpose of both supervising the recovery and outshipment of excess MDAP equipment in Viet Nam and of assisting in the improvement of Vietnamese logistical capabilities." The State Department informed the International Control Commission (ICC), an organization charged with enforcing the provisions of the Geneva Accords, that the total number of American servicemen in Vietnam would not exceed 740, allowing an overlap of 48 to account for those on leave, travel status, and so forth. As Dulles further directed, there would "not be actually more than 692 personnel physically present in Viet Nam at any one time, including TDY's [servicemen on temporary duty], but excluding overlaps."[42] Once again, it was the State Department, and not the Department of Defense, that was the driving factor in committing more resources to Southeast Asia.

Recognizing that this directive might violate the Geneva Accords, both the State and Defense Departments agreed to delay arrivals until 9 May, "thus leaving what appears to us reasonable time for Commission consideration." Regardless of the ICC's decision, the MAAG was going to get its increase in personnel. Although both the State and Defense Departments conceived the TERM as temporary in nature, the MAAG saw the additional authorizations as a way to reduce its focus on logistical requirements and to get back to the business of training. Never having received ICC approval or disapproval of the TERM, the MAAG completely absorbed it by 1960.[43]

ORIGINS OF THE PEOPLE'S LIBERATION ARMED FORCES

While organizing, training, and equipping an army are monumental tasks in themselves, they are made infinitely more difficult if undertaken while simultaneously attempting to defeat an insurgency. So it was with the ARVN. Although its early years were mainly occupied in assisting Diem to subdue his political enemies, by 1958 the ARVN began to face a larger threat: the PLAF, more commonly known as the Viet Cong (VC). So naming the insurgents to discourage the populace from associating them with the Viet Minh, the GVN sought to negate their reputation as nationalists who had triumphed over a colonial power. By renaming its opposition the Viet Cong, the GVN emphasized the communist heritage of the Viet Minh and not its victory over the French. Although the PLAF coalesced in South Vietnam, the organization inherited many of its characteristics and its members from the People's Army of Vietnam (PAVN), more commonly known as the North Vietnamese Army (NVA).

Tracing its birth to late 1944 in the mountains of northern Vietnam, the PAVN provided the bulk of the Viet Minh's fighting capability.[44] Facilitating the establishment of the Democratic Republic of Vietnam (DRV) on 2 September 1945 in Hanoi, the PAVN once again undertook a struggle for Vietnamese independence during the First Indochina War. Although suffering severe losses to the French during the war, particularly on the plains outside Hanoi in fall of 1951, the PAVN brought the war to a close by crushing the French at Dien Bien Phu in 1954. Following the French defeat and the division of Vietnam into two separate regions, the Geneva Accords authorized PAVN forces in South Vietnam to return to the north. This provision offered the DRV an opportunity to continue hostilities at a later time. Approximately 2,500 PAVN cadre remained in the south with caches of arms and ammunition. Although not officially named the "Liberation Army" until 15 February 1961, these cadres, or "armed propaganda units of former resistance members," in conjunction with cadres infiltrated from the north in the late 1950s, formed the skeleton of the PLAF.[45]

Following the Geneva Accords, the DRV encouraged its stay-behind cadres in the south to restrict themselves primarily to political activity while using violence selectively and judiciously. Although the northerners believed that

Vietnam was ultimately destined for unification under the control of the DRV, they also felt that their first priority was to develop North Vietnam's infrastructure before overtly attempting reunification. Suffering heavily during Diem's anticommunist drives in the countryside in the late 1950s, the southern guerrillas grew more impatient to liberate themselves, and their pressure upon the DRV's Politburo to do something tangible grew in strength. Recognizing that the insurgency required outside support to maintain its viability, Vo Nguyen Giap, the minister of defense, ordered the formation of Group 559 on 19 May 1959. Charged with opening a "modest track" to the south, the unit began secretly moving men and supplies toward South Vietnam through Laos and Cambodia. Two months later, Group 759 began its examination of how best to infiltrate personnel and equipment over the sea routes. Although what became known as the Ho Chi Minh trail did not support heavy infiltration traffic until some five years later, North Vietnam became committed to assisting the insurgency in the south well before the large deployment of American advisors and equipment in 1961.[46]

Before continuing this discussion, one must address the issue of the relationship between the PAVN and the PLAF. As noted earlier, the two armies shared a common heritage, particularly since many of the PLAF cadres were former PAVN veterans of the First Indochina War and stay-behinds after the Geneva Accords. Both subscribed to the idea of protracted warfare as the strategy of choice and organized themselves to conduct that type of combat. The extent to which the PLAF was an extension of the PAVN, however, is a matter of intense debate. Some historians and participants argue that the PLAF was simply a puppet of the PAVN. Colonel Bui Tin, a PAVN general staff officer, when asked if the NLF was an independent movement, stated plainly: "No. It was set up by our Communist Party. . . . We always said there was only one party."[47] At the other extreme, there are those who contend that the PLAF was completely independent of PAVN control and was uninfluenced by the Lao Dong. As with any issue, the truth lies somewhere between these two extremes.[48]

Most accounts place the beginning of PLAF activity in 1959, but some offer 1957 as the first year of increased PLAF terror and intimidation. Numbering some 9,000 guerrillas in 1959, the PLAF began in earnest to contest the GVN control of the South Vietnamese countryside.[49] In response to the rising number of violent incidents, the ARVN deployed in the field in July 1959 to prevent disruption of the scheduled 30 August elections. By this presence of its army in the field, the GVN signaled its rising level of concern for its security. The PLAF had simply grown too strong for the police to handle by itself. CHMAAG Williams later considered this deployment successful since the elections went as planned, but he also described what he considered an unfortunate side effect of the ARVN's success. Instead of operating in small harassing bands of three or four, the PLAF now massed in units of 30-, 50-, or 100-man elements to protect itself against the GVN forces. With their larger unit sizes, the guerrillas felt confident enough to attack Civil Guard (CG) detachments and isolated villages.[50] Gaining in strength, the insurgent cells coalesced into platoon- and company-size units, openly challenging Diem's control of the South Vietnamese countryside.

The selection of targets was not confined to GVN outposts or isolated Vietnamese villages (see Fig. 1.1). Although there were only a couple hundred American advisors in South Vietnam in 1959, they attracted the PLAF's attention. On the evening of 8 July, the members of the advisory detachment for the ARVN 7th Division settled down to watch a movie in the Bien Hoa officers' mess. At about 1900, Master Sergeant Chester M. Ovnand turned on the lights to change the movie reel. Taking advantage of the illumination, five to ten guerrillas, armed with French submachine guns and homemade bombs, opened fired, killing Ovnand. In the brief firefight that ensued, another American advisor, Major Dale R. Buis, died, as did an ARVN guard, a Vietnamese mess attendant, and a guerrilla. Also wounded in the attack were Captain Howard B. Boston and an eight-year-old Vietnamese boy who happened to be standing outside, watching the movie through a window.[51] Gaining confidence in its abilities, the PLAF was no longer satisfied to limit its attacks to Vietnamese outposts. Throughout the fall of 1959, PLAF assassinations and kidnappings continued to rise, prompting Ambassador Elbridge Durbrow to express his concern in cable traffic to the State Department.[52]

As 1960 began, the PLAF was preparing for yet another attack, this time against an entire ARVN infantry regiment. The 32nd Regiment had established a base camp near the village of Tran Sup, Tay Ninh Province, near the Cambodian border. All three of the regiment's battalions rotated in and out of the camp, conducting sweeps in the area. At 0230 on 26 January 1960, approximately four PLAF companies numbering some 200 guerrillas attacked the camp. Completely surprising the ARVN units, the PLAF ran completely through the 1st and 2nd Battalions, finally meeting resistance in the 3rd Battalion area. After a 60-minute firefight, the PLAF withdrew into the darkness, carrying its killed and wounded, as well as captured equipment.[53]

This attack was the most significant yet, both in terms of physical and psychological damage. The PLAF had destroyed two large barracks, the regimental headquarters, and four other buildings. It had also acquired a significant number of weapons and ammunition. The ARVN suffered 66 killed and wounded in action (KIA/WIA).[54] More disconcerting was the level of preparedness demonstrated by the PLAF and its effects on the confidence of the ARVN command. In a letter to a friend, General Williams noted that "[t]he VC had the place well reconnoitered. They knew most of the Regiment was gone, they knew exactly where the arms rooms were, they knew exactly which building individual officers slept in and they headed for them. This affair really put the [South] Vietnamese in a tizzy."[55] The PLAF was also becoming more brazen in its attacks. By the fall of 1960, Ambassador Durbrow cabled the State Department that the PLAF was even conducting terrorist attacks in Saigon itself, a clear sign of the growing threat to the GVN's internal security.[56]

With the increase in ARVN operations against the PLAF, the MAAG once again requested an increase in personnel authorization. Since the TERM personnel who had been absorbed by the MAAG were only in Vietnam on

Figure 1.1
South Vietnam

temporary duty, General Williams requested that the JCS raise the MAAG's assigned personnel from 342 to 685, nearly 200 less than the original ceiling placed by the Geneva Accords. On 5 May 1960, the Defense Department agreed, allowing yet another increment in the ever-increasing American presence in Vietnam.[57]

As 1961 progressed, the NLF and PLAF increased their pressure on the GVN. By late summer, the PLAF began to prepare for its largest offensive to this point in the war. In a memorandum to Admiral Felt, Lieutenant General Lionel McGarr, now CHMAAG, reported that the PLAF was massing battalion-sized elements along the Laotian border. Armed with a combination of captured and infiltrated weapons, including submachine guns, automatic rifles, machine guns, and mortars, the PLAF posed a significant threat.[58] The expected blow fell on 1 September 1961. Attacking with two to three battalions, the PLAF eventually occupied Poko and Dakha, which were villages in Kontum Province, some 300 miles north of Saigon. Wearing khaki uniforms into battle for the first time, the PLAF inflicted 19 ARVN KIA at an expense of 100 of its own dead. Offering his analysis to the State Department, H. Francis Cunningham, the counsel-general of the U.S. embassy, observed that the size of the attack and the use of uniforms indicated a possible massing of larger PLAF formations and signaled a prelude to larger attacks.[59] Cunningham's analysis proved accurate. On 17–18 September, the PLAF registered a "first" when, with three battalions, it captured and occupied Phuoc Thanh, the capital of Phuoc Thanh Province, approximately 50 miles north of Saigon, despite the two ARVN ranger companies in the area. Making the most of its occupation, the PLAF conducted a "people's trial" in the marketplace and executed the province chief and his assistant.[60]

ORIGINS OF THE MILITARY ASSISTANCE COMMAND, VIETNAM

After the September PLAF offensive, President John F. Kennedy dispatched to Vietnam his military representative, General Maxwell D. Taylor, to evaluate the situation. After numerous briefings and visits, Taylor on 3 November 1961 recommended that "[t]he MAAG, Vietnam . . . be reorganized and increased in size as may be necessary by the implementation of these recommendations [included in his report]."[61] Reacting to Taylor's observations, Secretary of Defense Robert S. McNamara called a meeting of senior commanders in Hawaii. There, on 16 December 1961, McNamara met with Ambassador Frederick Nolting, Deputy Assistant Secretary of Defense for International Security Affairs William Bundy, General Lyman L. Lemnitzer, CJCS, Admiral Felt, and General McGarr. Sensitive to the implications of Taylor's recommendations, the assembled leadership, in a closed meeting, agreed not to discuss a commander for U.S. Forces, Vietnam (USFV), during the open briefing that was to follow.[62] After opening the meeting to the lower-ranking staff, McNamara stressed the need for U.S. success in Vietnam. He continued that short of the already imposed exclusion of combat forces from Vietnam, no request was unreasonable because money was no object. Not surprisingly, the issue of the new command in Vietnam did not surface. Upon his return to Washington, McNamara sent a note on 18 December to Secretary of State Dean Rusk, asking to confirm Rusk's agreement with the creation of "U.S. Military Assistance Forces-Vietnam" and the duties and responsibilities of the new commander.[63] Because the MAAG was to retain direct responsibility for the advisory effort and remain a subordinate unit, the term "advisory" was not included in the new command's title.

The Defense Department saw the new command arrangement as the next logical step in directing American efforts in Vietnam, but State Department officials held mixed feelings about the introduction of a larger command, an interesting contrast to their previous arguments for a larger American military presence in South Vietnam. Earlier in December 1961, Rusk had agreed with Deputy Undersecretary of State for Political Affairs U. Alexis Johnson, who argued that the appointment of a U.S. "commander" would amount to an "irrevocable and 100% commitment to saving South Vietnam." This larger command was not simply the next logical step; it also implied that the GVN and ARVN efforts were insufficient, requiring increased American support and direction.[64] Rusk, responding to McNamara that same day, believed that the title "Commander, U.S. Military Assistance Command-Vietnam" was more appropriate; in Rusk's view, the term "forces" implied the presence of organized military units beyond which the U.S. planned to send to Vietnam.[65] Rusk got his way; President Kennedy confirmed General Paul D. Harkins as commander, U.S. Military Assistance Command, Vietnam (COMUSMACV), on 3 January 1962. One month later, on 7 February 1962, Military Assistance Command, Vietnam (MACV), took charge in Vietnam.[66]

The JCS envisioned MACV as a temporary headquarters that would supplement the MAAG and "enable the U.S. to carry out more effectively the expanded assistance and support requested by the Government of the Republic of Vietnam." Its formal mission, as directed by CINCPAC, was "to assist and support the Government of Vietnam in its efforts to provide for its internal security, defeat communist insurgency, and resist overt aggression." Authorized 216 personnel, 113 of whom belonged to the U.S. Army, MACV would disband after the GVN had brought the insurgency under control, thus restoring the MAAG to primacy in Vietnam.[67]

The MACV was not the only new command to come about in early 1962. Although the MAAG still possessed U.S. Air Force personnel in its headquarters, MACV's role required that it have its own U.S. Air Force command. As a result, the Pacific Air Forces established the 2nd Advance Squadron, redesignated shortly thereafter as the 2nd Air Division. Answering directly to COMUSMACV, the 2nd Air Division also responded to directives and received logistic and administrative support from the Pacific Air Forces. The U.S. Navy, on the other hand, did not receive a larger headquarters. Because waterborne operations had not increased with MACV's foundation, the MAAG's naval section did not increase in size, nor did MACV establish its own U.S. Navy subordinate command.[68]

Not surprisingly, command relationships between the various American units and agencies and the GVN became increasingly complex and ambiguous. Harkins, as COMUSMACV, oversaw the conduct of assistance to the GVN and U.S. military policy and operations in Vietnam. He was the senior military advisor to the Diem government and commanded all American troops assigned to the country. Although a subordinate to CINCPAC, he could direct messages through his higher command to the JCS and the secretary of defense. Harkins was not, however, the senior American official in Vietnam. The ambassador, as the agent for U.S. policy and political matters, also had the ability to refer his recommendations to Washington, but he could not issue directives to COMUSMACV. In essence, the command structure as it stood in 1962 did not provide for one senior American representative in Vietnam, a state that continued the tension between the military and civilian authorities that had already been present over the previous twelve years.[69]

The problems concerning relationships were not confined to the civil-military realm, but also applied to the military arena as well. Although overall commander in Vietnam, Harkins had delegated the majority of his command authority to Major General Charles Timmes, McGarr's replacement as CHMAAG, confusing an already complex chain of command. Harkins directly commanded Timmes's MAAG, but the CHMAAG administered the Military Assistance Program (MAP), a program that required him to answer directly to CINCPAC for its execution. The parallel structure of MACV and the MAAG caused a certain amount of duplication between the two headquarters. Further, MACV had to reestablish relationships already formed by the MAAG. These difficulties plagued MACV, the MAAG, and their subordinate commands until another reorganization in 1964.[70]

As the headquarters sought to sort out their roles and relationships, MACV sought to come to grips with another problem: The competence of its staff. While the company and field grade advisors were competent, as one State Department observer noted, "[t]he poorest people are at the staff level in all of the agencies."[71] In all fairness, building a large staff from scratch with few experienced personnel is not easy. The fact remains, however, that a complex chain of command, coupled with language difficulties, hampered the Americans' attempts to further assist the ARVN.

While MACV sought to establish itself, the ARVN continued to conduct combat operations against the PLAF, and the GVN seemed to be making gains. With the introduction of the strategic hamlet program in 1962, the insurgency's effects appeared to be diminishing as the number of villagers under GVN "control" rose ever higher. Pleasing to the MAAG, the number of ARVN combat operations were at an all time high. However, a troubling contradiction appeared. While PLAF losses mounted, so did the ARVN's; by February 1962, the ARVN was suffering nearly 3,000 casualties per month.[72]

By summertime, the GVN and MACV were guardedly optimistic about subduing the insurgency, but there were still troubling manifestations of the PLAF's strength. On 5 October, near Ap My Luong, Dinh Tuong Province, 40 miles south of Saigon, the PLAF withstood an air assault by eleven H-21s carrying a 90-man ranger company. Within minutes of landing, the rangers suffered 13 killed and 34 wounded, effectively decimating a platoon's worth of ARVN soldiers. Although the GVN claimed 100 PLAF dead, the insurgents disappeared into the countryside, frustrating yet another attempt to fix them in place. The Vietnamese were not the only ones to die; the crew chief of one of the H-21s was killed, bringing the total number of Americans killed in Vietnam since December 1961 to 13.[73]

As 1963 approached, each belligerent could look back upon its growing pains, successes, and failures of the previous fifteen years or so with mixed emotions. Both the ARVN and the PLAF had grown in size and sophistication. The American presence had also increased to the extent that the ongoing insurgency was no longer strictly a Vietnamese affair. In fact, by the eve of Ap Bac, these two Vietnamese military forces shared little in common, partly as a result of the outside forces that shaped them.

NOTES

1. Department of the Army, *Command and Control: 1950–1969* by George Eckhardt, Vietnam Studies (Washington, D.C.: U.S. Government Printing Office, 1974), 28–29.

2. In October 1955, Ngo Dinh Diem, prime minister of Emperor Bao Dai, declared Vietnam a republic. The VNA then became the ARVN. In many sources, "ARVN" is used interchangeably with "South Vietnamese army." For clarity, the term "VNA" will refer to the South Vietnamese army for periods before the declaration of the Republic of Vietnam and "ARVN" for periods after.

3. Ronald Spector, *Advice and Support: The Early Years of the U.S. Army in Vietnam, 1941–1960*, rev. ed. (New York: The Free Press, 1985), 134.

4. Department of State, *Foreign Relations of the United States, 1951*, vol. VI, *Asia and the Pacific* (Washington, D.C.: U.S. Government Printing Office, 1977), 159; Spector, *Advice and Support*, 154–155.

5. Department of State, *Foreign Relations of the United States, 1952–1954*, vol. XIII, *Indochina* (Washington, D.C.: U.S. Government Printing Office, 1982), 84–85.

6. *The Pentagon Papers: The Defense Department History of the United States Decisionmaking on Vietnam*, vol. I, the Senator Gravel edition (Boston: Beacon Press, 1971), 68.

7. Spector, *Advice and Support*, 225.

8. *Pentagon Papers*, vol. I, 72.

9. Department of State, *Foreign Relations of the United States, 1950*, vol. VI, *East Asia and the Pacific* (Washington, D.C.: U.S. Government Printing Office, 1976), 705.

10. Ibid., 744–747.

11. Ibid., 783–784, 817.

12. Department of the Army, *Command and Control*, 7; *Pentagon Papers*, vol. I, 197. Commanding in the Philippines before World War II, Brink served on various combined staffs in Southeast Asia during the war. These experiences, when coupled with his assignment as the chief of the U.S. Army advisory staff in China during 1948 and 1949, made him a logical choice as the first CHMAAG. Spector, *Advice and Support*, 116; *Who Was Who in America*, vol. 3, *1951–1960* (Chicago: A.N. Marquis, 1960), 104.

13. Department of State, *Foreign Relations of the United States, 1951*, vol. VI, *Asia and the Pacific*, 397.

14. Department of State, *Foreign Relations of the United States, 1952–1954*, vol. XIII, *Indochina*, 88, 116–117.

15. Ibid., 474.

16. Ibid., 455–456; Spector, *Advice and Support*, 193 and *passim*; Department of State, *Foreign Relations of the United States, 1952–1954*, vol. XIII, *Indochina*, 1151, 1161.

17. Even the Americans' technical visits to the French Union Forces were tightly controlled. In order to schedule end-use inspections (or checks to ensure the proper use of MDAP equipment), MAAG advisors had to submit detailed requests outlining the units to be visited, the desired visitation dates, the number of visitors, and any other "special requests" two months in advance. This request system effectively precluded "spot-checks" or any other type of unscheduled inspection. Memo Number 10, Headquarters, Military Assistance Advisory Group, Indochina, subject: Scheduling of End-Use Visits, 2 June 1954 (box 1; memorandums; Adjutant General Division; Military Assistance Advisory Group, Vietnam; Record Group 334; National Archives [hereafter AGD/MAAGV/RG 334]).

18. Department of State, *Foreign Relations of the United States, 1952–1954*, vol. XIII, *Indochina*, 1303, 1062. The American JCS were adamantly opposed to O'Daniel's reduction: "The Joint Chiefs of Staff hold it to be drastically detrimental to the prestige of the United States Military Services in general, and to the United States Army in particular to demote a distinguished senior United States Army officer already well and widely known in that region." *Pentagon Papers*, vol. I, 447–448. Despite their reservations, O'Daniel was reduced in rank for the billet. Spector, *Advice and Support*, 185.

19. Department of State, *Foreign Relations of the United States, 1952–1954*, vol. XIII, *Indochina*, 1358, 1600; William B. Rosson, "Four Periods of American Involvement in Vietnam: Development and Implementation of Policy, Strategy and Programs, Described and Analyzed on the Basis of Service Experience at Progressively Senior Levels" (Ph.D. diss., Oxford University, 1979), 62.

20. Department of the Army, *Command and Control*, 9–10; Department of State, *Foreign Relations of the United States, 1952–1954*, vol. XIII, *Indochina*, 1885; Rosson, "Four Periods of American Involvement in Vietnam," 63.

21. Department of State, *Foreign Relations of the United States, 1952–1954*, vol. XIII, *Indochina*, 1938–1939, 2089.

22. *Pentagon Papers*, vol. I, 216.

23. Spector, *Advice and Support*, 233; Stanley Karnow, *Vietnam: A History* (New York: Viking Press, 1983), 187, 219.

24. Edward G. Lansdale, *In the Midst of Wars: An American's Mission to Southeast Asia* (New York: Harper & Row, 1972), 172.

25. *Pentagon Papers*, vol. I, 219.

26. Although originally willing to allow Hinh to challenge Diem, the French finally submitted to American wishes and agreed to support Diem. Spector, *Advice and Support*, 237.

27. Department of State, *Foreign Relations of the United States, 1952–1954*, vol. XIII, *Indochina*, 2138.

28. Ibid., 2156–2157, 2161.

29. Ibid., 2366–2368, 2252; Department of State, *Foreign Relations of the United States, 1955–1957*, vol. I, *Vietnam* (Washington, D.C.: U.S. Government Printing Office, 1985), 31, 84–86.

30. Department of the Army, *The U.S. Adviser* by Cao Van Vien et al., Indochina Monographs (Washington, D.C.: U.S. Center of Military History, 1980), 3, 199. Because of the shortage of officers, the Americans did not replace the departing French in the TRIM as quickly as the MAAG would have liked. As a result, Vietnamese officers

trained in French methods filled the vacancies, making it more difficult for the Americans to supplant completely French doctrine with their own. Rosson, "Four Periods of American Involvement in Vietnam," 88.

31. Department of the Army, *The U.S. Adviser*, 199–200.

32. Spector, *Advice and Support*, 252; Rosson, "Four Periods of American Involvement in Vietnam," 87; Department of the Army, *Command and Control*, 12; General Orders Number 6, Headquarters, Military Assistance Advisory Group, Vietnam, subject: Redesignation of Unit, 1 November 1955 (box 1, general orders, AGD/MAAGV/RG 334). The inactivation of the French headquarters on 28 April 1956 also resulted in the dissolution of the TRIM and its reorganization as the Combat Arms Training and Organization Division (CATO) the following day. General Orders Number 1, Headquarters, Military Assistance Advisory Group, Vietnam, subject: Reorganization, 28 April 1956 (box 1, general orders, AGD/MAAGV/RG 334).

33. Spector, *Advice and Support*, 243.

34. *Pentagon Papers*, vol. I, 293–295; Department of State, *Foreign Relations of the United States, 1952–1954*, vol. XIII, *Indochina*, 1450.

35. *Pentagon Papers*, vol. I, 231–234, 303.

36. Ibid.; Department of State, *Foreign Relations of the United States, 1955–1957*, vol. I, *Vietnam*, 432, 511.

37. *Pentagon Papers*, vol. I, 298.

38. Department of the Army, *The Development and Training of the South Vietnamese Army* by James Collins, Vietnam Studies (Washington, D.C.: U.S. Government Printing Office, 1975), 9.

39. Ibid., 4–6.

40. Department of State, *Foreign Relations of the United States, 1955–1957*, vol. I, *Vietnam*, 52.

41. Ibid., 617–618.

42. This total of 692 included both the MAAG authorization (342) and the TERM authorization (350). Ibid., 640, 669–671.

43. Spector, *Advice and Support*, 261–262. Wishing to keep the dissolution of the TERM as quiet as possible, the MAAG's chief of staff directed his subordinates in April 1960 to brief their personnel that "[t]he facts that MAAG is being increased from 342 to 685 personnel and that the TERM is being phased out during 1960 will remain classified for the present. . . . The *manner* of the phase-out of TERM and the *manner* in which personnel are being added to MAAG by transfer from TERM will remain classified indefinitely" (emphasis in the original). Memo, Nathaniel P. Ward, III, Chief of Staff, to All Division Chiefs and Chief TERM, subject: Reorganization of MAAG, 4 April 1960 (box 2, memorandums, AGD/MAAGV/RG 334).

44. Thomas Hodgkin, *Vietnam: The Revolutionary Path* (New York: St. Martin's Press, 1981), 319–320.

45. Department of the Army, *U.S. Army Area Handbook for Vietnam* by George Harris et al., Pamphlet 550-40, rev. ed. (Washington, D.C.: U.S. Government Printing Office, 1964), 319; Le Hong Linh et al., *Ap Bac: Major Victories of the South Vietnamese Patriotic Forces in 1963 and 1964* (Hanoi: Foreign Languages Publishing House, 1965), 15.

46. Groups 559 and 759 were so named because of their organization dates—559 for the fifth month, 1959; 759 for the seventh month, 1959. Cecil B. Currey, *Victory at Any Cost: The Genius of Viet Nam's General Vo Nguyen Giap* (Washington, D.C.: Brassey's, 1997), 233–235.

47. Stephen Young, "How North Vietnam Won the War," *Wall Street Journal* (3 August 1995).

48. In 1945, Ho Chi Minh disbanded the Indochinese Communist Party, only to resurrect it in 1951 as the *Dang Lao Dong Viet Nam* (Vietnam Worker's Party), or Lao Dong. Douglas Pike, *Viet Cong* (Cambridge: MIT Press, 1966), 43, 137; Robert K. Brigham, *Guerrilla Diplomacy: The NLF's Foreign Relations and the Viet Nam War* (Ithaca, NY: Cornell University Press, 1999), 2–3.

49. The Congressional Research Service attributed the assassination of 400 minor GVN officials to the PLAF during 1957. Congressional Research Service, *U.S. Policy Toward Vietnam: A Summary Review of its History* by Ellen Collier et al. (Washington, D.C.: Library of Congress, 1972), 32 (folder 3, box 1, unit 2, Douglas Pike Collection, Vietnam Archive [hereafter DPC]); Department of the Army, *U.S. Army Area Handbook for Vietnam*, 320.

50. Department of State, *Foreign Relations of the United States, 1958–1960*, vol. I, *Vietnam* (Washington, D.C.: U.S. Government Printing Office, 1986), 320–321.

51. Ibid., 220; "Red Terrorists Kill Major and Sergeant—Captain Hit in Attack During Movie," *New York Times* (10 July 1959).

52. Department of State, *Foreign Relations of the United States, 1958–1960*, vol. I, Vietnam, 303.

53. Ibid., 343.

54. Ibid., 296.

55. Lieutenant General Samuel T. Williams, Saigon, Republic of Vietnam, to Major General Samuel L. Myers, Washington, D.C., 20 March 1960 (folder 6, box 2, Samuel T. Williams Papers, U.S. Army Military History Institute).

56. Department of State, *Foreign Relations of the United States, 1958–1960*, vol. I, *Vietnam*, 544.

57. The accords ceiling of 888 was the sum of both American and French advisors present in Vietnam in July 1954. Williams's rationale was that since the French were no longer present, their last advisors having left in late 1957, an increase in the MAAG was warranted. Department of the Army, *Command and Control*, 15. Official notification of the increase followed on 1 June and emphasized the primary role of the U.S. Army in the advisory effort. Of the 685 authorized advisors, almost three-quarters (508) were soldiers. General Orders Number 24, Headquarters, Military Assistance Advisory Group, Vietnam, subject: Reorganization of Military Assistance Advisory Group, Vietnam, 1 June 1960 (box 1, general orders, AGD/MAAGV/RG 334).

58. Department of State, *Foreign Relations of the United States, 1961–1963*, vol. I, *Vietnam, 1961* (Washington, D.C.: U.S. Government Printing Office, 1988), 297.

59. Ibid., 292.

60. Ibid., 305–306.

61. Ibid., 481.

62. Ibid., 679, 739.

63. Ibid., 740, 745.

64. Ibid., 702.

65. Ibid., 746.

66. Department of State, *Foreign Relations of the United States, 1961–1963*, vol. II, *Vietnam, 1962* (Washington, D.C.: U.S. Government Printing Office, 1990), 4; Department of the Army, *Command and Control*, 23.

67. Department of the Army, *Command and Control*, 23, 28–29; United States Information Service, Release P-22-62 (folder 9, box 2, unit 1, DPC); Department of State, *Foreign Relations of the United States, 1961–1963*, vol. II, *Vietnam, 1962*, 112.

68. Department of the Army, *Command and Control*, 29, 35.

69. Ibid., 29.

70. Ibid., 28–30, 38–39.

71. Department of State, *Foreign Relations of the United States, 1961–1963*, vol. III, *Vietnam, January–August 1963* (Washington, D.C.: U.S. Government Printing Office, 1991), 11.

72. Terence Maitland et al., *Raising the Stakes*, the Vietnam Experience (Boston: Boston Publishing Company, 1982), 14.

73. "American Killed in Vietnam Clash," *New York Times* (5 October 1962); United States Information Service, Release P-139-62 (folder 16, box 2, unit 2, DPC).

2

The Belligerents

It is our clear impression that, by and large, training and equipment of
the Vietnamese Armed Forces are still too heavily weighted toward
conventional military operations.[1]

Taylor Report
3 November 1961

Influenced by opposing doctrinal forces, the ARVN and the PLAF espoused
different conceptions of how to prosecute the war in South Vietnam. Steeped in
the traditions of victory through conventional war, U.S. advisors consistently
taught and encouraged the ARVN to employ strictly military strategies and
tactics. Although the MAAG began to dabble in counterinsurgency by the early
1960s, most senior advisors remained committed to defeating the PLAF through
conventional military operations. It is not surprising then that the ARVN closely
mirrored the U.S. Army, a conventionally oriented force, in doctrine, strategy,
tactics, and organization.

The PLAF, on the other hand, sought from the beginning to defeat the
ARVN through a combination of political and military means. The cadres'
experiences during the First Indochina War taught them that a military victory
without a corresponding success among the people was hollow. As a result, the
PLAF embraced a revolutionary doctrine, with a resulting unconventional
approach to strategy, tactics, and organization. Ap Bac not only demonstrated
the strengths and weaknesses of each belligerent's conception of warfare, but
also provided an indication of how each would continue to fight the Second
Indochina War.

THE ARMY OF THE REPUBLIC OF VIETNAM

Put simply, doctrine is how an army plans to fight. An army's doctrine is
influenced by its heritage, perceived role, recent experiences, and how it either
wants or expects to fight its next war. Doctrine influences all aspects of an army,
from how it trains to what it wears, and the U.S. Army is no exception to this
generalization. The U.S. Army's capstone document, Field Manual (FM) 100-5,

Operations, establishes the framework for all other documents and activities it produces or undertakes. As such, an examination of FM 100-5 provides an insight into the thoughts and actions of the U.S. advisors from 1954 to 1963 and how the MAAG envisioned the ARVN should prosecute the war and how it should be organized.

Without question, the U.S. Army of the late 1950s and early 1960s was an army imbued with an offensive and conventional nature.[2] After a major revision in September 1954 that incorporated the U.S. Army's perceived conventional warfare lessons from Korea, *Operations* received only minor changes in December 1954 (Change 1), July 1956 (Change 2), and January 1958 (Change 3). *Operations* was reissued in February 1962 to reflect innovations in technology and warfare, but it is similar in many respects to its 1954 predecessor.[3] Both the 1954 and 1962 versions, which the American advisors used as their doctrinal reference points, clearly embodied a traditional, conventional attitude.

The 1962 version of *Operations*, the governing edition during the Battle of Ap Bac, began its chapter on operational concepts with the principles of war, which were nine general axioms believed to govern the conduct of warfare. Listing the first as the "Principle of the Objective," the manual stated that "[t]he ultimate military objective of war is the destruction of the enemy's armed forces and his will to fight. The objective of each operation must contribute to this ultimate objective." In quite direct terms, *Operations* emphasized that the focus of any war should be the enemy's forces. Immediately thereafter, the "Principle of the Offensive" directed that "[o]ffensive action is necessary to achieve decisive results and to maintain freedom of action."[4] While it is preferable for a commander to maintain the initiative in any operation, conventional or unconventional, the principles of objective and offensive, when taken together, seemed to run counter to the precepts of a counterinsurgency. Instead of focusing the U.S. Army's efforts on maintaining the people's loyalties, they emphasized the urgency in aggressively targeting and destroying the enemy forces.

Although the U.S. Army was advising and organizing a force that was combating an insurgency, the 1954 version of *Operations* contained barely two pages of text devoted to defeating guerrillas.[5] Recognizing the recent innovations in warfare brought about by technology and the Soviet Union's promised "wars of national liberation," the 1962 edition of *Operations* expanded to include a new chapter on airmobile operations and a broader chapter on irregular warfare. While this latter chapter seemed to speak to the situation in Southeast Asia, it did little to provide authoritative or specific guidance to the American advisors in the field. Entitled "Military Operations against Irregular Forces," the chapter failed to mention the term "counterinsurgency," instead using the term "irregular" to "refer to all types of nonconventional forces and operations." In describing these operations, the manual suggested the "fundamental cause" of irregular activity was the populace's dissatisfaction "with the political, social, and economic conditions prevalent in the area." While acknowledging that irregular forces possessed both overt guerrilla and covert subversive elements, the chapter did little to describe what type of political activity other than propaganda these elements might undertake.[6]

Surprisingly, FM 100-5 conceded that "[i]mmediate decisive results of operations against irregular forces can seldom be observed," but the warning seemed to carry little weight and did not echo the overall tenor of the chapter. In the next section, the manual instructed its readers that "[o]perations to suppress and eliminate irregular forces are primarily offensive in nature. Thus, the conventional force must plan for and seize the initiative at the outset and retain it throughout the conduct of the operation."[7] This latter emphasis on seizing the initiative effectively nullified the earlier section's caution about maintaining tactical patience and not expecting immediate results against insurgents.

Operations recommended defeating irregular forces through continuous small-unit actions focused on destroying the guerrillas. Although insightfully recognizing that "[t]he irregular force itself is usually a result and not the cause of the problem . . . [and its] destruction . . . normally does not provide a complete solution," the manual did not offer any specific suggestions as to how best to gain the people's support.[8] This dearth of information about how best to enlist the populace's support lay at the heart of the Americans' doctrinal difficulties in Vietnam. The U.S. Army's focus during operations against irregular forces, as described by its capstone manual FM 100-5, was clearly upon the destruction of the armed guerrilla forces. Despite the intimation that elimination of the guerrillas might not solve a country's problems, *Operations*, with its aggressively offensive nature, pointed the advisors squarely at the PLAF guerrillas as their objective and not the South Vietnamese people.

This offensively oriented doctrine made perfect sense to the U.S. Army in 1962. Its primary focus was upon defending Western Europe and fighting, if necessary, the Red Army that lay waiting for it behind the Iron Curtain. To devote a significant portion of *Operations* to counterinsurgency warfare simply did not make sense, particularly since it had an entire manual devoted to this type of warfare, FM 31-15, *Operations against Irregular Forces*. Published in May 1961, FM 31-15 provided advisors with 47 pages of text and diagrams related to conducting operations against irregular forces and organizing friendly forces. Like FM 100-5, however, FM 31-15 did not use the term "counterinsurgency," instead relying upon the familiar all-inclusive term "irregular." *Operations against Irregular Forces* did expound on certain topics that *Operations* did not, but even then the discussion offered little specificity. In the section devoted to "Civic Action," FM 31-15 offered only five paragraphs about the subject and made clear the secondary role that civic projects played in defeating irregular forces. While encouraging commanders "to participate in local civic action projects," the manual specified that they were only to do so "whenever such participation *does not seriously detract from accomplishment of their primary mission*" (emphasis added), namely the destruction of the guerrillas. The primary responsibility of civic action, according to FM 31-15, lay with civil affairs and not combat units.[9] As such, the logical conclusion for the American advisor in Vietnam was that the mission of the combat forces, in this case the ARVN, was to target and destroy the guerrilla forces in the field; civic or political action was not a primary component of the ARVN's mission.

The Americans' manuals were not the only documents to encourage the South Vietnamese to focus upon the PLAF's destruction. Beginning in March 1962, the MAAG's U.S. Army Section (USASEC) began publishing a series of memoranda entitled "Lessons Learned" that were intended to provide "information and guidance."[10] A consistent theme running through these short 1962 papers concerned the necessity of aggressive, offensive action against the enemy guerrillas. In many instances, according to the memoranda, the ARVN had made contact with the PLAF only to allow it to escape, thus causing the advisors to consider those particular operations either "partially successful" or "unsuccessful."[11] To illustrate the importance of destroying the enemy, one memorandum cited an ARVN unit that had made contact with an enemy platoon but halted the pursuit when it reached its terrain objective, thus allowing the PLAF to escape. In commenting on this tendency, "Lessons Learned Number 9" noted that "[i]n counter-insurgency operations the capture of ground objectives does not contribute to the attainment of the mission. *The VC should be the primary objective of counter-insurgency operations* rather than a piece of real estate. . . . Once . . . contact is made, the mission becomes one of destruction" (emphasis added).[12] Even through informal channels, the American advisors clearly saw their efforts directed toward training and advising the RVNAF to attrit the PLAF's numbers.

The U.S. Army was not completely unaware of its doctrinal shortcomings with regard to this subject. As a result of President Kennedy's increased emphasis on developing counterinsurgency units and techniques, the U.S. Army began working on a new manual in 1962 to address some of the questions left unanswered by FM 31-15. As the authors struggled with this new manual, the editor of *Infantry* published sections of it to spur input from the field.[13] The resulting product was FM 31-16, *Counterguerrilla Operations*, published in February 1963. Although published after Ap Bac, this manual reflected the prevailing doctrinal beliefs of the U.S. Army for that time period. FM 31-16 was more than twice the length of FM 31-15 and served more as a supplement to the latter than a replacement. Unlike its predecessors, *Counterguerrilla Operations* more fully acknowledged the role of the civilian populace through its definition of terms. While continuing to identify a "guerrilla force" and a "resistance movement" (formerly the "underground" of FMs 31-15 and 100-5), the new manual introduced the definition of "civilian support" as "[t]he comparatively unorganized body of disaffected civilians which provides continuous support to the more organized elements of the resistance movement." Through this definition, the manual tacitly acknowledged the importance of the civilian populace in defeating a "resistance movement."[14]

Beyond these opening comments, FM 31-16, like its contemporary manuals, provided little guidance besides tactics and techniques for conducting combat operations against guerrillas. Nowhere did the manual address the term counterinsurgency, nor was there any detailed discussion of civic or political action. Given that FM 31-16's proponent was the U.S. Army Infantry School, and not the U.S. Army Special Warfare Center that was responsible for developing counterinsurgency doctrine, the manual's conventional orientation of closing with and destroying the enemy guerrillas should not be a surprise.[15] Despite the growing insurgency in South Vietnam, the U.S. Army was unable to provide its advisors with a manual that distinguished between counterguerrilla operations (small unit operations focused on militarily destroying guerrilla units) and counterinsurgency operations (operations involving both military and political means to defeat an insurgency).[16] As a result, American advisors in Vietnam, in keeping with their doctrinal references, focused the ARVN on destroying the PLAF in the field.

As the agents of doctrinal transmission, the American advisors played a key role in the development of the ARVN, but how they fit into the South Vietnamese efforts was a consistently troubling subject for both military and civilian leaders, American and Vietnamese alike. With the establishment of the TRIM in 1955, Americans began to have a direct impact on the ARVN. How direct those effects needed to be, however, changed as the American presence in Southeast Asia increased. As late as 1959, the MAAGV and CINCPAC still believed that an advisory role was best accomplished at Vietnamese higher headquarters. General Williams felt that an advisor's duties included taking to the field with the headquarters he advised, offering assistance in tactical and logistical questions, and submitting training equipment requests. At no time, however, was the advisor to accompany small units in combat: "It has never been my intent to suggest that advisors accompany attacking units or get into firefights."[17] To Williams, the prosecution of combat was best left to Vietnamese officers and NCOs.

Attempting to codify the advisor's role, Admiral Felt issued a directive to Williams on 25 May 1959, ordering that "[t]he activities of MAAG Advisors must be limited to advisory functions and *under no circumstances shall they participate directly in combat operations* nor will they accompany units on anti-guerrilla operations in areas immediately adjacent to national boundaries" (emphasis added). In quite direct terms, CINCPAC echoed Williams's earlier sentiments and directed that American advisors not take part in combat actions with the South Vietnamese. Yet in the very same cable, Felt also ordered the MAAG to "[p]rovide MAAG Advisors down to and including Infantry Regiment level and Artillery, Armored and separate Marine Battalion level," effectively nullifying the proscription of combat involvement by authorizing Americans below the divisional level of command.[18] This increase of advisors, coupled with the growing PLAF activity in 1960 and 1961, contributed to the tendency of American advisors to accompany small units in combat. Wishing to support the MAAG's desire for increased ARVN combat operations, the advisors took to the field in an attempt to stimulate South Vietnamese aggressiveness.

This movement of Americans closer to combat had unintended side effects. Arguably, members of the MAAG at the lower levels were crossing the line from "advisor" to "fighter," particularly since many ARVN commanders considered their advisors to be their deputies. This perceived change in status may have contributed to the guerrilla attack on the 7th Division Advisory Detachment at Bien Hoa in July. With Americans taking a more active role in the war, the insurgents most likely believed that the advisors were worthwhile targets.[19]

Worse, with advisors appearing at the smaller unit level, tensions between Vietnamese and Americans often increased. Assigned to Vietnam for only a year, the Americans had a short period of time in which to make tangible gains in their areas. As a result, many tended to become impatient with what they considered the ARVN commanders' "seemingly sluggish approach" to the task at hand. Advisors often inundated their counterparts with recommendations and lists of improvements, many times frustrating the Vietnamese officers. Compounding this problem was the lack of experience among the advisors. Most ARVN commanders had already seen a fair amount of combat; the majority of American company grade officers, on the other hand, had not seen any combat unless they were Korean War veterans. In many cases, ARVN commanders could not help but feel that a junior American captain or first lieutenant with almost no combat experience had little to offer them in the way of worthwhile advice.[20]

As the number of air assets increased, however, most Vietnamese commanders were happy to have an American present since the advisor was the direct link to close air support. Of course, the increased firepower brought its own set of problems, not the least of which was the perception that American airpower, controlled by the advisor, was the key to success in the field, rather than disciplined, trained leaders and soldiers. As American advisors and assets played a larger role at the tactical level, the ARVN dependence upon them increased. Consequently, the opportunities for Vietnamese commanders to develop initiative and prestige in the field decreased. In short, instead of increasing the ARVN's effectiveness and encouraging its development, the U.S. Army unwittingly "produced over-reliance and sometimes total dependence on US advisors," effectively undercutting their purpose for being in Vietnam.[21]

American advisors assumed their positions with little training in advising or Vietnamese language and culture. There was no formal schooling for advisors until January 1962, when the U.S. Army Special Warfare Center at Fort Bragg, North Carolina, established the Military Assistance Training Advisors (MATA) Course. A four-week program, it addressed recent counterinsurgency operations in Greece and Malaya but offered no instruction on Indochina. Focusing primarily upon conventional infantry tactics, the course offered little in the way of Vietnamese language or culture, and its early iterations suffered from a lack of qualified language instructors. Despite the programmed 25 to 30 hours of language instruction, advisors learned little conversational Vietnamese, usually gaining their insights about their counterparts' culture and language only after arriving in Vietnam. Some advisors were lucky enough to attend a nine-week language course at the Defense Language Institute at Monterrey, California, but they were a clear minority. Difficulties in communicating with the Vietnamese, however, were not insurmountable. Since many ARVN officers spoke French, the U.S. Army could have easily trained many of its advisors in this language, but inexplicably it did not, adversely affecting their ability to communicate with those they were to assist.[22]

At the same time, however, if one considers the U.S. Army's greater view of the world, the lack of cultural and language training does seem to make a certain amount of sense. In its view, cultural and linguistic proficiency were not the most important skills an American advisor needed to pass along tactical wisdom. As long as he possessed the requisite motivation, technical, and tactical skills to advise the ARVN on how best to close with and destroy the enemy guerrillas, the advisor would achieve his purpose. With the increased influx of American personnel and equipment, many believed that the insurgency would be quickly over, just as it had been against the North Korean guerrillas some ten years before. Once the GVN had its insurgency under control, the Americans could get back to the serious business of defending Europe. In an already fiscally constrained environment, the U.S. Army simply did not see any long-term gains in training Vietnamese experts who would soon find themselves out of a job, choosing instead to rely upon all-purpose, motivated combat arms officers and NCOs to bring about success in Southeast Asia.

Although perhaps lacking in some respects, the officer and NCO advisors were highly trained professionals in conventional tactics. Responding to President Kennedy's call for volunteers to serve as advisors in Vietnam, many answered their commander in chief's request. While Washington ordered officers and NCOs to Vietnam, the MAAG actually assigned them to advisory duty with ARVN units, usually after they had served at the MAAG for a period of time.[23] These soldiers served with distinction, causing a visiting State Department observer to note that "[t]he quality of our people in the field is high. . . . [T]he lower ranking officers, from lieutenant to major, are proving themselves adaptable and imaginative." Roger Hilsman, the State Department's director of intelligence and research and a veteran of the China-Burma-India theater of World War II, was even more direct by noting that "what is really saving us out here is the high quality of the sergeants, lieutenants, and captains."[24]

Being a professional soldier, however, did not necessarily equate to being a suitable advisor because, as one former advisor observed, "[a]djusting to advising is a greater individual challenge than can be easily imagined by anyone who has not tried it. . . . Skill in advising is a reflection of one's own ability to influence other individuals."[25] Having no formal command authority, the advisor could only make suggestions to his counterpart; he could cajole, plead, or beg, but the decision ultimately fell to the unit commander. In essence, the advisor had no real leverage over his counterpart other than personal persuasion.[26] This command relationship, or more accurately, the lack thereof, was a source of constant friction between the Americans and South Vietnamese.

Further complicating the advisor's role was that although he had no authority, the MAAG held him responsible for his unit's performance. Just as General Marshall had asked of General Stilwell's headquarters some twenty years before, the chain of command, which included the MAAG, CINCPAC, the JCS, and the executive branch, expected the advisors to maintain a positive outlook. The senior leadership encouraged advisors to cast the best possible light on their units. Reporting unsavory, yet truthful facts became known as "negativism."[27] Because the MAAG and, later, MACV required positive reports, what they received was what they expected of the advisors: upbeat, yet "truthful" reports. Since most advisors were professionals and wished to make the U.S. Army their career, few were willing to address their units' problems directly in their monthly reports.

Although the advisors did not actually deceive their higher command, their emphasis on the positive aspects tended to cloud over the more troubling difficulties of the ARVN. One advisor, in describing this indirect pressure, made the connection between progress and advancement quite clear: "There was pressure for good reports. I don't mean that it was said, 'I want you to report good.' But it's very obvious that you've [the subordinate] got to show some progress or I'm [the higher commander] going to take you out of your position." More telling, as another former advisor pointed out, was the simple fact that a general officer can resign in protest and look forward to retirement pay; a company grade officer who resigns can look forward to the unemployment line, a reality that most likely remained in the back of most junior officers' minds.[28]

The difficulties the advisors faced with the Vietnamese often bred what David Halberstam called the "Asian reality."[29] A type of cynicism, the "Asian reality" caused the advisors to realize the truth in Rudyard Kipling's warning that

> It is not good for the Christian's health
>   to hustle the Asian brown,
> for the Christian riles and the Asian smiles
>   and he weareth the Christian down.[30]

Yet the Americans approached their task with a sense of humor and commitment.[31] Completely defeating totalitarian regimes twenty years earlier, maintaining Korean safety only ten years earlier, and embodying the Kennedy "can-do spirit," American advisors sought to superimpose their way of conducting war on the Vietnamese. Confident of the righteousness of their cause and of ultimate victory, the advisors sought to steer the ARVN to victory.

American advisors initially remained at higher ARVN command levels. As described earlier, the MAAG maintained advisors at the army, corps, division, and regimental levels in 1959. Additional advisors oversaw the artillery and tank battalions.[32] With the change of American presidents in early 1961, advisors continued to work their way down to the smaller unit level. Shortly after Kennedy's inauguration, advisors appeared in infantry battalions and armor companies, since these were the smallest ARVN combat units to operate independently. Not surprisingly, by the following year the number of advisors had increased significantly to more than 3,000. From the ARVN general staff level to the regimental level, the advisory detachment contained a senior advisor and a staff to mirror the ARVN staff. At the battalion level, two company grade officers (a captain and a lieutenant) and an NCO composed the advisory team.

Beginning in 1962, 36 of the 43 Vietnamese provinces also received advisory teams consisting of a field grade senior advisor, an intelligence NCO, a light weapons advisor, an administration specialist, a communications specialist, and a medical specialist.[33] As more advisors appeared at the lower unit levels, the character of ARVN operations increasingly reflected American doctrine, at least on the surface.

Doctrine was not the only influence to color the Americans' perspective; their previous experiences also played a role in how they envisioned what the ARVN should accomplish. Some advisors had World War II experience; many more had experience fighting the North Koreans and Chinese in Korea. Major General Thomas Trapnell, the second CHMAAG, exemplified the type of soldiers sent to the MAAG in Vietnam. Commissioned as a cavalry officer, Trapnell held various command and staff positions before World War II. Surviving the Bataan Death March and his imprisonment by the Japanese, he commanded the 505th Parachute Infantry Regiment and the 187th Regimental Combat Team before assuming command of the MAAG. Perhaps as a result of having witnessed the Japanese invasion of the Philippines firsthand and his experiences in Korea, Trapnell firmly believed that the greatest threat to South Vietnam's security lay in the potential invasion from the north. Arguing for a "Korea model" upon which to base a reorganization of the VNA, Trapnell consistently reminded his staff to "remember the lessons of Korea."[34]

General O'Daniel, Trapnell's successor and also a World War II and Korea veteran, matched his predecessor in both previous experiences and future outlook toward the VNA. While visiting Indochina in early 1953 as CINCUSARPAC, O'Daniel seemed perplexed by French explanations of why pacification of the countryside was so difficult. His response to those briefing him was direct, in keeping with his personality. Dismissing their concerns, O'Daniel responded that the U.S. did not have the same difficulties with pacification in Korea, clearly intimating that the French could stand to learn from the American experiences with the North Korean guerrillas. This overgeneralization caused the American chargé, Robert McClintock, to comment that the general "conceive[d] of the war in Indochina largely in terms of the war in Korea," a tendency that was not lost on Ambassador Heath. Shortly after O'Daniel's assumption of command as CHMAAG the following year, Heath, while "lik[ing] him as an individual and admir[ing] him as a soldier . . . [did] not value him as a military advisor for the strategic and tactical conduct of this particular war," a judgment based upon O'Daniel's statements during his previous four visits to Indochina. In Heath's final analysis, "Iron Mike" did not stand a "good" chance of helping French efforts against the Viet Minh because of the general's attempts to apply his experiences in Korea to Southeast Asia.[35]

The senior French leadership in the region also echoed its doubts about O'Daniel's ability to provide valuable advice concerning its conduct of the war. General Navarre, the French commander in Indochina, while also "personally liking" O'Daniel, expressed his reservations about the CHMAAG's knowledge of how to fight an insurgency. Navarre spoke to Heath of his "very low opinion of O'Daniel's understanding of the peculiar problems of this war and of his solutions for overcoming them." At the heart of this matter lay O'Daniel's tendency to bombard the French with "annoying" solutions to their problems, from immediately undertaking an all-out offensive against the Viet Minh to reorganizing the VNA. To the CHMAAG, far too many army units, both French and Vietnamese, were conducting pacification operations instead of offensively seeking out and destroying the Viet Minh. The solution, O'Daniel believed, was to use the paramilitary organizations for providing internal security against the sporadic violence in the countryside, freeing up the regular army units for conventional combat operations, a course of action one might expect to find in an American field manual.[36]

This tendency to oversimplify Vietnam's political and military complexity and look back to Korea for inspiration continued with O'Daniel's successor, Lieutenant General Samuel T. Williams. Despite the National Intelligence Estimate of 17 July 1956, which stated that "[w]e believe that the Communist 'Democratic Republic of Vietnam' [DRV] will not attempt an open invasion of South Vietnam . . . during the period of the estimate," Williams continued to organize, equip, and train the ARVN along the lines of a conventional army.[37] True to their experiences, the Americans looked to their immediate martial past to bring success to the South Vietnamese, a past that did not even remotely resemble the realities of Indochina.

Despite the intelligence reports that the DRV was more concerned with focusing inward and the rising number of violent incidents in the South Vietnamese countryside, the MAAG focused the ARVN's training efforts toward repelling a conventional invasion. Almost a full year after the National Intelligence Estimate discounted an invasion by the DRV, the ARVN's 1st Field Division prepared for a four-phased unit field exercise. Once deployed to its positions, the division was to screen another division's withdrawal and conduct a delay to another defensive position. Once in the defense, the division was to improve its defense and prepare to conduct an attack. After the unit's preparations and before actually conducting an attack, the American advisors were scheduled to conduct a critique of the 1st Division's performance. At no time was the division scheduled to attack, nor was there any time allotted for training or evaluating domestic security tasks.[38] Quite clearly, the scenario driving the division's exercise might well have been conducted on the Korean peninsula five or six years earlier while facing either the North Korean or Chinese offensives. Worse, as one ARVN commander later observed, not only were these large scale exercises "irrelevant but they diverted the troops from active combat responsibilities," a genuine concern given the increasing number of incidents in the South Vietnamese countryside.[39] Organization and training to repel a conventional invasion was certainly the MAAG's focus for its client the ARVN, regardless of the political realities in North Vietnam or in the South Vietnamese countryside.

The MAAG's attempts to train and organize a thoroughly conventional army continued through the next two years, but by early 1960, Diem began to resist the MAAG's efforts. Perhaps realizing that a force trained and organized along conventional lines could not defeat the insurgency or possibly resenting the rumors that he submitted to every American recommendation, Diem suggested including counterguerrilla training in the MAAG's scheduled program. The president was not alone in his concerns. Some senior ARVN commanders later commented that

[t]he nature and purpose of . . . [the American] training effort . . . was purely conventional; it did not help combat units cope with the unconventional requirements of counterinsurgency warfare and fight it effectively. Many unit commanders in effect complained of having to "learn one way and practice another way." Naturally, U.S. Army doctrine and field manuals served as the guide and yardstick in developing ARVN combat capabilities.[40]

Whether out of self-interest or true concern for domestic tranquility, the GVN's senior leadership was clearly reaching its limits of tolerance toward American training efforts.

What ensued over the next several months was a running debate between the CHMAAG, General Williams; Ambassador Elbridge Durbrow; and Diem over the focus of the ARVN. In a February 1960 conversation, Diem expressed to Durbrow his concern about the growing number of PLAF incidents and had come to the conclusion that "he now believed [that] too much attention had been given to training the ARVN along conventional lines." A visiting Central Intelligence Agency official concurred with Diem's observation. In summarizing his visit, Sherman Kent, the assistant director of intelligence for national estimates, wrote that the ARVN's training focus was incorrect; instead of training for the insurgency contingencies of the recent intelligence estimates, the ARVN was conducting division and corps maneuvers more suitable for a conventional invasion, just as it had in previous years.[41]

State Department officials were not the only ones to express a desire to reorient the MAAG's training program for the ARVN. After a visit to Vietnam in March 1960, General Lyman L. Lemnitzer, the U.S. Army chief of staff, submitted a report to the JCS concerning the ARVN's training orientation. His concern was that the ARVN was lacking training in counterguerrilla tactics, a belief shared by CINCPAC. Both suggested that "an anti-guerrilla capability can be developed within the regular armed forces by changing the emphasis in the training of selected elements of the Vietnamese Army and other security forces from conventional to anti-guerrilla warfare." The report went on to recommend that the best means to this end was the introduction to Vietnam of selected U.S. Army Special Forces, psychological warfare, civil affairs, and intelligence and counterintelligence teams.[42] In essence, Lemnitzer's recommendations intimated that perhaps Williams's strictly conventional approach to the situation in Vietnam might not be the most appropriate.

General Williams placed little stock in the expected gains from changing the South Vietnamese training focus. He firmly believed that the ARVN's difficulty lay not in the type of training but in its poor training or complete lack thereof. In a response to Tran Trung Dung, the GVN's assistant secretary of national defense, the CHMAAG dismissed the importance of antiguerrilla training: "As you will know, it is an established military fact that well trained soldiers, with good leadership and sound plans can successfully fight any kind of enemy on any kind of terrain." In Williams's estimate, the ARVN's poor performance was a direct result of not preparing its soldiers for war: "In too many cases little or no worthwhile training of any kind is being done. . . . Typical demands cited [for not training] are for security operations, guard, housing construction, and ceremonies [rather than individual or collective military training]."[43] The CHMAAG's response illustrates the dichotomy between the U.S. Army's doctrine and the war it was preparing the ARVN to fight. A conventional soldier, Williams expected large ARVN units to defeat a DRV invasion in the field. By intimating that "security operations, guard, [and] housing construction" were detracting from the ARVN's overall effectiveness, he demonstrated his complete misunderstanding of the situation in South Vietnam and his disregard for the importance of civic action among the people. In short, an army's focus was the enemy; everything else, which included winning the support of the people and building their confidence in the central government, was secondary.

Despite the CHMAAG's reservations, Lemnitzer's report did have some effect upon the MAAG. In response to the U.S. Army chief's concerns, the MAAG submitted to CINCPAC a plan for conducting antiguerrilla training at the beginning of April 1960. Requiring three ten man Special Forces teams, two or three counterintelligence instructors, and two or three psychological operations specialists, the program proposed to train the senior ARVN leadership in how guerrillas fight and how best to combat them. By the following month, 30 Special Forces soldiers began training Diem's newly formed ARVN ranger companies at Nha Trang, Da Nang, and Song Mao. The MAAG's new effort in offering the ARVN unconventional training, however, was shallow at best. Relying upon a "train the trainer" concept in which selected individuals attended the training and then returned to their units, it did not directly affect the individual ARVN soldier. As originally briefed, the antiguerrilla program only envisioned training approximately 2,000 ARVN leaders, less than 2% of the South Vietnamese army's end strength, and suggested the true level of the MAAG's interest in training for unconventional warfare.[44]

The use of Special Forces soldiers to train the ARVN was not without precedent. In 1957, two officers and ten NCOs from Okinawa's recently organized 14th Special Forces Detachment, 1st Special Forces Group, conducted training exercises for 58 ARVN soldiers at Nha Trang's Commando Training Center through the summer and early fall. This deployment, like the later iteration in 1960, contributed little to the overall American training effort, but it earned the unfortunate distinction of resulting in the first death of a Special Forces soldier in Vietnam. Near the end of the scheduled training period, Captain Harry G. Cramer died as a result of injuries suffered during a training accident on 21 October 1957, almost four months after America's first deaths to guerrilla activity at Bien Hoa.[45]

Despite Lemnitzer's intimation that the CHMAAG's training focus was not completely appropriate for Vietnam, this is not to say that the U.S. Army chief was significantly closer to being correct in his recommendation that there be an increase in "anti-guerrilla" training for the ARVN. As discussed earlier, counterguerrilla operations, as the U.S. Army understood them, focused upon destroying guerrillas primarily through small unit combat actions. In essence, Lemnitzer was simply suggesting that the MAAG refocus its efforts from training the ARVN to repel a conventional invasion to training it to destroy the increasingly active guerrillas by conducting ambushes and other small unit actions, operations that are arguably still conventional. He did not recommend any organizational or equipment changes for the ARVN, nor did he spend much time describing any necessary civic action or security training above sending a civil affairs team to provide advice. While Lemnitzer may have believed he was recommending a significant reorientation of the MAAG's focus, he was actually not doing so. Again, the gaps in U.S. Army doctrine with regards to the ill-defined concepts of conventional and irregular warfare hindered the MAAG's efforts to train and organize the ARVN to combat the growing insurgency.

Despite the MAAG's training initiative that included Special Forces soldiers, Durbrow was not convinced that the MAAG's concept satisfied his concerns. A week after the plan's submission to CINCPAC, Durbrow wrote to a friend in the State Department that perhaps the Americans "were . . . doing too much conventional war training to fight another World War II." The same day, the ambassador requested that Williams provide him a "full and detailed briefing" of the MAAG's plans to alter the ARVN's training programs.[46] Responding in June, Williams reemphasized his belief that "[a]s stated many times by MAAG as proven doctrine, the primary combatant role in anti-guerrilla warfare operations is performed by well-trained Army units." With regard to the MAAG's role in developing an ARVN training program, the CHMAAG noted that the MAAG only made suggestions to the Vietnamese concerning training and that the Republic of Vietnam Armed Forces (RVNAF) could conduct its own counterguerrilla training if it so desired. In sum, despite Durbrow's concerns, Williams believed that "the RVNAF, on balance, possesses an excellent state of combat readiness to combat guerrilla terrorist attacks within South Vietnam."[47] While entirely correct in embracing the tenet that a disciplined and well-trained army is imperative, the CHMAAG continued to hold fast to his misplaced emphasis on training the ARVN to repel a conventional invasion from the north.

This ongoing tussle over the ARVN's focus highlighted the tension between the State and Defense Department representatives in Vietnam. As ambassador, Durbrow was technically senior to Williams, but he did not have the authority to order Williams to change the MAAG plans and programs. Although both Durbrow and Williams informed their superiors in the State and Defense Departments of their opinions and actions in Vietnam, both departments preferred to allow the country team (headed by Ambassador Durbrow and CHMAAG Williams) to sort out its problems. While both departments recognized the growing threat of insurgency by October 1960, their response consisted of simply issuing a "joint State-Defense message directing the country team to develop an overall plan to support the Diem government." Instead of clarifying the situation, "[t]hese instructions simply transferred back to the country team the long-standing State and Defense debate about the best means for dealing with the Vietnam situation."[48]

By the end of October, the MAAG believed that the antiguerrilla training provided to the ranger companies had better prepared the ARVN for the insurgency. In its estimate, "the regular military establishment of South Vietnam has the capability to fight either guerrillas or external aggressors." Lieutenant General Lionel McGarr, Williams's replacement, continued this trend of presenting the MAAG's training program as capable of handling an insurgency while at the same time reinforcing the advisors' tendency to stress conventional operations. Despite distributing a manual to all American advisors entitled *The Tactics and Techniques of Counter-Insurgency Operations*, a pamphlet developed during McGarr's tenure as the chief of the U.S. Army's Command and General Staff College, the new CHMAAG at the same time instructed his subordinates to "'outconventional' the unconventionalists!"[49] By the following spring, Ambassador Frederick Nolting, Durbrow's successor, assessed the MAAG's counterguerrilla training as "excellent." Even General Lemnitzer, who had expressed concern the year prior, assured General Maxwell D. Taylor in October 1961 that the progressively larger PLAF attacks countered the argument that the MAAG was training the ARVN for "the wrong war." Despite these favorable reports, even a traditional soldier like General Taylor observed upon his return from Vietnam in his report of 3 November 1961 that "[i]t is our clear impression that, by and large, training and equipment of the Vietnamese Armed Forces are still too heavily weighted toward conventional military operations."[50]

These conflicting reports illustrated one of the greatest challenges faced by the MAAG's advisors. U.S. Army doctrine did not provide any clear separation between what constituted "conventional" and "irregular" warfare, and it had not yet even offered definitions for the terms "insurgency" or "counterinsurgency" in its manuals. The MAAG, the embassy, and the visitors from Washington all offered their assessments of what the ARVN's training focus should be, and, to a certain extent, all were to some degree correct in their positions. Because there was no clear delineation between "conventional" and "irregular," each group could rightfully claim its recommendations were appropriate. In most cases, these groups' analyses resembled each other except for their language since there was no common understanding of the terms. This was certainly a serious problem, exacerbated by the lack of consensus concerning the relative importance of military and political factors to bringing about success in Vietnam.[51] In essence, doctrinal omissions and ambiguities in terminology prevented the U.S. Army from clearly defining exactly what it needed to be doing in Vietnam.

To some Americans, simply training the ARVN in antiguerrilla tactics was not enough; the GVN needed a comprehensive counterinsurgency plan. Roger Hilsman, in February 1962, submitted to the president a paper entitled "A Strategic Concept for South Vietnam." Essentially a paraphrased version of the recommendations of Sir Robert Thompson, a British counterinsurgency expert who had played a key role in the Malayan crisis, it was met with a warm reception by the Kennedy administration.[52] Conceptually, the plan revolved around pacification, or denying the NLF/PLAF access to the people. By establishing government control in the villages, and denying access to the enemy, the plan sought to reestablish GVN control and legitimacy in the rural areas.

Ngo Dinh Nhu, Diem's brother, was the program's champion and "was the real driving force behind the GVN's uneven but discernible movement toward adoption of the strategic hamlet."[53] Mirroring a similar program used by the British in Malaya in the 1950s, the hamlets concentrated the people in fortified and defended villages.[54] This type of village defense, however, was not new to Vietnam:

The strategic hamlet concept itself, however, was not necessarily an adaptation of British strategy in Malaysia despite apparent similarities. This concept had antecedents in Vietnamese history which dated back to the period of Chinese domination, but the most striking and recent precedent was perhaps the "combat village" defense system established [by the Viet Minh] during the 1946–1954 war of resistance against the French.[55]

Only three years before, in 1959, the GVN had attempted to build "80 'prosperity and density centers.'" First known as "agglomerations" and then "agrovilles," these population centers sought to segregate villagers and families with known PLAF associations from the other citizens and required the relocated families to build new homes with no compensation other than a one-time grant of $5.50. Put simply, the agrovilles were a "complete reversal of tradition and the social and economic pattern of the people affected." Suffering from peasant resistance and PLAF attacks, the program ended in early 1961, only to reappear in a slightly different form the following year during Operation SUNRISE, a GVN attempt to gain control of the provinces north of Saigon.[56]

Composed of an inner fence of bamboo spikes and thorn bushes; a moat with sloped, mined sides; an outer barrier of barbed wire; and cement or brick watchtowers, the strategic hamlet sought to protect the villagers from the PLAF and to establish social programs for their benefit. In reality, the villages were for control and not for building the GVN's legitimacy through civic action. The people once again resented building new homes with no compensation and being herded into the fortified stockades every evening. In many instances, the local population had to buy the materials for the hamlet's defense, such as barbed wire, while others had to pay a fee for their government-issued identification card.[57] Further, many farmers now had to walk a significant distance to their fields.

Although somewhat successful at first in disrupting the PLAF's contact with the villagers, the program rapidly spiraled downward. Province chiefs, vying for Diem's favor, eagerly "secured" more people and constructed additional strategic hamlets with the peasants' labor, while at the same time failing to provide the necessary materials and support, a shortcoming that did not escape American notice.[58] By forcing the people to live in hamlets and not funding the promised social benefits, the province chiefs created increasing numbers of potential PLAF members. Fostered by overeager American advisors with a penchant for statistics, the province chiefs continued to herd the people into hamlets, causing the program to collapse under its own weight, although the deaths of Diem and Nhu signaled the program's actual demise.[59] In summarizing the strategic hamlet program, two senior ARVN generals observed that "[t]he end result was that instead of voluntary participation, a primordial condition for this national policy to achieve success, the strategic hamlet people found themselves living in a state of represeed [*sic*] feelings, suspicion, and frustration."[60]

The strategic hamlet program was only one example of how the U.S. attempted to combat the PLAF through the "importation" of counterinsurgency techniques. In establishing Diem as the central political figure in South Vietnam, the Americans sought to emulate the example set by Ramon Magsaysay in the Philippines, but the South Vietnamese president was not Magsaysay in either charisma or personality. There existed a similar problem in attempting to apply the "lessons" of Malaya to South Vietnam. The ethnic Chinese, from whom the Malayan insurgents gained their support, had no familial ties to the land. When the British relocated them into the so-called New Villages, the Chinese, so long as they could earn wages in the tin mines or on the rubber plantations, did not "care much where they lived."[61] For the uprooted South Vietnamese, the relocation was emotionally traumatic. Believing in ancestral worship, abandoning their ancestors' burial grounds was an extremely heavy price to pay for ensuring the GVN's security. In many instances, instead of developing new techniques for defeating the insurgency, the U.S. used "ready made" answers for the growing problems in Vietnam.

While influenced by the MAAG's firm belief in conventional warfare, by 1962 the GVN's overall strategy included a combination of conventional (ARVN combat operations) and unconventional warfare (establishment of strategic hamlets). Tactically, the ARVN relied on two general types of operations to support their strategy: the sweep and the sweep and hold. First used in 1959 against the PLAF, the sweep, also called "mopping-up operations" consisted primarily of daylight patrolling through the contested countryside.[62] Leaving soon after daylight, ARVN units conducted roadmarches through the villages, looking for PLAF guerrillas. As night approached, they returned to their encampments, leaving the villages open to insurgent influence.[63] With the ARVN approaching on foot, the PLAF, with ample warning, frequently eluded its enemies. As Roger Hilsman observed in late 1962 to Secretary of State Rusk, "Tactically, the operating units on patrol tend to gain the impression that they are in enemy territory and they act accordingly," suggesting the GVN forces' unwillingness to remain in contested areas.[64] The arrival of American air assets in 1961 and the increased mobility they offered initially boosted the effectiveness of the sweep, but the PLAF soon developed methods to counter the helicopters.

The real victims of the sweeps were the villagers. Although they suffered at the hands of both sides, the people frequently bore the brunt of "mischievous acts" committed by the ARVN. As one village elder lamented, "We fear Saigon troops more than we fear provincial troops. They seem to create havoc wherever they go."[65] Unfortunately, this type of conduct had the secondary effects of pushing the villagers into the arms of the PLAF and reinforcing one of the NLF's propaganda themes of equating the ARVN with the French. When asked about the effects of the ARVN's sweeps on the PLAF, one villager observed that "[e]very time the Army came they made friends for the V.C." Another peasant standing near by chimed in, "Cruel like the French." As two senior ARVN generals later commented, "[r]arely, if ever, was the problem of winning the people's hearts and minds taken into serious consideration."[66]

A second tactic, the sweep and hold, sought to reduce the nighttime control of the PLAF in the villages. Recognizing that the sweeps did little to break the guerrillas' hold on the villages, the GVN sought to combine military with political activity. Initially conducting a sweep, the ARVN cleared the PLAF out of a region or area. The GVN then implemented the "hold" portion, consisting of establishing local officials and strategic hamlets.[67] Conceptually more sound than the sweep alone, the sweep and hold also suffered from its inability to destroy the PLAF initially or to prevent the guerrillas from infiltrating the hamlets during the sweep phase of the operation.

As combat with the PLAF became more intense in the early 1960s, the ARVN came to rely heavily on field artillery and fighter-bomber preparations before launching any attacks, a tendency that the American advisors struggled to prevent. Rather than close with the enemy to engage in hand-to-hand combat, the ARVN preferred to stand off and pummel its opponents with rockets and artillery rounds. This reliance on firepower, while allowing the commander to reduce "friendly" casualties, worked to the ARVN's disadvantage as well. Not only was the PLAF able to counter this massive firepower, but also serious collateral damage resulted from its indiscriminate use. Vietnamese civilians suffered horribly, resulting in a populace extremely unfriendly toward the GVN.[68]

The growing American concern about the ARVN use of firepower and its potential collateral damage resulted in an August 1962 "Lessons Learned" memorandum that specifically addressed this issue. Describing the potential adverse effects, the paper observed that

[t]he indiscriminate use of firepower, regardless of caliber, type or means of delivery cannot be condoned in CI [counterinsurgency] operations. . . . Unless targets are positively identified as enemy or completely clear of non-combatants, casualties among the people, rather than the VC, will result. This will only serve to strengthen VC influence over the population with the final result that the fundamental task of separating the guerrilla from the people will be far more difficult.[69]

Despite the Americans' attempts to encourage discretion in the use of the ARVN's available weapon systems, the South Vietnamese continued to employ significant quantities of ordnance before and during their operations.

Not only did the MAAG struggle to develop a strategy in Vietnam that followed American doctrine, but it also fought to organize the ARVN into an army that could conduct it successfully. Even before the MAAG started training the VNA in 1955, the Americans sought to impose their doctrinal belief upon the French that the division, and not the battalion, was the true basic unit for combat. In 1953, both Generals Collins and O'Daniel attempted to impress upon the French the inherent weakness of individual battalions engaging in combat. Upon his return to Washington, D.C., Collins characterized the French belief in their organizational basis as "fallacious," but it took the departure of the French from Indochina to allow the U.S. Army to organize the Vietnamese as it saw fit.[70]

This process of molding the ARVN culminated in a sweeping reorganization in 1959. Championed by General Williams to bring the ARVN in line with FM 100-5, the ARVN's reorganization in September established the general framework that was in place during Ap Bac. Diem, as president, held the position of commander in chief of the RVNAF. He also maintained the portfolio for the secretary of state for national defense, effectively combining the two positions. The chief of the Joint General Staff (JGS), answering to Diem, was the senior military commander of the RVNAF. Within his staff was the ARVN commander, who also acted as the assistant chief of staff, army. The JGS maintained five staff sections: J1, personnel; J2, intelligence; J3, operations; J4, logistics; and J5, civil operations.[71]

With the reorganization, the ARVN now fielded three corps headquarters, a fourth being added 14 December 1962, and seven infantry divisions. With 10,450 soldiers each, the divisions consisted of three infantry regiments, an artillery battalion, a mortar battalion, an engineer battalion, and various support companies.[72] Within the corps regions were divisional tactical zones, the boundaries of which were generally superimposed upon the existing civil provinces. The province chiefs, charged by law to provide security for their provinces, were often ARVN officers. Although military officers, the province chiefs were responsible to the Department of the Interior, not the Department of Defense. Thus, although province chiefs might be junior to other ARVN commanders operating in their provinces, they were not subject to ARVN orders and could deploy the Civil Guard (CG) units as they saw fit.[73]

The province chiefs' independence of ARVN command was the bane of the MAAG, which stressed unity of action between the ARVN and CG, and was a point of contention among visitors from Washington, among them Maxwell Taylor. On numerous occasions, the province chiefs failed to deploy their units to support ARVN operations in their provinces, thus depriving the ARVN commanders of unity of command. The ARVN tactics for fighting the guerrillas were cumbersome enough, but the South Vietnamese inability to concentrate forces rapidly because of a divided command structure only exacerbated the problem. In his report to the president in 1961, Taylor recommended that "the U.S. government insist that a single inviolate chain of command be established and practiced. This must include removal of Province Chiefs from the [CG] chain of command."[74] Regardless of the obvious benefits to the commanders in the field, Diem refused to act on this recommendation of placing the CG under direct ARVN control. By placing CG units with personally loyal ARVN officers under the Department of the Interior, Diem had at his disposal a ready-made countercoup force, since the CG units were not Department of Defense, and hence JGS, assets.

Reflecting the differences between conventional and internal security operations, armed South Vietnamese units were of three types: the regular army (ARVN), the CG or *Bao An*, and the Self-Defense Corps (SDC) or *Dan Ve*. Despite the Western influences of the MAAG, the GVN maintained these three branches that reflected the Vietnamese tradition of dividing their armed forces into main force, regional, and local units. As described earlier, ARVN units focused on destroying the enemy's forces through conventional strategy and tactics. The CG and SDC, on the other hand, were products of Diem's desire to maintain stability in the countryside since the MAAG was orienting the ARVN to repel a conventional invasion from the north. On 5 May 1955, Diem established the CG by presidential decree to provide internal security, and it remained a completely presidential asset until 1958, when the Department of the Interior took over administrative and technical support to reduce the burden on Diem's office.[75]

Diem's direct control over the CG caused the MAAG great concern, and General McGarr in particular. With the CG outside the JGS's authority, coordination between the CG and the ARVN was almost nonexistent. After campaigning through the summer of 1960, the CHMAAG won a minor victory in December when the CG finally became a Department of National Defense asset. This realignment, however, did little to solve the unity of effort problems in the field. While the Department of National Defense was now in charge of organizing and administering the CG units, these units still fell under the command of province chiefs who were personally responsible to the president. As a result, the single chain of command that the MAAG wished to encompass the ARVN, CG, and SDC units still had not come to fruition.[76]

The CG units were the equivalent of Italy's *carabinieri*. Charged with enforcing the law and maintaining public order and security in the rural areas, the CG soldiers were uniformed and lightly armed. Unlike the ARVN, the CG's primary focus was to conduct counterinsurgency operations and collect information, participate in civic action programs, and foster the population's confidence in the GVN. Organized into 160-man companies composed of four platoons and a headquarters section, the CG usually assigned platoons to guard posts along key routes.[77] These units did not possess the same level of training and readiness as their ARVN counterparts and often acted accordingly when in contact with the PLAF.

The SDC, established in 1956, assisted regular security forces to maintain public order and security at the village and hamlet level. Originally a Department of the Interior asset, the SDC, like the CG, became a Department of National Defense asset in October 1961. More concerned with static defense, the SDC was not uniformed and lightly armed. Consisting of three platoon companies, the SDC could apprehend suspected PLAF guerrillas but had to surrender them to the CG for action.[78] If properly trained, the SDC soldiers actually possessed the potential to be extremely effective against the PLAF. Since the SDC soldiers defended their own homes and villages, the GVN stood to gain staunch defenders against guerrilla infiltration. Unfortunately, the GVN placed little emphasis on training and equipping the SDC, and, not surprisingly, their performance against PLAF attacks was extremely poor. In many cases, American advisors referred to the SDC outposts as "VC supply points" because of their recurrent loss of weapons.[79]

In line with U.S. Army doctrine, the basic unit of employment for the ARVN was the squad, usually consisting of nine to eleven men. Maintaining a triangular configuration, typical of conventional warfare, three squads composed a platoon, and three platoons a company. Originally, four rifle companies plus a headquarters company rounded out a battalion, but, after Diem established the ranger companies in 1960, this number dropped to three.[80] Just as in American infantry regiments, the ARVN regiments possessed three battalions, but unlike American divisions, the ARVN divisions only possessed one battalion of 105mm howitzers and one battalion of 4.2-inch mortars, a rather slim fire support organization by American standards. By 1961, the ARVN still fielded seven divisions, the 1st, 2nd, 5th, 7th, 21st, 22nd, and 23rd, but it also gained an airborne brigade of five battalions.[81] The Americans' transformation of the ARVN from a colonial leftover to a modern, conventionally equipped and oriented army was near total. The South Vietnamese carried American weapons, wore American uniforms, and mirrored American organizational structure and traits right down to their vehicle drivers' bad habits. By late 1960, the ARVN had become, in the words of a former advisor, "a nifty miniature copy of the U.S. military establishment."[82]

Despite the MAAG's ongoing efforts to create the ARVN in its own image, Diem had his own ideas about how his army should be organized. Shortly after expressing to Ambassador Durbrow his concern about the overly conventional nature of the ARVN, Diem issued directives on 18 and 24 February 1960 ordering the formation of seventy-five 150-man commando companies (11,250 soldiers total). Later known as ranger companies, Diem expected these units to focus on commando, guerrilla, and antiguerrilla operations associated with pacification of the countryside. A hidden benefit to these new companies was their potential to act as additional anticoup insurance, a subtlety not lost on the increasingly insecure president. Diem informed neither the ambassador nor the CHMAAG of his intentions to establish the new units, and it was not until some time later that Durbrow caught wind of this development. Despite the ambassador's differences with the CHMAAG over ARVN training, he supported Williams's protests to Diem about the potentially detrimental effects on the ARVN by forming the ranger companies. By removing one company's worth of soldiers per battalion, the formation of the new units effectively reduced the infantry battalion's combat strength by one-fourth. Worse, by selecting the best officers and NCOs for the ranger companies, the standard ARVN battalions suffered the worst possible fate: The loss of their strongest and best-trained leaders. These new companies also represented a net gain in the

ARVN's total number, an intimation that Diem expected the U.S. to fund his armed forces' expansion above the current MAP projection. By April, Williams had successfully convinced Diem to hold the commando forces down to 3,000 or 4,000, but the Vietnamese president also demonstrated once again his increasing willingness to act on his own against American advice.[83]

Although the U.S. wanted the South Vietnamese to defeat the PLAF on their own, the Americans realized as 1961 progressed that the ARVN did not possess adequate mobility to counter the guerrillas' agility. Staying true to the U.S. Army's offensively oriented doctrine and wishing the ARVN to regain the initiative in seeking out the PLAF, the U.S. acted on Taylor's recommendation that it "rais[e] the level of the mobility of Army Forces by the provision of considerably more helicopters and light aviation."[84] Approximately one month later, a U.S. Navy ship arrived in Vietnam with its cargo of U.S. Army H-21s, thus introducing the first of many American helicopter companies to Vietnam. Between the 8th Transportation Company (Light Helicopter) of Fort Bragg, North Carolina, and the 57th Transportation Company (Light Helicopter) of Fort Lewis, Washington, the newly arrived American units reported to Southeast Asia with 32 H-21s and soon saw action. Within twelve days of arrival, Majors George D. Hardesty, Jr.'s, and Robert J. Dillard's 8th and 57th Companies participated in Operation CHOPPER, the first ARVN airmobile operation of the Second Indochina War. Transporting more than 1,000 ARVN paratroops, the helicopter companies distinguished themselves in an operation that the ARVN, and later the U.S. Army, repeated countless times throughout the war.[85]

The H-21 was one of the many types of helicopters used by the U.S. Army in Southeast Asia. Officially nicknamed the "Shawnee," the H-21 possessed dual rotors, powered by piston engines, and an angular fuselage, lending itself to the derisive moniker "The Flying Banana." Despite a relatively slow cruising speed of 101 miles per hour, the H-21 could carry 20 passengers, plus crew, and provided the ARVN with a heretofore-unknown degree of mobility. Where before the PLAF had time to react to the ARVN foot or vehicle patrols, now it had little advance warning of its opponent's approach. One critical shortcoming, however, was the aircraft's lack of any weaponry. Once the guerrillas began to adapt to the Shawnees' presence and fire at them, the aircrews had no way of returning fire, although they did later mount one .30 caliber machine gun with limited traverse in the crew chief's window. Another difficulty was the H-21s' age, which resulted in numerous mechanical problems for the aircraft. Despite their relative durability, the Shawnees did not command the aircrews' unreserved confidence. As one pilot phrased it, the aircraft was simply "an accident looking for a place to happen."[86] The crews' concerns aside, the H-21s remained the principal transport helicopter in Southeast Asia until their replacement by the UH-1s in late 1963.

Soon after the deployment of the H-21s, the U.S. introduced another technologically advanced weapon to assist the ARVN: the M113 armored personnel carrier (APC). Organizing two M113 companies in April 1962, the ARVN assigned them to the 7th and 21st Divisions. Originally called mechanized rifle companies, they fielded fifteen M113s organized into three platoons of three APCs, a support platoon of four APCs, and a headquarters section of two APCs. Boasting fifteen .50 caliber and eighteen .30 caliber machine guns, these companies brought heavy firepower and mobility to the battlefield.[87] With their amphibious capability, the APCs could cross the rice paddies with ease, but they were also limited by their difficulties in crossing the canals that bounded the paddies. Since many of the canals possessed high banks with vegetation firmly rooted in them, it was difficult, if not impossible, for the APCs to climb up and over them. This liability was a serious one, particularly in the rich rice areas of the Mekong Delta, given the canals that crisscrossed the region.

As 1962 progressed, the number of American helicopters in Vietnam grew. In January, the 93rd Transportation Company arrived, followed shortly thereafter by the 45th Transportation Battalion from Fort Sill, Oklahoma, a headquarters element charged with taking command of the three helicopter companies now based in South Vietnam. By the summer, two more companies arrived, the 33rd and the 81st, bringing the total to five. With the growing number of aircraft and the decreasing shock resulting from the airmobile operations, the PLAF gradually developed tactics to counter the H-21s effectively, resulting in mounting helicopter losses. In an attempt to maintain the ARVN's mobility and to protect the five H-21 companies that were now in Vietnam, the U.S. deployed in early 1962 the Utility Tactical Transport Helicopter Company (UTTHC), the U.S. Army's first gunship company, with 15 UH-1As. Its prototype flying only six years earlier, the UH-1A was armed with sixteen 2.75-inch rockets and two .30 caliber machine guns. The "Iroquois," or "Huey" as it was commonly called, provided protection for the slower and less well-armed H-21s.[88] While maintaining that it did not have combat forces in Vietnam, the U.S. subtly changed its role by introducing the UTTHC, technically a combat force by today's doctrine.

Throughout the fall of 1962, the gunships suppressed the PLAF at the landing zones with a fair amount of success. Continuing to hone its airmobile capabilities, the U.S. Army introduced to Vietnam in late 1962 11 UH-1Bs, an improved version of the original Huey. First tested in November 1960 and rushed into production, the UH-1Bs were armed with sixteen 2.75-inch rockets and four 7.62mm M60 machine guns.[89] Within a year of Taylor's visit, the profound effect of his November 1961 report was clear. By the end of 1962, the U.S. had provided the ARVN enough M24 tanks, M8 armored cars, and M113 APCs to field two armored cavalry regiments (1st and 2nd ACRs). The CG now fielded 77,000 soldiers; the SDC, 99,500; and the ARVN, 218,000. Standing behind these forces were the five American transport helicopter companies and the UTTHC, ready to support their operations against the PLAF.[90] Previously content to increase the ARVN's strength without committing additional American assets, the U.S. by 1962 made it clear that it would provide its own assets commensurate with South Vietnamese personnel increases.

Despite the ARVN's increase in size and quality of equipment, its effectiveness remained questionable. Among the greatest hindrances to its efficacy was its poor leadership. Burdened by its political nature under Diem, the ARVN's officers not only had to worry about success in the field, but also the political climate of the GVN. Diem's influence over the ARVN and his ability to ensure that loyal subordinates occupied key positions were clear from General Nguyen Van Hinh's dismissal as chief of staff in 1954. Favoring central Vietnamese who were Roman Catholic, Diem played a personal role in the appointment of most senior commanders and staff officers:

[T]he authority to promote company grade officers rested with the Minister of Defense [the portfolio of which Diem maintained]. The promotion of field grade and general officers was the sole prerogative of the President. . . . The rumor circulated among military officers that the decisive factors were the three Ds, the Vietnamese initials for Party, Religion, and Region. An officer had to possess one of these three qualifications for promotion or a good position. . . . Promotion was restricted, hard to obtain, and highly opportunistic; it often did not bear any relation to military needs.[91]

At a time when the ARVN desperately required competent officers to fill its expanding needs, the president, through his patronage, actually undermined the MAAG's efforts at developing a professional South Vietnamese officer corps by failing to use a merit-based promotion system.

The arbitrary and restrictive nature of the promotion system not only applied to the senior officers, but also reached down to the lowest NCO level. In late 1961, Ton That Dinh, II Corps commander, petitioned the president to reevaluate his promotion policies because they adversely affected his units' readiness. Dinh wrote that his two divisions, the 22nd and 23rd, were sorely understrength at the lowest NCO levels, and, as a result, soldiers went unsupervised and untrained. As evidence, the corps commander stated that the 22nd Division possessed only 29% of its authorized number of corporals and 69% of its sergeants. The 23rd Division was little better off, maintaining 31% and 70%, respectively. Because the president would not allow the divisions to promote deserving soldiers on their own, the NCO positions went unfilled. Compounding this problem was the penchant of Nhu, the president's brother, to interfere in ARVN promotions as well.[92]

An example of this influence and maneuvering by the Ngo Dinh clan concerned General Duong Van Minh. At a rally to celebrate a GVN victory, an orator pronounced Minh as the "Hero of the Nation." The Ngo Dinhs, feeling slighted at this elevation of Minh, immediately organized the Army Field Command and appointed Minh as commander. This new organization commanded no units, acting strictly as an inspectorate for the I and II Corps. In essence, Diem had pigeon-holed Minh for being successful.[93] As General Huynh Van Cao, a Diem appointee to the newly formed IV Corps, observed: "It does not pay to be too successful, for you then become a threat," a belief that did little to encourage aggressive action among the senior officers in combating the insurgency.[94]

Even the U.S. Army's *Area Handbook for Vietnam* admitted the adverse effects of Diem's centralized control. In its discussion of the South Vietnamese government, the handbook stated that "President Ngo's [sic] exercise of personal power and reluctance to delegate authority beyond a small circle of relatives and close friends . . . deny the government the services of some able men . . . [and] tend to convert constructive opposition into hostility."[95] While Diem was not successful in dominating all aspects of the government and the military, as evidenced by his inability to change initially General Williams's conventional training program, he certainly exerted influence in most all areas of South Vietnamese life through his civil and military appointments. Politically adept or "loyal" officers advanced to senior positions instead of officers possessing true military skill, thus reducing the ARVN officer corps' overall quality.

Lack of combat experience among the leadership was also a grave liability, and seasoned leaders were few and far between in the line units for a number of reasons. First, there was little martial experience among the officers from which the units could draw. The French, at all levels, officered the VNA, effectively depriving the Vietnamese of opportunities to gain command experience in combat. With the rapid expansion of the VNA, and later the ARVN, officer training simply could not keep up with the units' requirements because of the time it took to train the officer candidates. To deal with these shortcomings, the JGS promoted junior leaders with no combat experience to higher command and staff positions just to fill a new unit, a tendency that further exacerbated the problem. Second, staff officers received the majority of promotions, discouraging the better officers from serving in combat units.[96] As the better officers gravitated to the staffs, they took with them their experience and abilities, thus leaving the weaker officers in the combat units.

Third, the Ngo Dinhs valued officer loyalty over proficiency. Although it is difficult to assess their effects on later ARVN officer actions, the coup attempts against Diem in 1960 and 1962 demonstrated the precarious position of the Vietnamese political leadership. As a result, the president rotated commanders regularly to prevent camaraderie and the formation of cliques that might lead to possible future coup attempts.[97] An officer's experience gained in a particular position, therefore, was lost from the unit upon his rotation. Finally, since the better combat leaders exposed themselves and took more risks, their casualty rate was higher than the less aggressive officers, and they could not be immediately replaced. As General J. Lawton Collins sagely observed about the shortage of competent ARVN officers: "[C]ombat operations often eliminated the best commanders."[98]

Diem's guidance to his officers concerning "defeats" further served to hamper ARVN officer aggressiveness. The president had made it clear time and again to his senior officers that the GVN never suffered a defeat "but only one long series of victories." Even the loss of an officer in the field constituted a defeat. As a result, this emphasis on only victorious engagements and battles resulted in "excessive caution" on the part of the ARVN officers. To some of the American advisors, the Vietnamese commanders were "hamstrung," fearful that Diem would "remove or demote any officer who suffers heavy losses, even though he is successful."[99]

ARVN officer timidity resulted in part from Diem's guidance, but in many instances the officers simply could not lead their men effectively. A portion of this difficulty resulted from the traditions the ARVN officers inherited from their earlier experiences with the French. The French system of command embraced a vastly different set of precepts from those of the American advisors, often causing tension between counterparts. Vietnamese officers, while under French tutelage, learned such maxims as:

> "A 2nd lieutenant knows nothing, and does nothing
> A 1st lieutenant knows nothing, but does everything
> A captain knows everything, but does nothing" . . .
>
> or . . .
>
> "A leader does not have to do anything, lets nothing disturb him, and makes others work" . . .
>
> or even . . .
>
> "Do what I say but not what I do"[100]

While the French never officially offered these cynical precepts as formal teachings, their sentiments nevertheless found their way into the culture of the ARVN officers. With no experience to temper these sentiments, many "unsophisticated Vietnamese officers who looked up to their French commanders as tutors . . . might have . . . construed [them] as wisdom."[101] No matter how much the Vietnamese may have wanted to distance themselves from their former colonial masters, this skewed vision of leadership had a profound effect on the ARVN officers and haunted American advisors for the entire Second Indochina War.

Further, most ARVN officers were from the middle and upper classes, while their soldiers were from the lower strata of society. The inability on the part of the officers to relate to their subordinates who came from the lower social classes and their unwillingness to share their soldiers' hardships, a shortcoming that Halberstam called the "mandarin legacy," only exacerbated their problems in attempting to influence their men. To many ARVN officers, the whole point of achieving rank was to preclude their presence in the field, a privilege many believed was a result of promotion to higher grades.[102] In a 1962 report to COMUSMACV, Australian Colonel F. P. Serong summarized this attitude among South Vietnamese officers rather bluntly when he wrote that

[t]he officer in the field believes that all reward and professional satisfaction exists only in Saigon. . . . Consequently, except for the rare dedicated fighting man, the aim of the officer is a steady escalation up the formation headquarters to the Promised Land. He doesn't want to fight, because, if he does, he may spoil his record, and his Saigon chances; and he may be killed.[103]

Rather than viewing a promotion as an opportunity to lead and inspire larger units of soldiers, many sought it as a reward for their service and a way to separate themselves from "the dirty aspects or the dangers of war," a belief that further widened the gap between the officers and their men.[104]

Given the difficulties with its leadership, the ARVN's morale and motivation not surprisingly varied during the war. In some instances, South Vietnamese units were highly trained, disciplined, and motivated, but, more often than not, motivation was lacking among the officers and soldiers, resulting in poor performance in combat. The South Vietnamese soldiers' reasons for fighting contributed little, if any, to their desire to close with and destroy the guerrillas. While some volunteered out of a personal tragedy suffered at the hands of the PAVN or PLAF, most fought because they had been drafted. Feeling little loyalty to the GVN, the ARVN soldiers did not often place themselves at risk for the Ngo Dinhs' sake. Throughout the war, even better trained and equipped ARVN units repeatedly showed an unwillingness to engage the insurgents in sustained combat.[105]

Another facet of this reluctance to engage the enemy stemmed from the poor medical attention wounded ARVN soldiers received. With a rudimentary medical evacuation (medevac) and treatment system, the South Vietnamese were unable to provide their soldiers with quality health care. Since the Vietnamese air force had few rotary wing aircraft, Vietnamese soldiers could not expect aero-medevac unless an American advisor was nearby and the wounded ARVN soldiers could get to the pickup zone (PZ).[106] Upon becoming a casualty, most soldiers expect some type of medical treatment; when they do not receive it, and they do not firmly believe in the cause for which they fight, they may avoid heavy combat to preserve themselves. Understandably, the poor prospects of surviving heavy combat weighed upon the ARVN soldiers and dampened their fervor.

Family considerations only made matters worse for the ARVN. Organized by geographical region, ARVN units suffered heavy desertion rates when they deployed away from the soldiers' home areas.[107] The pull of family was stronger than that exerted by the GVN, and the government only worsened its plight by never systematically returning or prosecuting deserters. In essence, Saigon tacitly acknowledged a soldier's right to desert, fostering many ARVN soldiers' lack of belief in the GVN's legitimacy.[108] Organized along conventional lines and well equipped, but suffering from poor leadership and reservations about their government, the ARVN soldiers approached 1963 with something significantly less than a whole-hearted enthusiasm for defeating the PLAF.

THE PEOPLE'S LIBERATION ARMED FORCES

Arguably, the PLAF's strategy and tactics better addressed the nature of the conflict in South Vietnam during this period because they dealt with more than just the military dimensions of the insurgency. The basis of their strategy revolved around the politico-military concept of *dau tranh* (struggle). An extremely emotional term for Vietnamese, *dau tranh* formed the groundwork for all Vietnamese revolutionary thought. One PAVN defector put this seemingly exaggerated assertion into perspective when he said that "*[d]au tranh* is all important to a revolutionary. It shapes his thinking. . . . [H]is whole world is *dau tranh*." This concept of struggle possessed two components: *dau tranh chinh tri* (political *dau tranh*) and *dau tranh vu trang* (armed *dau tranh*).[109] Instead of clearly delineated elements, these two components were intertwined and complementary. A master at coordinating *dau tranh*'s two components, Vo Nguyen Giap wrote during the Second Indochina War that "[t]he military and political struggles are closely coordinated, assist each other, and encourage each other to develop." Like ice tongs, the two arms of *dau tranh* gripped the enemy from both the political and military sides.[110]

Within political *dau tranh* (what Douglas Pike termed "politics with guns" since the political cadres were also armed), there were three *van* (action) programs: *dich van* (action among the enemy) or nonmilitary activities among the population controlled by the enemy; *dan van* (action among the people) or administration and other activities in the "liberated area"; and *binh van* (action among the military) or nonmilitary action among the enemy's troops. In most cases of political *dau tranh*, influencing the people—friendly, antagonistic, or neutral—was through nonviolent means. Propaganda, threats, mass organizations, plays, and meetings were the political programs' methods of influencing the people. Critical to the success of political *dau tranh* was the targeting of all Vietnamese. All three *van* programs focused upon a different group and ensured that all inhabitants of both the "liberated" and "occupied" areas of South Vietnam were subject to political struggle.[111]

The complement and equal to political *dau tranh* was armed *dau tranh*, also known as the "violence program."[112] The objectives of armed *dau tranh*, according to Vo Nguyen Giap, were "to destroy the enemy military force, to defend the people, to attract the people's sympathy, to coordinate with the political struggle, and to serve and help the political struggle score the greatest victories for the resistance."[113] Given their weakness and their opponents' strength, the insurgents could not hope to achieve these objectives in a short period of time. As a result, the NLF came to the conclusion that a successful outcome lay in making the war last as long as possible. As many of the cadres had discovered during their experiences during the First Indochina War against the French, the best method to prolong the war was through the military strategy of protracted conflict paired with the tactics of guerrilla warfare. Put simply, their protracted conflict, or long-term war, sought to counter their larger enemy's strength by wearing down his resolve. As the insurgents eroded the enemy's morale, they also built their strength by involving the people in the struggle. In protracted warfare, time was on the side of the insurgent. The longer the struggle, the more time the insurgents had to build strength, and the more time the enemy had to tire of the fight.[114]

The involvement of the people was critical to a protracted war's success, because without the people, the guerrillas were unable to draw supplies, manpower, or moral support to build their strength. By making the conflict a "people's war," the insurgents drew upon a large resource base that they might not otherwise have had, which allowed them to prolong the conflict.[115] Given the people's importance to its concept of protracted warfare, it should not be surprising then that the PLAF viewed all people as legitimate tools (and targets) of war. This difference in perspectives and definitions between the insurgents and the U.S. and GVN concerning the role of the population overshadowed the Second Indochina War. Accustomed to "fighting by the rules," the U.S. often exercised restraint in areas that the PLAF did not, particularly when it came to interacting with the South Vietnamese people.

By conducting the insurgency in terms of *dau tranh*, the NLF also dramatically differed from the U.S. Army and the ARVN in their perceptions of what constituted "success" or "victory." Despite a military defeat or setback, the NLF could still view an engagement in terms of political success or gains among the people. The PLAF's ambush of an ARVN ranger company near Ap My Luong in October 1962 illustrated this concept. Militarily, one could view the engagement as a draw. The PLAF, while destroying an ARVN platoon, withdrew soon thereafter, surrendering the field to the rangers. From a political perspective, however, the insurgents' actions reaped significant dividends. By engaging the ARVN, the PLAF demonstrated to the South Vietnamese villagers its resolve and growing strength by not running at the sight of helicopters. This subtlety in defining terms was lost on the Americans and South Vietnamese, who usually viewed engagements and battles strictly in terms of military success (destruction of so many guerrillas, retention of a terrain feature, and so forth). As illustrated at Ap Bac and countless other battles, what the insurgents considered a victory was not necessarily what the Americans or South Vietnamese considered success.

Dau tranh provided the strategic framework for the insurgency, encompassing a people's war that was protracted in nature. The best methods to prolong the conflict and exhaust the enemy, as demonstrated during the First Indochina War, were guerrilla tactics. According to the Vietnamese framework of protracted warfare, the guerrilla tactics followed three stages: the contention stage, the equilibrium stage, and the counteroffensive stage.[116] In the contention phase, the PLAF restricted itself to small unit actions against the ARVN. Not requiring large numbers, assassinations of GVN officials and small ambushes against the ARVN, CG, and SDC were the prevalent forms of armed *dau tranh* in the early years of the insurgency. As the PLAF gained strength in the field and transitioned to the equilibrium phase, the guerrillas conducted progressively larger ambushes and raids against the RVNAF. These first two phases allowed the insurgents to build their infrastructure in the villages, organize larger units, and stockpile weapons and munitions. They played to the strengths of the insurgents and the weaknesses of the enemy. The PLAF found security in its dispersal; the GVN had to concentrate its forces in the villages, thereby inviting attack. The insurgents lived with the people and exerted influence on a daily basis; the ARVN only maintained a presence as it passed through the villages. The guerrillas gained logistical support from the people, making it difficult for the GVN to interdict their lines of supply; the ARVN, heavily reliant upon logistical bases, begged attack on its lines of communication.[117]

As the insurgents gained power, they shifted to mobile warfare, or the counteroffensive stage. As defined by Giap, "[m]obile warfare is the fighting way of concentrating troops, of the regular army in which relatively big forces are regrouped and operating on a relatively vast battlefield, attacking the enemy where he is relatively exposed with a view to annihilating enemy manpower, advancing very deeply then withdrawing very swiftly."[118] In essence, mobile warfare involved large units conducting operations against the enemy, but it did not direct fighting set-piece battles, nor was it an end unto itself. While the PLAF expected to fight in the open with large units, it also expected tactics of the first two phases to wear down and destroy the enemy's reserves. Put simply, mobile warfare and guerrilla were inseparable and mutually supporting.[119] At no time did the NLF expect, or want, to fight a large scale, conventional battle against the ARVN without also pairing it with guerrilla operations. This recognition that the phases overlapped and were mutually supporting provided the PLAF with unbelievable flexibility in conducting operations in the field. If the insurgents met stiff resistance in a certain region, they might fall back to the phase of contention and concentrate only upon small unit actions. In areas where the GVN was weak, the PLAF could easily jump ahead to the counteroffensive and mass its units for large operations. In short, the NLF matched its operations to the specific conditions in each region, an approach that effectively confused American strategists and policymakers who tended to view South Vietnam in overall, general terms.[120]

The Vietnamese framework of the three phases of a protracted struggle resembled quite closely the writings of Mao Tse-tung, but they were not identical, particularly in regards to the first phase. Mao's conception of an insurgency reflected his experiences against the Japanese Imperial Army during the Sino-Japanese War and how he believed his army would bring about success against the invaders. In his writings, the Chinese leader defined his stages as the strategic defensive, the strategic stalemate, and the counteroffensive. During the first phase of strategic defensive, Mao expected his forces to conduct a spirited defense against the Japanese through mobile warfare, contesting each of the enemy's thrusts and movements, particularly in the urban areas. As the Japanese took over the larger cities and ventured into the countryside, Mao expected his insurgents to transition to small unit guerrilla actions. For the Chinese, mobile warfare was the primary method of contesting the Japanese advance; guerrilla and positional warfare (fighting from trenches or other static positions) were clearly secondary.[121] For the PLAF, the first phase did not involve mobile warfare, nor did the guerrillas defend the urban areas according to Mao's model. The simple reality for the South Vietnamese insurgents was that the GVN already occupied and controlled the cities, with its influence extending out into the countryside, at the outset of the insurgency. For the Vietnamese, their first phase encompassed only guerrilla, and not mobile or positional, warfare. Without a doubt, the Vietnamese owed much of their revolutionary doctrine to the Chinese, particularly since Mao provided advisors to the Viet Minh during the First Indochina War, but the concept of *dau tranh*, coupled with the idea of protracted warfare, gave the insurgency in the south a distinctly Vietnamese character.

Although the PLAF expected to reach the stage of counteroffensive at some point, it did not believe that the insurgency would end as a result of a purely military victory. To the contrary, the NLF believed that the people themselves would end the struggle through a general uprising, or *khoi nghia*. In keeping with the communist principle of a general strike, *khoi nghia* espoused the belief that at some precipitous moment, the people, under the leadership of the NLF, would rise up to take control of South Vietnam, similar to what purportedly happened during the August Revolution of 1945. Besides the belief that it was certain to occur, the NLF was vague in its descriptions of this momentous event, primarily because the leadership was itself unsure *how* the general uprising would transpire. The idea that the people, and not military action, would end the insurgency reinforced the PLAF's focus on the political effects of its operations on the populace.[122]

Militarily, the PLAF knew that it could not counter the ARVN's strength in the field, and it sought to lessen the effects of the enemy's combat power, particularly the growing South Vietnamese capability to bring its massed firepower to bear. To neutralize the enemy's advantage, the PLAF closed with the enemy forces any time it wanted to maintain contact. By intermingling with the enemy, the PLAF knew that the enemy, fearing fratricide, could not call for close air support (CAS) or field or rocket artillery. If the PLAF wished to avoid contact and the fire support that went with it, the guerrillas broke contact and melted into the jungle. Properly employed, the "bear hug"/break contact tactics prevented unnecessary PLAF casualties.[123]

The PLAF generally relied on two specific tactics when initiating contact with the ARVN: the ambush and the raid. Usually employing either an "L" shaped or a "V" shaped ambush, the PLAF sought through this tactic to acquire weapons, harass and demoralize the ARVN, delay or block reinforcing troops or supplies, destroy or capture enemy troops, or undermine the enemy's confidence.[124] Maintaining the element of surprise, the PLAF regularly inflicted casualties on the poorly trained ARVN patrols.

When targeting outposts or fixed positions, the PLAF employed the raid to destroy or damage equipment or supplies, capture enemy or inflict casualties, or harass and demoralize the enemy.[125] Also called sapper operations, the PLAF's raids were often devastating, as witnessed by the 32nd Infantry Regiment in 1960. Prior to a raid, the cadres sent out extensive reconnaissance patrols to determine the locations of enemy positions, the strengths and weaknesses of the defenses, and the routes to and from the objective. After digesting this information and developing a plan, the cadres constructed a sandtable—that is, a three-dimensional model of the terrain—and conducted a thorough backbrief, or talk-through, before the attack. If time permitted, the sappers constructed actual mock-ups of the enemy's positions and rehearsed on them.

After each man thoroughly understood his role, the sappers began their infiltrations just after dark, capitalizing on the ARVN's usual reduction of security at sunset. Sappers emphasized camouflage, sometimes taking three hours to prepare themselves. Stripped to only shorts, weapons, and explosives, the sappers crawled through the enemy wire. If a sapper needed to cut the barbed wire, he only cut two-thirds of the way through the strands. After wrapping them in cloth, he then broke them by hand to reduce the amount of noise produced.[126] Once through the wire, each sapper proceeded to his assigned objective. Destroying the crew-served weapons first to reduce the enemy's defenses, the sappers then either planted their explosives or tossed their satchel charges to destroy other objectives. Once a sapper had completed his assigned mission, he returned through his breach to a rally point outside the wire.[127]

The aggressive nature of the ambushes and raids served to keep the ARVN off balance, but the PLAF was not immune to the effects of the increasing number of American technological advances. With the ARVN's increased use of APCs and helicopters in mid-1962, the PLAF faced the challenge of developing tactics to reduce these technological advantages. At the outset, the guerrillas did not fully understand how to engage the helicopters and inflicted little damage on them. Soon after the American helicopters arrived in Vietnam, one pilot recalled how the guerrillas, thoroughly trained to "lead" the helicopter, massed their fire at a point 20 yards in front of the helicopter, even though it was on the ground.[128] Experience with the helicopters was a harsh teacher, however, and the PLAF soon developed a counter to the ARVN's now airmobile sweeps. Called "counter mopping-up operations," these tactics sought to capitalize on the perceived weaknesses of the ARVN. First used with success in the fall of 1962, these tactics involved employing sound defensive and improved antiaircraft techniques:

Defensive works were consolidated, and camouflage discipline strictly observed. Guards were positioned around our quarters to detect enemy surprise attacks. AAA [antiaircraft artillery] cells were activated and trained in the proper techniques to down enemy aircraft and helicopters. Our units were notified of the weaknesses of amphibious M113's. Proper firing and combat techniques as well as camouflage of fortified works were taught to units.[129]

The PLAF conducted "successful" counter mopping-up operations in Cai Nai and Phu Phong on 13 September, Vinh Kim on 23 September, and My Hanh Dong (reported as Ap My Luong by American sources) on 5 October.[130] Although the PLAF initiated contact in each instance, it broke contact soon thereafter. By January 1963, these counter mopping-up operations involved remaining in contact with the ARVN for longer periods of time, with telling results.

One PLAF tactic essential to all units, whether main force, regional, or local, was *vu trang tuyen truyen*, or armed propaganda. Not a new innovation particular to the Second Indochina War, armed propaganda was one that has been present throughout Vietnamese history. The PAVN perfected armed propaganda's modern form during the First Indochina War.[131] Put simply, armed propaganda was a political-military tactic used to integrate armed action with the political ideal. Although a program of violence was an integral part of this tactic, terror was not its sole basis. It was the daily interaction with the people to reinforce their indoctrination continually that was critical. As a Viet Minh manual prescribed in 1945, "[p]ropaganda teams must work hard. Sometimes they must help our people in their work or work their way into a crowd of people who are harvesting or transplanting in the fields to propagandise them."[132] This combination of physical presence, indoctrination, and actual or implied violence against government supporters was extremely effective. As a villager told an ARVN commander in 1962: "You came here with artillery, trucks, and well-equipped soldiers to fight against our own people. . . . You blame us for giving the NLF soldiers rice, but you must remember that they are living here with us, sharing our poor lot and protecting us [from ARVN misconduct]. They are our own children and brothers and belong to our village."[133] Once again, the PLAF's focus on the political aspects of the insurgency heightened the contrast with the almost purely military approach of the GVN and its American advisors.

Just as the ARVN followed American doctrine to organize, the PLAF looked to the doctrine of protracted conflict for answers. Fighting a conflict similar to the First Indochina War, the PLAF's organization resembled the Viet Minh's and the PAVN's, although the clandestine nature of the PLAF and its organization defy precise description. The PLAF maintained the same general organization from its inception and organized itself into main force and paramilitary units like the ARVN. The *Than Phan Quan Su* (regular military forces) were divided into two sections, the *Quan Doi Chu Luc* (main force) and the *Bo Doi Dia Phuong* (regional force). The three-man cell was the basic unit of all PLAF units, whether military or paramilitary. Led by an experienced cadre member, the cell served well the guerrilla nature of the insurgency and also provided the party with the means of maintaining control over its members. The PLAF organized these cells into squads and platoons. Platoons formed companies, some of which were independent units that reported to the NLF district, while others were organic to battalions. Battalions were also of two types: the *tieu doan co dong* (independent battalion) and the *tieu doan tap trung* (concentrated battalion). The *tieu doan tap trung* composed *trung doan* (regiments), which formed divisions, the largest PLAF units organized.[134]

The paramilitary branch of the PLAF was the *Dan Quan Du Kich* (Guerrilla Popular Army). The PLAF further divided the *Dan Quan Du Kich* into three sections: the *Du Kich Chien Dau* (combat guerrillas), the *Du Kich Xa* (village guerrillas), and the *Tu Va Nhan Dan* (self-defense militia).[135] The *du kich* was the PLAF's full-time presence in the hamlet and village. Poorly armed, the *du kich*'s focus was on psychologically influencing the people, not military action. The *du kich* also formed a manpower pool for the main force units.[136] The basic *du kich* element was the three-man *du kich bi mat* (secret guerrilla cell). Depending upon the population of the hamlet or village, the PLAF organized the *du kich bi mat* into squads and platoons, which peaked at 36 to 48 men, although some reportedly reached sizes of 100.[137] Given the sheer number and types of units, it is easy to see the tremendous task that faced any ARVN or American intelligence officer who attempted to maintain a current and accurate enemy order of battle.

Americans have not yet systematically studied the PLAF leadership, but one may certainly make some observations. Given their experiences gained during World War II and the First Indochina War, the PLAF officers who remained in the south were certainly not new to insurgency warfare. This knowledge served as the basis for their competence in executing tactical missions during the Second Indochina War. Because the party maintained a presence at almost every level of command vis à vis the political officer, the PLAF did not have to rotate its officers for fear of coups or cliques like the ARVN. By staying in the same position for lengthy periods of time, the officers honed their skills, rather than having to learn new ones continually. This stability contributed to the combat effectiveness of the guerrilla units.

Like his ARVN counterpart, a PLAF soldier joined the insurgency for various reasons. The NLF terror in the villages and hamlets was an effective means of recruiting, but sometimes it did not have the desired effect. In one instance, the PLAF assassinated a local official, spurring five village members to join. At the same time, five other men joined the ARVN, effectively nullifying the NLF's gain.[138] While some became guerrillas because of coercion, others had a desire to avenge personal loss. As described earlier, the ARVN treatment of the villagers during its sweeps through the countryside served to alienate the people. As a result, many PLAF soldiers simply joined as a means to avenge mistreatment at the hands of the GVN.

For other PLAF soldiers, joining the struggle offered an opportunity for a better life. Not concerned with ideological concepts, numerous recruits wanted only to own the land that their families had farmed for generations. As one PLAF senior captain, who had been a tenant farmer and had suffered at the hands of his landowner, stated: "We had to get rid of the regime that allowed a few people to use their money and authority to oppress the others. So I joined the Liberation Front. I followed the VC to fight for freedom and prosperity for the country. I felt that this was right."[139] Focusing on the possibility of a better life, much of the PLAF indoctrination emphasized patriotic themes and the expulsion of the Americans without touching on Marxist doctrine.[140]

The PLAF possessed a valuable asset to maintain the guerrillas' motivation: the *chinh tri vien* (commissar or political officer).[141] A party member, the commissar was present at every command level, down to company, similar to the Soviet Red Army and the Chinese People's Liberation Army. In essence, the commissar "mobilized the spirit." He conducted political indoctrination, solved personal problems, and generally attended to the unit's morale.[142] An editorial in *Quan Doi Nhan Dan* (*People's Army*) outlined the duties of the political officer in October 1962: "The role of the political commissar has been very clearly defined: They are responsible for the political attitude of their companies, they must look after the intellectual training of the servicemen and continuously help them to develop their thinking habits."[143] Responsible to the party for his unit, the political officer ensured unit cohesion and morale.

The PLAF also conducted extensive indoctrination of its soldiers to stiffen their resolve. As noted earlier, the concept of *dau tranh* permeated the soldiers' views of themselves. This almost mythical concept provided purpose to their existence. Indoctrination reinforced the sense of purpose in its members. Far from receiving indoctrination only as a part of basic training, PLAF soldiers continually underwent political education in their units in the field. A captured guerrilla training schedule from the Chau Thanh District listed combat or political training daily from 0630 to 1000.[144]

A third influence in maintaining morale was the self-criticism session. Held at varying intervals, but usually weekly, these sessions gave an outlet to the PLAF soldiers' emotions. The political officer conducting the session encouraged criticism, even of superiors. He would not, however, accept a superficial answer for a criticism. An accusation of a shortcoming, for example, resulted in continued probes of a soldier until he admitted fully to his faults. Although being praised in front of peers was not unpleasant, the soldiers feared being the subject of criticism. While it is impossible to quantify the effectiveness of these sessions, the focus on introspection and public admission of fault must have influenced many soldiers not to be the subject of criticism. At the same time, this adversarial forum may have influenced some PLAF guerrillas to distance themselves from their comrades. As one American who analyzed these sessions observed: "Probably this form of psychological control —which is distantly related to, but entirely different from, indoctrination—is one of the principal bonds by which the . . . army . . . is held together."[145]

One other influence affecting the PLAF soldiers' motivation was their nationalistic commitment to drive the U.S. from Vietnam. Many PLAF soldiers, characterizing the GVN and ARVN as "lackey forces" or "puppets," simply viewed the southern regime as a symbol of American imperialism.[146] To these soldiers, the Americans, like the French before them, had no right to influence the Vietnamese government or its affairs. Le Thanh, a North Vietnamese, summarized his feelings toward the GVN and the U.S.: "We understood that the Americans were behind Diem and that they were exactly like the French. . . . I associated the Americans with the French. Both of them were imperialists. . . . I was enraged about the Southern regime and the Americans. I hated them."[147] This fervent desire to rid Vietnam of foreign influence bonded soldiers of a wide ideological spectrum into units with a common purpose.

Despite all the motivating factors—coercion, better opportunities, nationalistic fervor, and so on—this is not to suggest that the PLAF did not face challenges in maintaining its soldiers' morale, recruiting new guerrillas, or training its leadership. To the contrary, the casualties inflicted through the summer and fall of 1962 by the ARVN's airmobile operations and M113s had telling effects on the guerillas' motivation and fervor, particularly in the Delta region. In reviewing its situation on the eve of Ap Bac, the local PLAF leadership noted that in one of its regional companies, the "[s]oldiers had no confidence in their cadre and were afraid of mopping up [operations], enemy weapons and technique, M113's, air shelling and heliborne operations." As a result of these fears, "[s]ome men requested discharge, while others lacked a sense of responsibility and failed in their mission of leading their men."[148] Despite the seeming invincibility of the South Vietnamese insurgents, they suffered from the same privations and fears of war as their ARVN counterparts did. Unlike the ARVN, however, the PLAF possessed the leadership capable of neutralizing and correcting these deficiencies in a relatively short period of time. As the company in question, 1st Company, 261st Regional Battalion, demonstrated some three months later, the insurgent leadership overcame these shortcomings, and the company ably stood its ground against both helicopters and M113s at Ap Bac.

Whatever the relative influence of the above factors, they bonded the PLAF into a tough, focused enemy. Despite the effects of setbacks on morale and recruitment, heavy casualties generally did not lessen the guerrillas' allegiance to their cause, an indication of their devotion to their perceived purpose and mission.[149] While the PLAF fought with outdated or captured weapons against a numerically larger foe and continually reorganized its units to preserve their security against the larger and better-armed GVN forces, it possessed attributes that the ARVN seemed to lack: a coherent plan for victory, thorough training, and a will to fight. The American advisors in Vietnam believed they were there for just those reasons. An example of how well the belligerents and their systems did against each other in the field was demonstrated at Ap Bac, a small village outside of My Tho, on 2 January 1963.

NOTES

1. Department of State, *Foreign Relations of the United States, 1961–1963*, vol. 1, *Vietnam, 1961* (Washington, D.C.: U.S. Government Printing Office, 1988), 497–498.

2. For the purposes of this work, conventional warfare refers to traditional methods of fighting, similar to the U.S. Army's experiences during the world wars and Korea.

3. Because the manual's original issue date is 1954, the term "1954 version" refers to the 1954 base document with posted changes. Department of the Army, *Field Service Regulations-Operations*, Field Manual 100-5, rev. ed. (Washington, D.C.: U.S. Government Printing Office, 1958), inside front cover.

4. Department of the Army, *Field Service Regulations-Operations*, Field Manual 100-5 (Washington, D.C.: U.S. Government Printing Office, 1962), 46.

5. Department of the Army, *Field Service Regulations-Operations*, 1958, 171–173.

6. Department of the Army, *Field Service Regulations-Operations*, 1962, 106–109, 136–138.

7. Ibid., 137, 139.

8. Ibid., 139–140.

9. Department of the Army, *Operations against Irregular Forces*, Field Manual 31-15 (Washington, D.C.: U.S. Government Printing Office, 1961), 3, 18.

10. Memo, H. K. Eggleston, Chief, USASEC (CHUSASEC), to Distribution "B," subject: Lessons Learned Number 2, 30 March 1962 (U.S. Army Military History Institute Digital Library [hereafter USAMHIDL]).

11. Of the 11 "Lessons Learned" memoranda issued between March and May 1962 that described ARVN operations, two were listed as "successful," seven as "partially successful," and two as "unsuccessful." For examples of each, see Memo, H. K. Eggleston, CHUSASEC, to Distribution "B," subject: Lessons Learned Number 1, 30 March 1962; Memo, H. K. Eggleston, CHUSASEC, to Distribution "B," subject: Lessons Learned Number 7, n.d.; and Memo, H. K. Eggleston, CHUSASEC, to Distribution "B," subject: Lessons Learned Number 4, 11 April 1962 (USAMHIDL).

12. Memo, H. K. Eggleston, CHUSASEC, to Distribution "B," subject: Lessons Learned Number 9, 27 April 1962 (USAMHIDL).

13. "The Nature of the Beast," *Infantry* 52 (May–June 1962): 7–8, 60–61; "Characteristics of Guerrilla Operations," *Infantry* 52 (May–June 1962): 9, 64–66; "Considerations in Fighting Irregular Forces," *Infantry* 52 (July–August 1962): 8–9, 39–

41; "Military Operations Against Irregular Forces," *Infantry* 52 (July–August 1962): 12–13, 44–46.

14. Department of the Army, *Counterguerrilla Operations,* Field Manual 31-16 (Washington, D.C.: U.S. Government Printing Office, 1963), 2.

15. Ibid.

16. Cable's work discusses these doctrinal oversights in depth. Larry Cable, *Conflict of Myths: The Development of American Counterinsurgency Doctrine and the Vietnam War* (New York: New York University Press, 1986), 111–201.

17. Department of State, *Foreign Relations of the United States, 1958–1960,* vol. I, *Vietnam,* 182–183.

18. Ibid., 200, 199.

19. John Coleman, "Advisors to Fighters: America's First Combat Soldiers of the Vietnam War" (paper delivered at the Vietnam Center's Third Triennial Symposium, Lubbock, TX, 1999), 17–18. Coleman argues that when advisors facilitated ARVN operations by coordinating fire support or providing tactical intelligence that resulted in the death of guerrillas, they became "legitimate target[s] of war." While this participation directly affected the insurgents in the field and may have made the Americans more "fighters" than "advisors," the issue of whether they were legitimate targets or not is immaterial. To the insurgents, all personnel, whether civilian, military, Vietnamese, or American, were legitimate targets if their deaths served a political purpose.

20. Department of the Army, *The U.S. Adviser* by Cao Van Vien et al., Indochina Monographs (Washington, D.C.: U.S. Army Center of Military History, 1980), 72–74.

21. Department of the Army, *RVNAF and U.S. Operational Cooperation and Coordination* by Ngo Quang Troung, Indochina Monographs (Washington, D.C.: U.S. Army Center of Military History, 1980), 163.

22. Andrew F. Krepinevich, *The Army and Vietnam* (Baltimore: Johns Hopkins University Press, 1986), 48; Department of the Army, *Mounted Combat in Vietnam* by Donn Starry, Vietnam Studies (Washington, D.C.: U.S. Government Printing Office, 1978), 19–20; Department of the Army, *The U.S. Adviser,* 31; Colonel Andrew P. O'Meara, Riyadh, Saudi Arabia, to author, West Point, NY, 8 February 1999. Interestingly, an officer writing in 1962 about assignment to a MAAG characterized the potential language barrier as "a formidable obstacle to the advisor." The editor discounted the author's obvious concern by noting that "the author may have made too much of the 'language barrier.' It *is* readily soluble if the advisor so desires" (emphasis in the original). What, exactly, the editor believed the solution to be is left to the reader to decide. Leonard D. Chafin, "Assignment: MAAG," *Infantry* 52 (January–February 1962): 52–53.

23. Colonel Andrew P. O'Meara, Riyadh, Saudi Arabia, to author, West Point, NY, 8 February 1999; Chafin, "Assignment: MAAG," 52–53; Department of the Army, *Mounted Combat in Vietnam,* 20. This desire to volunteer for advisory duty evaporated after the arrival of American tactical units in late 1965. Many Americans believed that holding advisory positions reduced their chances for advancement and sought to avoid them if possible. Krepinevich, *The Army and Vietnam,* 207–208.

24. Department of State, *Foreign Relations of the United States, 1961–1963,* vol. II, *Vietnam, 1962* (Washington, D.C.: U.S. Government Printing Office, 1990), 772; Department of State, *Foreign Relations of the United States, 1961–1963,* vol. III, *Vietnam, January–August 1963* (Washington, D.C.: U.S. Government Printing Office, 1991), 10.

25. Dave R. Palmer, *Summons of the Trumpet,* rev. ed. (New York: Ballantine Books, 1984), 38–39.

26. David Halberstam, *The Making of a Quagmire* (New York: Random House, 1965), 139.

27. Guenter Lewy, *America in Vietnam*, rev. ed. (New York: Oxford University Press, 1980), 168.

28. Thomas J. Lewis, "Year of the Hare: Bureaucratic Distortion in the U.S. Military View of the Vietnam War in 1963" (M.A. diss., George Washington University, 1972), 76.

29. Halberstam, *The Making of a Quagmire*, 108.

30. Lewy, *America in Vietnam*, 168.

31. Halberstam, *The Making of a Quagmire*, 108.

32. Department of State, *Foreign Relations of the United States, 1958–1960*, vol. I, *Vietnam*, 182; Department of the Army, *RVNAF and U.S. Operational Cooperation and Coordination*, 152.

33. *The Pentagon Papers: The Defense Department History of the United States Decisionmaking on Vietnam*, vol. II, the Senator Gravel edition (Boston: Beacon Press, 1971), 454; Terrance Maitland et al., *Raising the Stakes*, the Vietnam Experience (Boston: Boston Publishing Company, 1982), 11; Department of the Army, *The U.S. Adviser*, 46.

34. Association of Graduates, *Register of Graduates and Former Cadets* (West Point, NY: Association of Graduates, 1993), 208; General William B. Rosson, U.S. Army (Retired), interview by author, 15 April 1997, Lubbock, TX.

35. Department of State, *Foreign Relations of the United States, 1952–1954*, vol. XIII, *Indochina* (Washington, D.C.: U.S. Government Printing Office, 1982), 465, 467, 1076. Interestingly, Walter B. Smith, the undersecretary of state, responded to Heath with his own "misgivings" about O'Daniel's appointment as CHMAAG, a surprising fact given that Smith and O'Daniel had served together in Europe during World War II. Ibid., 1077.

36. Ibid., 1076; Ronald Spector, *Advice and Support: The Early Years of the U.S. Army in Vietnam, 1941–1960*, rev. ed. (New York: The Free Press, 1985), 272–273.

37. Department of State, *Foreign Relations of the United States, 1955–1957*, vol. I, *Vietnam* (Washington, D.C.: U.S. Government Printing Office, 1985), 720; General William B. Rosson, U.S. Army (Retired), interview by author, 15 April 1997, Lubbock, TX. Williams outlined his belief in the inevitability of a North Vietnamese invasion of South Vietnam in his "Chief's Bulletin Number 3": "It must be remembered that the Viet Minh have declared their intention to bring South Vietnam under their control. . . . Historically, worldwide, the Communists use two methods to gain their objective; subversive action leading to infiltration of the government or failing that, conquest. They have been unable to infiltrate and overthrow the Government of South Vietnam. We may expect then that their alternate method will be to attempt to gain their objective by force of arms. . . . Hostile operation[s] on a Division and Corps level . . . may be expected if and when the Vietminh attack. The enemy will move suddenly and with speed." S. T. Williams, Chief's Bulletin Number 3, 21 June 1956 (box 1; issuances; Adjutant General Division; Military Assistance Advisory Group, Vietnam; Record Group 334; National Archives [hereafter AGD/MAAGV/RG 334]).

38. Memo, J. N. Pearman, Executive Officer, CATO Division, to Senior Advisors, subject: Field Exercise, 1st Field Division, 5 July 1957 (folder 3, box 1, Samuel T. Williams Papers, U.S. Army Military History Institute [hereafter USAMHI]).

39. Department of the Army, *Strategy and Tactics* by Hoang Ngoc Lung, Indochina Monographs (Washington, D.C.: U.S. Army Center of Military History, 1980), 69.

40. Department of the Army, *Reflections on the Vietnam War* by Cao Van Vien and Dong Van Khuyen, Indochina Monographs (Washington, D.C.: U.S. Army Center of Military History, 1978), 10 (part 1, reel 2, *U.S. Armed Forces in Vietnam, 1954–1975*).

41. Department of State, *Foreign Relations of the United States, 1958–1960*, vol. I, *Vietnam*, 283, 293.

42. Ibid., 346–348.

43. Ibid., 291–292.

44. Ibid., 394; Shelby L. Stanton, *Green Berets at War: U.S. Special Forces in Southeast Asia, 1956–1975* (Novato, CA: Presidio Press, 1985), 36–37; Department of the Army, *U.S. Army Special Forces, 1961–1971* by Francis Kelly, Vietnam Studies (Washington, D.C.: U.S. Government Printing Office, 1973), 5.

45. Stanton, *Green Berets at War*, 35; Department of the Army, *U.S. Army Special Forces*, 4.

46. Department of State, *Foreign Relations of the United States, 1958–1960*, vol. I, *Vietnam*, 396, 403.

47. Ibid., 474–475, 482.

48. Spector, *Advice and Support*, 365.

49. Department of State, *Foreign Relations of the United States, 1958–1960*, vol. I, *Vietnam*, 620; Department of State, *Foreign Relations of the United States, 1961–1963*, vol. II, *Vietnam, 1962*, 19; Krepinevich, *The Army and Vietnam*, 56–58.

50. *Pentagon Papers*, vol. II, 650–651; Department of State, *Foreign Relations of the United States, 1961–1963*, vol. I, *Vietnam, 1961*, 279, 497–498.

51. As late as November 1962, some of the senior U.S. Army leadership still believed that political factors in Vietnam were secondary. In speaking at Fordham University, General Earle G. Wheeler stated his position quite clearly: "It is fashionable in some quarters to say that the problems in Southeast Asia are primarily political and economic rather than military. I do not agree. The essence of the problem in Vietnam is military." Roger Hilsman, *To Move a Nation: The Politics of Foreign Policy in the Administration of John F. Kennedy*, rev. ed. (Garden City, NY: Doubleday & Company, 1967), 426.

52. *Pentagon Papers*, vol. II, 142. For copies of both Thompson's and Hilsman's reports, see Department of State, *Foreign Relations of the United States, 1961–1963*, vol. II, *Vietnam, 1962*, 102–109 and 73–90, respectively.

53. *Pentagon Papers*, vol. II, 145.

54. Tran Van Don, *Our Endless War* (San Rafael, CA: Presidio Press, 1978), 81.

55. Department of the Army, *Reflections on the Vietnam War*, 19.

56. *Pentagon Papers*, vol. II, 256, 313; Department of State, *Foreign Relations of the United States, 1958–1960*, vol. I, *Vietnam*, 487; Memo, H. K. Eggleston, CHUSASEC, to Special Distribution, subject: Lessons Learned Number 19, 31 July 1962 (USAMHIDL).

57. Department of the Army, *U.S. Army Area Handbook for Vietnam* by George Harris et al., Pamphlet 550-40, rev. ed. (Washington, D.C.: U.S. Government Printing Office, 1964), 315; Lewy, *America in Vietnam*, 25; Department of State, *Foreign Relations of the United States, 1961–1963*, vol. II, *Vietnam, 1962*, 359.

58. In assessing Operation SUNRISE, one American memorandum observed that "[i]n spite of specific Presidential directives, the required level of support and assistance from responsible GVN agencies, including national ministries, were difficult to obtain and were, in some instances, late and inadequate." Memo, H. K. Eggleston, CHUSASEC, to Special Distribution, subject: Lessons Learned Number 19, 31 July 1962 (USAMHIDL).

59. Palmer, *Summons of the Trumpet*, 158–159.

60. Department of the Army, *Reflections on the Vietnam War*, 21.

61. Richard Clutterbuck, *The Long, Long War: Counterinsurgency in Malaya and Vietnam* (New York: Praeger, 1966), 67.

62. Department of the Army, *Reflections on the Vietnam War*, 31.

63. Department of State, *Foreign Relations of the United States, 1961–1963*, vol. III, *Vietnam, January–August 1963*, 9. For a narrative of a typical sweep, see Halberstam, *The Making of a Quagmire*, 89 and *passim*.

64. Department of State, *Foreign Relations of the United States, 1961–1963*, vol. I, *Vietnam, 1961*, 624.

65. Department of the Army, *Reflections on the Vietnam War*, 32.

66. James W. Trullinger, *Village at War: An Account of Revolution in Vietnam* (New York: Longman, 1980), 85; Department of the Army, *Reflections on the Vietnam War*, 31.

67. Department of State, *Foreign Relations of the United States, 1961–1963*, vol. III, *Vietnam, January–August 1963*, 9.

68. Neil Sheehan, *A Bright Shining Lie* (New York: Random House, 1988), 107; Department of State, *Foreign Relations of the United States, 1961–1963*, vol. II, *Vietnam, 1962*, 790.

69. Despite the stated requirement for a positively identified target, the memorandum did allow for "[c]ontrolled reconnaissance by fire . . . provided there is little or no possibility that non-combatants will become involved." Memo, H. K. Eggleston, CHUSASEC, to Special Distribution, subject: Lessons Learned Number 20, 27 August 1962 (USAMHIDL).

70. Department of State, *Foreign Relations of the United States, 1952–1954*, vol. XIII, *Indochina*, 466, 473.

71. Department of the Army, *U.S. Army Area Handbook for Vietnam*, 476, 478.

72. Department of the Army, *The Development and Training of the South Vietnamese Army* by James Collins, Vietnam Studies (Washington, D.C.: U.S. Government Printing Office, 1975), 9; Spector, *Advice and Support*, 297.

73. Department of the Army, *U.S. Army Area Handbook for Vietnam*, 478; Lieutenant Colonel John Vann, briefing notes, n.d., 2 (folder 3, box 39, Vann-Sheehan Vietnam War Collection, Library of Congress Manuscript Division [hereafter VSVWC]).

74. Department of State, *Foreign Relations of the United States, 1961–1963*, vol. I, *Vietnam, 1961*, 504.

75. Department of the Army, *U.S. Army Area Handbook for Vietnam*, 274.

76. *Pentagon Papers*, vol. II, 436–437; Department of the Army, *U.S. Army Area Handbook for Vietnam*, 274.

77. Ibid.

78. Ibid., 275.

79. Sheehan, *A Bright Shining Lie*, 100.

80. Department of the Army, *The Development and Training of the South Vietnamese Army*, 17.

81. United States Military Assistance Advisory Group, "ARVN Order of Battle Report, April 1961," NLK 81-197 (folder 8, box 1, unit 2, Douglas Pike Collection, Vietnam Archive [hereafter DPC]).

82. In early 1962, the senior II Corps advisor sent a memorandum to his counterpart that described ARVN drivers who were exceeding posted speed limits, overloading vehicles, and failing to use cargo straps. According to his statistics, "vehicle accidents each month are causing more casualties in troop units of II Corps than are VC combat actions." His solution was to enforce the speed limits ruthlessly and establish ordnance checkpoints to ensure driver compliance. Almost any living American soldier who served in Vietnam can readily provide a firsthand experience that reflects these observations.

Memo, Senior Advisor, II Corps, to Commanding General, II Corps, subject: Safe Driving Practices II Corps Zone, 14 February 1962 (folder 2, box 2, Wilbur Wilson Papers, USAMHI). Palmer, *Summons of the Trumpet*, 17.

83. Department of State, *Foreign Relations of the United States, 1958–1960*, vol. I, *Vietnam*, 329, 352–353, 374. Durbrow's cable of 28 March 1960 describes "75 15-man commando companies," but given the TOE for the units that provided for 129 weapons, 15 is most likely a typographical error.

84. *Pentagon Papers*, vol. II, 89.

85. Department of the Army, *Airmobility, 1961–1971* by John Tolson, Vietnam Studies (Washington, D.C.: U.S. Government Printing Office, 1973), 3.

86. Barry Gregory, *Vietnam Helicopter Handbook* (San Bernadino, CA: Bargo Press, 1988), 144; Department of the Army, *Airmobility*, 29; Memo, H. K. Eggleston, CHUSASEC, to Special Distribution, subject: Lessons Learned Number 22, 8 September 1962 (USAMHIDL); Halberstam, *The Making of a Quagmire*, 84.

87. Department of the Army, *Mounted Combat in Vietnam*, 21–22.

88. The original designation of the Iroquois was HU-1 (helicopter, utility, model 1), but the U.S. Army later changed its nomenclature to the more recognizable UH-1. While many documents from this period refer to the Huey as "HU-1," this study will only use "UH-1" to avoid confusion. Department of the Army, *Tactical and Materiel Innovations* by John Hay, Vietnam Studies (Washington, D.C.: U.S. Government Printing Office, 1974), 14–16; Gregory, *Vietnam Helicopter Handbook*, 55, 148; Department of the Army, *Airmobility*, 15–16, 28.

89. Department of the Army, *Airmobility*, 28, 30.

90. Colonel Andrew P. O'Meara, Riyadh, Saudi Arabia, letter to author, West Point, NY, 8 February 1999; Office of the Secretary of Defense, "U.S. Military Advisory Effort," in *United States-Vietnamese Relations, 1945–1967*, Book 3, Part IVB, Section 3, 132 (folder 6, box 1, unit 2, DPC).

91. Sheehan, *A Bright Shining Lie*, 77; Department of the Army, *The RVNAF* by Dong Van Khuyen, Indochina Monographs (Washington, D.C.: U.S. Army Center of Military History, 1978), 86 (part 1, reel 3, *U.S. Armed Forces in Vietnam, 1954–1975*).

92. Memo, Ton That Dinh, Commander, II Corps and 2nd Tactical Zone, to President of the Republic of Vietnam, subject: Promotion of NCO's and Platoon Leaders in Combat Units, 3 November 1961 (folder 1, box 1, WW); Department of the Army, *The RVNAF*, 86.

93. Tran Van Don, *Our Endless War*, 78.

94. Palmer, *Summons of the Trumpet*, 42.

95. Department of the Army, *U.S. Army Area Handbook for Vietnam*, 312.

96. Lewy, *America in Vietnam*, 170–171.

97. Ibid., 19.

98. Ibid., 171.

99. Department of State, *Foreign Relations of the United States, 1961–1963*, vol. II, *Vietnam, 1962*, 776; Department of State, *Foreign Relations of the United States, 1961–1963*, vol. III, *Vietnam, January–August 1963*, 9. Diem's treatment of Huynh Van Cao, the 7th Division's commander, illustrates the president's reaction to perceived setbacks. When Diem heard of the engagement at Ap My Luong and the resulting casualties, he immediately summoned Cao to Saigon. After spending almost the entire day outside the president's office, Cao received of one of Diem's famed monologues. If Cao wished to receive a promotion to general and a corps command, Diem told his subordinate, Cao had to exercise more caution in conducting operations. Diem's admonition had the desired effect. Between October and December 1962, Cao's division conducted 14 operations but only suffered three killed, purportedly to "friendly fire." Sheehan, *A Bright Shining Lie*,

120–121. Diem's demand for casualty reduction may also offer an explanation for the ARVN's reliance upon firepower instead of close combat to destroy the PLAF.

100. Department of the Army, *Leadership* by Cao Van Vien, Indochina Monographs (Washington, D.C.: U.S. Army Center of Military History, 1978), 15 (part 1, reel 4, *U.S. Armed Forces in Vietnam, 1954–1975*).

101. Ibid.

102. Lewy, *America in Vietnam*, 170; Halberstam, *The Making of a Quagmire*, 165.

103. David Kaiser, *American Tragedy: Kennedy, Johnson, and the Origins of the Vietnam War* (Cambridge, MA: The Belknap Press of Harvard University Press, 2000), 162.

104. Lewis, "Year of the Hare," 25.

105. Department of State, *Foreign Relations of the United States, 1961–1963*, vol. III, *Vietnam, January–August 1963*, 8; George Herring, *America's Longest War*, rev. ed. (New York: McGraw-Hill, Inc., 1996), 256.

106. Lewy, *America in Vietnam*, 173.

107. Bruce Palmer, *The 25-Year War: America's Military Role in Vietnam*, rev. ed. (New York: Touchstone, 1985), 104.

108. Lewy, *America in Vietnam*, 177.

109. Douglas Pike, *Viet Cong* (Cambridge: MIT Press, 1966), 85; Douglas Pike, *PAVN: People's Army of Vietnam* (Novato, CA: Presidio Press, 1986), 217.

110. Vo Nguyen Giap, *Big Victory, Great Task* (New York: Praeger, 1968), 52; Pike, *PAVN*, 233.

111. Pike, *PAVN*, 216; Pike, *Viet Cong*, 86.

112. The concept of a "violence program" is often misleading because many believe it includes the military or guerrilla actions of the PLAF. In actuality, it encompassed all forms of violence, including assassinations, kidnappings, executions, and sabotage. Pike, Viet Cong, 86.

113. Vo Nguyen Giap, *Big Victory, Great Task*, 54.

114. Vo Nguyen Giap, *People's War, People's Army* (New York: Praeger, 1962), 46.

115. Although Chinh was describing the Viet Minh's activities during the First Indochina War, his narrative spoke directly to the situation in South Vietnam during the early 1960s. Troung Chinh, *Primer for Revolt: The Communist Takeover in Viet-Nam*, rev. ed. (New York: Praeger, 1966), 168–169.

116. Vo Nguyen Giap, *People's War, People's Army*, 46–47.

117. Ibid., 104.

118. Ibid., 106.

119. Ibid., 107–108.

120. This ability to adapt the insurgency to the local conditions while at the same time maintaining political pressure throughout the struggle is perhaps the primary reason why Pike wrote that *dau tranh* "is a strategy for which there is no known proven counterstrategy." Pike, *PAVN*, 213.

121. Mao's model did apply to the First Indochina War, since the Viet Minh fought the French for the urban centers before withdrawing to the countryside. Mao Tse-tung, *On Protracted War*, rev. ed. (Beijing: Foreign Languages Press, 1966), 34–39.

122. The concept of *khoi nghia* was to play a critical role in the DRV's decision to launch the 1968 Tet Offensive. Pike, *Viet Cong*, 76–77.

123. David Chanoff and Doan Van Toai, *Portrait of the Enemy* (London: I. B. Taurus & Company, 1987), 108.

124. Department of the Army, *Human Factors Considerations of Undergrounds in Insurgencies* by Andrew Molnar, Pamphlet 550-104 (Washington, D.C.: U.S. Government Printing Office, 1966), 213–216.

125. Ibid., 218.

126. Chanoff and Doan Van Toai, *Portrait of the Enemy*, 162–163.

127. Ibid., 161–166.

128. Department of the Army, *Airmobility*, 15.

129. U.S. Military Assistance Command, Vietnam, *Ap Bac Battle, 2 January 1963; Translation of VC Document, 20 April 1963*, C0043021, 4 (hereafter *Ap Bac*) (Vietnam Archive).

130. Ibid., 2.

131. Greg Lockhart, *Nation in Arms* (Boston: Allen and Unwin, 1989), 92.

132. Ibid., 94.

133. Tran Van Don, *Our Endless War*, 82.

134. Pike, *Viet Cong*, 234–237; William Henderson, *Why the Vietcong Fight: A Study of Motivation and Control in a Modern Army in Combat* (Westport, CT: Greenwood Press, 1979), 120–121; Palmer, *Summons of the Trumpet*, 67.

135. William Andrews, *The Village War* (Columbia: University of Missouri Press, 1973), 105.

136. Pike, *Viet Cong*, 234–235.

137. Ibid., 234–235; Andrews, *The Village War*, 105.

138. Ibid., 58.

139. Chanoff and Doan Van Toai, *Portrait of the Enemy*, 42–43.

140. Truong Nhu Tang et al., *A Vietcong Memoir* (New York: Harcourt, Brace, Jovanovich, 1985), 164.

141. Department of the Army, *The Communist Insurgent Infrastructure in South Vietnam: A Study of Organization and Strategy* by Michael Conley, Pamphlet 550-106 (Washington, D.C.: U.S. Government Printing Office, 1967), 150.

142. Pike, *PAVN*, 164.

143. Department of the Army, *The Communist Insurgent Infrastructure in South Vietnam*, 140.

144. Andrews, *The Village War*, 107.

145. Edward Doyle et al., *The North*, the Vietnam Experience (Boston: Boston Publishing Company, 1981), 48.

146. Tran Van Tra, *Vietnam: History of the Bulwark B2 Theater*, vol. 5, *Concluding the 30 Years' War* (Berkeley: University of California Indochina Archive, 1995), 3, 17, and *passim*.

147. Chanoff and Doan Van Toai, *Portrait of the Enemy*, 59–60.

148. *Ap Bac*, 4.

149. Frank H. Denton, *Some Effects of Military Operations on Viet Cong Attitudes* (Santa Monica: Rand Corporation, 1966), 24.

3

The Fight

It is better to die than to leave one's post.[1]

a PLAF commander at Ap Bac

A battle's outcome is the result of numerous influences and variables. The opponents' doctrine, training, organization, and equipment; the commanders' personalities and previous experiences; the terrain; and, in many cases, plain chance all affect the unfolding and decision of a battle. Ap Bac was no different from any other battle in these respects. Both belligerents came to Ap Bac inspired or burdened by their pasts, how they expected to fight, and how they organized their units. Given the nature of the insurgency, the PLAF's performance did not seem as dependent upon the personalities of the commanders and their advisors as the ARVN's, but neither army could avoid the terrain's influence.

THE TERRAIN AND THE BELLIGERENTS' PLANS AND TASK ORGANIZATIONS

In any engagement or battle, the terrain is a neutral. It does, however, favor the commander who is best able to turn it to his advantage. As George Marshall observed in *Infantry in Battle*, "The ground is an open book. The commander who reads and heeds what it has to say is laying a sound foundation for tactical success."[2] The ARVN and the PLAF units had met each other on numerous occasions throughout the Dinh Tuong Province over the previous year. Both armies knew the advantages and disadvantages the terrain had to offer through the hard teacher of experience, and both initially planned to use the terrain to their gain.

Ap Bac lay approximately 20 kilometers northwest of My Tho (see Fig. 3.1).[3] Located in the Mekong River Delta, the village was nestled amidst rice paddies and swamps. Canals crisscrossed the region, dividing it into numerous island-like sections. Although many of the canals were both narrow and shallow, some of the larger canals, like the Ba Beo Canal to the north, supported boat

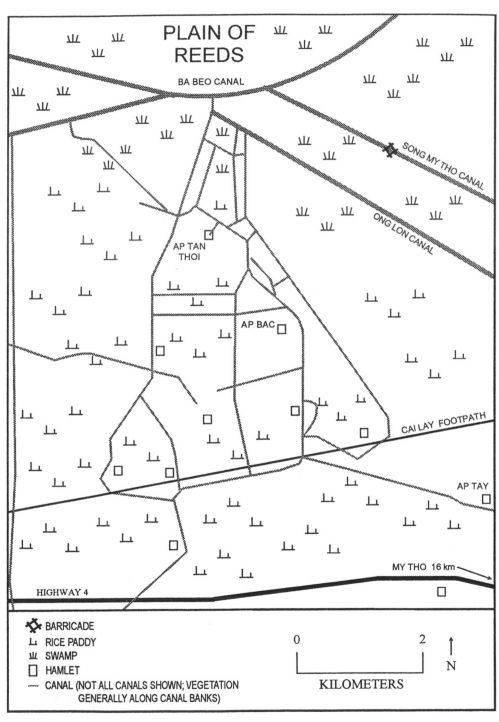

Figure 3.1
Ap Bac and Vicinity

movement. Some canals were dug below the level of the surrounding area, while others required dikes to transport their water. Along the canals, trees and scrub vegetation further reinforced the image that each paddy or section was its own isolated world.

Movement by either foot or vehicle was difficult, as few large roads crossed the canals. Footpaths and cart trails connected the many hamlets and villages, but they crossed the canals only by precarious footbridges. For mounted movement, wheeled vehicles were restricted to the few suitable roads in the area. The tracked M113s easily traversed the rice paddies, but, though amphibious, met with difficulties when trying to cross the canals. Once the carriers were in the canal, the steeply sloped sides made it difficult for the APCs to pull themselves up and out the other side. In some cases, if the carriers dived too deeply into a canal, the water would rush through the air intakes, possibly flooding the engine compartment and potentially killing the engine or sinking the vehicle. As a result, if the APCs were not able to cross a canal at a bridge or suitable ford, their speed of movement was drastically reduced. Solutions to the crossing dilemma lay in the cutting into the sides of the canals by hand or piling brush in the channels but were oftentimes not sufficient and caused the carriers to work in pairs or larger groups to pull each other across the obstacle. Depending upon the APC crews' level of training, the size of the canal, and the thickness of the vegetation, a crossing could take anywhere from 15 minutes to an hour or more.[4] In this region of Vietnam, air assets provided the ARVN with the only true means of rapid mobility that did not require large canals for the boats or unimproved roads for the carriers.

The canals and their vegetation not only restricted movement, but they also degraded observation as well. When crossing the knee-deep paddies, a unit could only observe as far as the next canal or woodline, adversely affecting its ability to direct fires, both indirect and air delivered. Command and control were adversely affected as well; unless a commander were airborne, it was nearly impossible for him to see other units beyond his paddy. Further, since the paddies themselves were flat and unobstructed, soldiers caught in the open while crossing the rice fields had neither cover from enemy fire nor concealment from observation. A unit dug in along a canal or treeline not only had the advantage of concealment and surprise, but of cover and protection as well.[5] While possessing advantages for both attacker and defender, the terrain at Ap Bac better favored the PLAF's plans for the coming engagement, as the ARVN soldiers, particularly those of the 7th Division, soon discovered.

As 1962 came to a close, the PLAF received reports from its agents throughout Dinh Tuong Province that the ARVN was conducting preparations for yet another sweep operation. In the last two months of the year, the guerrillas observed more than 70 supply trucks moving into My Tho, the home of the 7th Division's base camp. Further, with Diem's birthday on 3 January, the PLAF suspected that the ARVN units would conduct operations on either 1 or 2 January 1963 in order to gain a victory just prior to the president's birthday.[6] As a result of these indicators, the senior party committee member in the area, Hai Hoang, acting as the de facto PLAF commander, outlined four plans to counter the imminent ARVN attack, all of which were offensive, and not defensive, in nature.[7] Wishing to take advantage of the ARVN's lack of precise intelligence, the guerrillas anticipated striking at the CG forces massing along Highway 4 before they could mount a coordinated attack.

Why the PLAF chose to dig in at this particular village and time remains unclear. One explanation may lie with the increased training the guerrilla units received in the latter stages of 1962. Although suffering serious defeats earlier in the year at the hands of the heliborne and armored ARVN units, the PLAF had conducted what it believed to be four successful counter mopping-up operations between September and December 1962.[8] This perceived efficacy against the ARVN's sweeps may have emboldened Hai Hoang enough to choose to fight it out instead of breaking contact because he believed himself strong enough and his troops well trained enough to do so. In essence, a successful fight at Ap Bac would "proof" the PLAF's tactics against helicopters and APCs.[9]

Another possibility is that the commander sought to build his units' morale and provide a victory that would attract recruits from the region. Both of the companies that fought at Ap Bac had suffered heavy casualties through the previous fall, resulting in soldiers having "no confidence in their cadre" and others "request[ing] discharge." After the party committees took the "[n]ecessary corrective action," in which training played a major part, the units' morale by the end of the year was "very high." By taking on the ARVN 7th Division, the PLAF stood to reverse the GVN's gains in the province, demonstrate to the peasants its ability to counter the South Vietnamese APCs and the American helicopters, and rebuild the units' confidence in their leadership.[10]

A third prospect is that what happened at Ap Bac was simply the result of a serious miscalculation on the part of the PLAF commander that resulted in the guerrillas having no other option but to stand and fight. Of the four plans that Hoang outlined prior to the battle, all targeted only the CG units approaching along Highway 4; none discussed a recommended action in the case that the M113s attacked Ap Bac. Perhaps believing that he could ambush the CG companies in the south and then escape before the arrival of the remaining ARVN units, it is possible that the PLAF commander waited too long before ordering a withdrawal. Unable to escape the ARVN units that were closing in on them and faced with the prospect of becoming a lucrative target for close air support (CAS) and artillery, the guerrillas may have chosen to meet their fate in their prepared positions.[11] Whatever the reason, the commander's decision to remain in and around Ap Bac ushered in a new phase of the Second Indochina War in which the PLAF no longer broke contact shortly after sighting helicopters or APCs.

Taking advantage of the surrounding terrain, the PLAF commander arrayed his forces along the canals to the north, east, and south of Ap Bac (see Fig. 3.2). To the north, the 1st Company, 514th Provincial Battalion (C1/514), under the command of San Bich, anchored its right flank in Ap Tan Thoi, oriented to the southwest. Further to the south along the canal, the 1st Company, 261st Regional Battalion (C1/261), under the command of Nguyen Bay, formed a semicircle

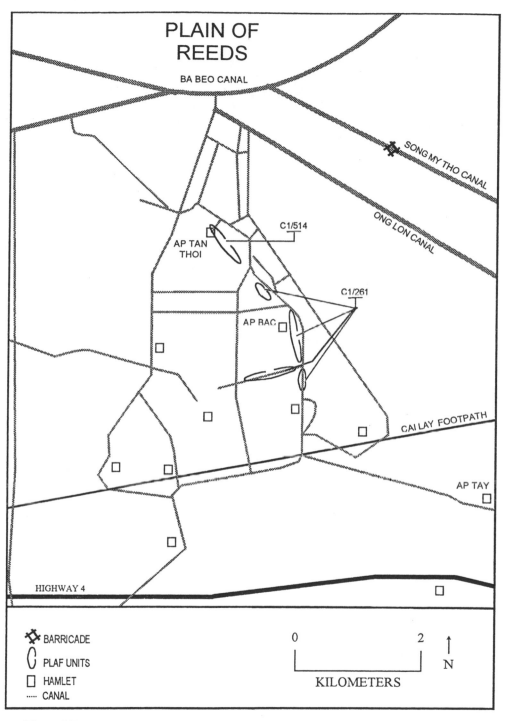

Figure 3.2
PLAF Defensive Positions, 1–2 January 1963

around Ap Bac. Tied in to C1/514's left flank, C1/261's elements to the north and east of Ap Bac oriented to the southwest and west. The company's southern-most platoon, defending along the east-west treeline below Ap Bac, oriented due south.[12] Reinforcing these two companies were two squads of the 5th Company, 261st Battalion, and the 13th Support Unit, both main force units, and guerrillas from both regional and local PLAF units. Although estimates vary, the commander at Ap Tan Thoi controlled at least two companies with reinforcements numbering some 340 guerrillas in all.[13]

As described earlier, the PLAF guerrillas' level of experience and readiness varied between units. Some of the leaders, particularly those of C1/261, were hardened veterans. Nguyen Bay had fought for the Viet Minh during the First Indochina War. A fair portion of the remaining cadre had seen some combat, and many had participated in earlier counter mopping-up operations. There were many guerrillas, however, who would see shots fired in anger for the first time. C1/514, the locally recruited provincial company, had recently replaced "up to 1/3 of its strength . . . after its previous operations and losses." Most of the new recruits benefited from the previous months' increased training on defensive tactics and techniques for use against helicopters and APCs. Results of the training efforts, however, were not uniform. In assessing its overall unit readiness, the PLAF leadership admitted that the militia and local guerrillas "were not well trained in combat." To their credit, however, "they were familiar with the maintenance of security" as demonstrated by their ability to prevent the ARVN or CG from establishing security posts in the local area. On the whole, Hoang had under his command a sufficiently trained and motivated ad hoc battalion.[14]

The PLAF units around Ap Bac mustered small arms of primarily American manufacture, two or three locally produced rifle grenades, one 60mm mortar with three rounds, approximately 12 Browning Automatic Rifles (BARs), four .30 caliber machine guns, and at least one heavy machine gun.[15] Recognizing the potential air threat to his position, Hoang directed that "[e]ach unit . . . form an anti-aircraft cell responsible for the security for their area . . . [and] must dig gun emplacements beforehand." Burrowing into the sides of the dikes, the guerrillas emplaced near-perfect fighting positions that took advantage of the cover the banks provided them and the concealment offered by the vegetation. To maximize the effectiveness of their weapons, the PLAF soldiers set out aiming stakes for the automatic weapons, which were small posts marked with white tape that designated each weapon's sector of fire. With their positions along the canals, the guerrillas also did not have to worry about resupplying themselves during the coming battle. Since the water level in the canals was well below the tops of the dikes because of the dry season, the insurgents could safely use sampans to move supplies without exposing themselves to enemy fire. Beginning their preparations early, the units completed their positions by 2200 on 1 January. Although not knowing the exact time and location of the ARVN approach, the PLAF units in and around Ap Bac and Ap Tan Thoi were dug in and prepared for the attack that was certain to come.[16]

Facing Hoang was Lieutenant Colonel Bui Dinh Dam, the newly appointed
7th Division commander. Unlike his guerrilla counterpart, who knew exactly
where Dam was, the ARVN commander, although aware of the PLAF units in
the area, did not know where Hoang was. Despite his experiences as the division
chief of staff, Colonel Dam lacked the skills necessary to lead a division in
combat. Although a dedicated professional and an able administrator, he was ill
suited for command.[17] One contemporary characterized him as "a nice little man
and good staff officer, but [he] did not want responsibility. . . . [He was] terrified
of battle, helicopters, and [General Huynh Van] Cao [the IV Corps
commander]."[18] Given these characteristics, Dam was an odd choice for division
command. When one takes into account the political climate and machinations
of the ARVN officer corps, however, Dam's appointment was perhaps a logical
one. By recommending to Diem that Dam command the 7th Division, Cao,
formerly the 7th's commander, prevented an able rival from commanding one of
the ARVN's premier divisions.[19]

Between 28 and 30 December 1962, the division had received reports that a
PLAF radio station was operating in the vicinity of Ap Tan Thoi, a small village
several kilometers to the northwest of My Tho. These intercepted transmissions,
when paired with the additional reports of some 50 to 60 sampans moving
toward the area, indicated to Colonel Dam that a reinforced company of roughly
150 guerrillas guarded the station. Acting on the division commander's estimate,
on 30 December a small American-Vietnamese joint planning staff began
developing the operation's concept around an expected enemy strength of one
company.[20] The staff's reliance upon a doctrinal template (an estimate based
upon the enemy's doctrine, his past activities, and the staff's experience and
intuition) illustrated the covert nature of the war and the difficulties in painting
an accurate portrait of the PLAF, its activities, and its intentions. As with so
many other operations, the division staff did not know how many of the elusive
guerrillas were on the ground, nor did they know how they were deployed. This
nagging inability to fix the enemy's disposition, composition, and strength with
any certainty plagued both American and South Vietnamese efforts throughout
the Second Indochina War.[21]

Planning for the operation did not proceed without difficulty. When Major
Herbert Prevost, the advisory detachment's air liaison officer (ALO), attempted
to verify that the joint air operations center had received his CAS requests for
the operation, the officer on duty responded that the JGS had cancelled all the 7th
Division's air requests. Because the JGS planned to use all available air assets in
support of a larger operation in another tactical zone, the 7th Division's attack
would proceed without any preplanned air sorties. Worse, with less than 18
hours remaining before the mission, the JGS had also taken the helicopter
company slated to transport the 7th Division for the larger operation to the north.
Instead of the 57th Transportation Company, now the 93rd Transportation
Company would fly the mission. While both companies possessed H-21
Shawnees, a fair portion of the liaison officer's plan was no longer accurate.
The 93rd only had ten available helicopters to fly the mission, six less than the
57th planned to fly. Within five hours of notification, Captain Richard Ziegler,

the 7th Division's operations advisor, and the 93rd's liaison officer had identified the new landing zones (LZs) and had finalized their plans for the next day's mission.[22]

After the planners ironed out the operation's final details and the difficulties with the helicopters, the American advisors received their full briefing concerning Operation *DUC THANG* 1 at seven in the evening on 1 January. The 7th Division's mission was straightforward and reflected once again the American advisors' offensive mindset. The ARVN unit was to attack at 0630 on 2 January 1963 "to seize or destroy a VC radio and a VC company in the vicinity of" Ap Tan Thoi. The staff's concept to achieve this mission was simple. A provisional regiment of CG units would attack from south to north, oriented on Ap Tan Thoi; an ARVN infantry battalion would move by helicopter to an LZ to the north of Ap Tan Thoi and then attack south; and a mechanized company would attack from the west. To help prevent the guerrillas from escaping the cordon, two CG companies would establish a blocking position almost five kilometers to the west of the village, and a ranger company would establish another such position along the Ba Beo Canal to the north. The ranger company acting as the northern blocking force, an infantry company, and a support company would serve as the division's reserve.[23] In essence, the 7th Division would establish a three-sided cordon around Ap Tan Thoi. The fourth side of the encirclement, to the east, was left open. If the PLAF chose to retreat to the east, the ARVN would use artillery and air assets to destroy the guerrillas caught in the open. At no time did it cross anyone's mind that perhaps the insurgents might not run from the helicopters and APCs.

Dam had significant forces at his disposal to conduct this operation. The Dinh Tuong Regiment (Provisional), under the command of Major Lam Quang Tho, the province chief of Dinh Tuong Province, would attack from the south and west. As indicated by its provisional status, the Dinh Tuong Regiment was an ad hoc unit and comprised units of the 17th Civil Guard Battalion and the 4th Mechanized Rifle Squadron, 2nd Armored Cavalry Regiment (4/2 ACR). For the coming attack, Tho divided his attacking forces into two wings, placing the CG battalion in the south and his mechanized unit to the west. The southern force, massing some six companies, would attack with two task forces abreast: Task Force A (TF A), consisting of the 174th, 842nd, and 892nd CG Companies under the command of Captain Tri in the east; and Task Force B (TF B), consisting of the 171st, 172nd, and 839th CG Companies under the command of Lieutenant Thi in the west. Another two CG companies, the 173rd and 175th, would occupy the far western blocking position as Task Force C (TF C). As with most CG units, the 17th was poorly trained, but the division commander believed that its numbers were sufficient for the task.[24]

Without question, Tho's most powerful asset was 4/2 ACR, commanded by Captain Ly Tong Ba. Previously designated the 7th Mechanized Company, Ba's unit would attack from the west with 13 APCs, two less than authorized by the TOE.[25] Organized in April 1962, 4/2 ACR completed its nine-week training program in June and had seen combat throughout the summer and fall. Although relatively successful against the PLAF in September, Ba's company still demonstrated a need for additional training. Despite the unit's training deficiencies, the aggressive leadership that Ba demonstrated throughout the fall of 1962 inspired the confidence of the American advisors in the APC unit.[26]

Tho's regiment clearly represented the tangled and ambiguous South Vietnamese command structure, a testament to Diem's successful machinations to frustrate the MAAG's efforts at streamlining the chain of command. As commander of the 2nd ACR, Tho was Ba's immediate superior. At the same time, Tho, as province chief, also commanded the CG units assigned to Dinh Tuong Province. The difficulty with this command structure was not an issue of Tho commanding both 4/2 ACR and the 17th CG Battalion but one of who actually commanded Tho. Despite the fact that both the CG battalion and the M113 company were Department of Defense assets, Tho, as province chief, answered to the Department of the Interior and was outside the formal ARVN chain of command. As a result, the Dinh Tuong Regiment and Major Tho were technically outside of Dam's jurisdiction as the 7th Division commander. In essence, Dam's orders to Tho during the upcoming operation were more suggestions than directives, a fact that was not lost on the province chief.

The 7th Division's only organic unit slated to participate in *DUC THANG* 1 was the 2nd Battalion, 11th Infantry Regiment (2/11 IN). Moving to the LZ north of Ap Tan Thoi in ten H-21s of the 93rd Transportation Company, the infantry battalion formed the northern portion of the cordon around the village. Originally scheduled to make its assault in one serial with sixteen H-21s from the 57th Transportation Company, the battalion would now require three serials to get its three rifle companies and headquarters on the ground.[27] Once the three serials reached the LZ, each of the battalion's three companies would move along a separate axis toward Ap Tan Thoi. To support the infantry battalion's landings and provide overwatch for the operation, the Utility Tactical Transport Helicopter Company (UTTHC) would provide five UH-1s.[28] In all, 15 American helicopters would participate in the Ap Bac operation.

The division could look forward to a relatively significant amount of artillery support. Six 4.2-inch mortars from A Battery, 7th Artillery Battalion, two 105mm howitzers from B Battery, 7th Artillery Battalion, two 105mm howitzers from C Battery, 28th Artillery Battalion, and four 155mm howitzers from 1st Battery, IV Corps Artillery stood by to provide the indirect fire support.[29] As noted earlier, although Major Prevost, the ALO, was unable to obtain approval for preplanned air sorties for the operation, he did request that the air operations center be prepared to divert assets in the "event of an emergency."[30] As for advisory representation, each independent ARVN maneuver unit would have at least one American officer or NCO with it.[31] In short, Dam's plan envisioned assaulting the expected PLAF company at Ap Tan Thoi from three directions with over 1,200 soldiers, APCs, gunships, and indirect fire. To the American and ARVN officers alike, it appeared that Operation *DUC THANG* 1—in English, Operation VICTORY 1—would be a walkover. The guerrillas dug in around Ap Bac and Ap Tan Thoi, however, thought otherwise.

THE BATTLE OF AP BAC

Before dawn on 2 January 1963, the ARVN and CG units participating in Operation *DUC THANG* 1 moved to their positions in preparation for the attack at 0630. As with any mounted movement in limited visibility, not all the troop movements went smoothly, particularly those of the CG task forces. Because its attack position was farther west along Highway 4 than that of TF A, TF B was to lead the CG convoy of trucks out of My Tho, but the movement did not proceed as planned. After disrupting an armored column shortly after leaving its base camp and waiting unsuccessfully for its sister task force to arrive and take the lead, TF A left for its attack position on its own. Arriving near his appointed start point shortly after 0600, Captain Tri aligned his companies to cross the line of departure (LD), an imaginary line that designates the start of an attack. Organizing his unit into two separate elements, the task force commander placed the 842nd and 174th CG Companies in the eastern portion of his zone and the 892nd CG Company some 700 meters to the west. Despite the rough start, Tri's TF A was prepared to cross the LD at the scheduled time, much to the relief of the American advisor traveling with the CG units, First Lieutenant Arthur L. Bloch. For Bloch, the preceding hour and a half must have seemed high adventure, particularly since this was his first operation in Vietnam, but within the next hour and a half, the movement to begin the attack would seem almost pedestrian by comparison.[32]

Although TF B did not take its correct place in the convoy leaving My Tho, it did manage to find its position in enough time to organize itself before beginning the attack. After dismounting from the trucks, the CG soldiers formed into their companies and prepared themselves for the movement north. Unlike his compatriot Tri, who split his unit into two elements, Lieutenant Thi placed his three companies abreast, with the 171st Company in the west, the 839th Company in the center, and the 172nd Company in the east. Once aligned, the western task force waited for the appointed hour to cross the LD.[33]

At about the same time the CG units moved into position along Highway 4, a naval task force from the 21st River Assault Group (21st RAG) proceeded out of My Tho with one landing craft, mechanized (LCM), 13 landing craft, vehicle and personnel (LCVP), and four STCAN/FOMs.[34] The Vietnamese naval captain in command of the task force took his mission seriously. Besides the embarked 352nd Ranger Company, also based in My Tho, the task force also had with it five engineers and two tons of explosives to deal with any obstructions in the canals that might have been placed by the insurgents. Not willing to allow his unit to fall victim to a PLAF ambush, the Vietnamese commander directed his lead craft to "shoot at every bush" once it came to a certain location some six kilometers from the rangers' blocking positions. Avoiding the barricade that obstructed the Song My Tho Canal, the convoy proceeded to the north. Stretching several hundred meters, the task force carried the 352nd to its assigned blocking positions along the canals adjacent to Ap Tan Thoi.[35]

The noise resulting from the movement of the trucks, APCs, and landing craft did not go unnoticed by Ap Tan Thoi's defenders. Not surprisingly, the

PLAF units clearly heard "the noises of enemy vehicle [*sic*] and boats." Reacting to the reports and sounds of enemy movements, the guerrilla battalion commander ordered his units to their fighting positions. Having finished their preparations the night before, all the PLAF units had to do was crawl into their holes and steel themselves for the coming fight. Although it is unclear exactly when the insurgents occupied their positions, they were well established by the time of their first contact with the ARVN and CG units later that morning.[36] During this operation, unlike earlier ARVN sweeps, the PLAF would not be surprised by the arrival of helicopters and APCs, nor would it find itself in the open with no protection.

While the naval task force wound its way along the canals, Lieutenant Colonel John P. Vann took off in an L-19, a light, two-seat observation aircraft, at 0630. As the 7th Division's senior advisor, Vann planned to supervise 2/11 IN's aerial insertions and observe and relay information to Colonel Dam, who chose to remain at the division command post (CP) located at the Tan Hiep airstrip.[37] Vann was a career officer who had entered the U.S. Army during World War II and trained as a navigator for B-29s but never saw combat.[38] Having fought in Korea, he understood and embodied the U.S. Army's offensive and aggressive spirit.[39] Without question, he believed his primary role as the senior division advisor was to goad his ARVN counterpart into action, continually urging him to engage and to destroy the PLAF through sustained combat operations. Halberstam remembered him as having "little polish"; he was "blunt . . . [and] at times reactionary."[40] These traits were apparent in a discussion Vann had with Harkins during a briefing about an ARVN operation. COMUSMACV had cautioned Vann about his aggressive, and potentially offensive, nature, and, true to character, Vann's response was direct: "I'm not here to save their [Vietnamese] face, I'm here to save their ass."[41] As one former State Department official observed: "He didn't stand much on formality. . . . He told it like it was."[42]

An intense man, Vann was energetic, always in motion, and "evoked strong reactions in all who met him."[43] Yet for all his bluster and aggressiveness, Vann understood that certain aspects of American doctrine did not address the difficulties of fighting an insurgency. He consistently fought against the ARVN's penchant for indiscriminate use of artillery and CAS. As he saw it, such tactics only alienated the people and pushed them farther from the GVN and into the arms of the PLAF.[44] Vann intimated his understanding of the situation in South Vietnam when he related that "[t]his is a political war and it calls for discrimination in killing. The best weapon for killing would be a knife, but I'm afraid we can't do it that way. The worst is the airplane. The next worst is artillery. Barring a knife, the best is a rifle—you know who you're killing."[45] Despite his belief in reducing collateral damage, however, Vann still believed that the final measure of success in defeating the insurgency was the destruction of the guerrillas and not the building of the GVN's legitimacy. Vann maintained a clear image in his mind of how the 7th Division and its commanders should set about to destroy the PLAF, and he took every opportunity to express his views. As an advisor, however, he was not the commander; Colonel Dam was.

Although Vann "was as good as we [the Americans] had out there," his abilities alone would not be enough to bring the ARVN victory at Ap Bac.[46]

At about the same time that Vann took off from Tan Hiep, the Dinh Tuong Regiment reported to the 7th Division's CP that its units had crossed the LD. In the east, TF A crossed Highway 4 with the 842nd CG Company in the lead, followed by the 174th. Tri's other company, the 892nd, moved along its own axis farther to the west. Treating it almost as an administrative movement, the CG unit did not send out any elements to act as frontal or flank security, and it was only after Lieutenant Bloch pointed out the deficiency to the task force commander that these elements provided any type of local security. At the same time, some three kilometers farther west, Lieutenant Thi's TF B also crossed Highway 4 with its three companies still on line.[47] 4/2 ACR began its attack as scheduled as well, but within 15 minutes it had run into difficulties. Having already crossed many of the smaller irrigation canals with ease, this time Ba's company was now faced with a rather formidable obstacle. With no other option, 4/2 ACR's soldiers dismounted and began crossing their vehicles, a task that took almost a full hour.[48]

As the mechanized company struggled to get its vehicles moving again and the two CG task forces continued their northerly movement, the first of the three planned serials of 2/11 IN left the airstrip at Tan Hiep in ten H-21s. Despite a building ground fog, the transports, escorted by the UTTHC's five UH-1s, flew to the LZ north of Ap Tan Thoi. Landing just after 0700, the first company on the ground, Captain Chin's 2nd Company, did not meet any resistance (see Fig. 3.3). Shortly after touching down, the American advisor for 2/11 IN, Captain Kenneth Good, established communications with Vann and reported his arrival and the absence of enemy contact. For Dam, the operation was shaping up nicely. He now had portions of his three wings closing in on the transmitter at Ap Tan Thoi, and, as yet, none had experienced any enemy contact. All he had to do now was insert the remainder of 2/11 IN and close the cordon. Unfortunately for the 7th Division commander, however, nature did not cooperate with his plans. After the helicopters returned to Tan Hiep to pick up the second serial, the ground fog became too dense for the H-21s to lift off safely. For almost two hours, the helicopters sat at Tan Hiep as prisoners of the weather. While the remainder of the battalion waited at the airstrip, Good and the forward elements of 2/11 IN continued south to Ap Tan Thoi.[49]

Although the division plan called for all three of 2/11 IN's companies to land within a short time of one another to preclude the PLAF from engaging them individually, the ground fog did not seriously undermine the 2nd Company's security. The 352nd Ranger Company's positions along the Ba Beo Canal were only 1,200 meters north of the infantry company. Originally intended as a blocking force to prevent the PLAF from escaping north to the Plain of Reeds, the rangers received orders to move south, link up with the 2nd Company, and remain until the arrival of the second and third serials. Landing at 0800 at its assigned position along the canal, the ranger company began its move south but made little progress. Just as at Tan Hiep, a heavy ground fog blanketed the area, making the rangers' movement painstakingly slow. Exercising caution, the 352nd

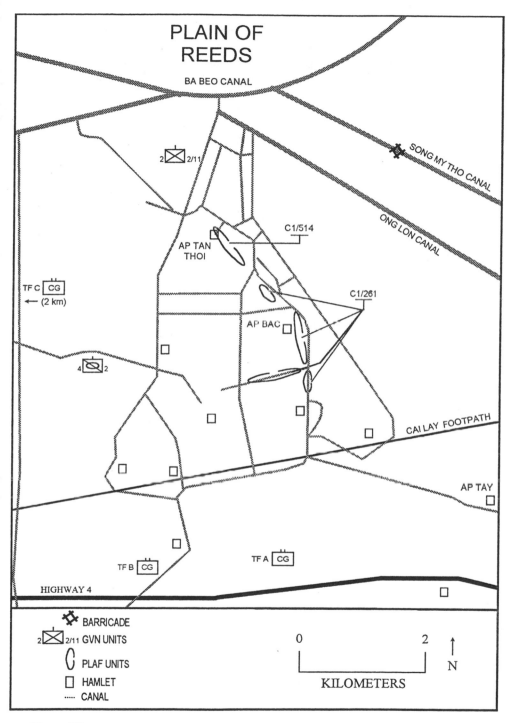

Figure 3.3
Unit Locations, 0700 Hours, 2 January 1963

took approximately one hour to travel some 500 meters, at which point the company lost one man (KIA) to a mine. Enveloped by fog and finding itself in a possible minefield, the company abruptly stopped to wait for visibility to improve. This half-kilometer movement was basically the company's sole contribution to *DUC THANG* 1. Despite its mission to support 2/11 IN, the ranger company did not continue its movement south, even after the fog lifted. Remaining in position until about 1600, the 352nd received orders to reembark on the naval task force's vessels, move south, and provide security for the 11th Infantry Regiment's CP.[50] Despite the company's relative proximity to Ap Tan Thoi (approximately 1,700 meters), its failure to move farther south deprived Colonel Dam of approximately 150 rangers, a force that might have made a difference in the outcome of the battle.

At about the same time the rangers neared their debarkation point, Dam's plan met its second and more serious hitch of the day. By this point, TF A had moved to within one kilometer of Ap Bac. To its front and right flank were two treelines, each approximately 150 meters away from the column. Concerned about a possible ambush, Captain Tri halted the task force and sent forward elements of the 842nd CG Company, which was still in the lead, to check for guerrillas who might be hidden in the vegetation. As the reconnaissance elements closed to within 30 meters of the east-west treeline, sporadic firing broke out. Dug in along the dike, C1/261 engaged the CG soldiers while holding its positions among the trees. After exchanging fire for some 15 minutes, the lead elements of the CG company began to withdraw. As they did so, the guerrillas located in the trees to the task force's right flank opened with a withering fire. Following their compatriots' lead, the insurgent platoon located to the north of the 842nd Company also increased its volume of fire. Within the opening minutes of the engagement, the lead company's commander and executive officer both fell dead from the small arms fire. Worse, a PLAF round also struck one of the task force radios, effectively cutting Bloch off from Vann and any assistance the advisory chain of command might have rendered.[51]

While Tri sought to make sense of the situation confronting him, his opponent, C1/261's commander, received reports that the platoon facing the CG units was not only holding its own but could also potentially capture enemy weapons, always a lucrative reward for the poorly equipped insurgents. Not yet in contact with any enemy troops around Ap Bac, Bay dispatched his assistant political officer, Vo Phuong, to the action with a squad and charged him with the mission of suppressing the enemy's flank. Moving rapidly along the main north-south canal, the squad moved south past the lead CG company in order to carry out its superior's directive. Avoiding the few CG soldiers located to the east of the canal, the insurgents made rapid progress.[52]

After gaining his bearings, Tri attempted over the ensuing hour and a half to break the hold the guerrillas had on his task force. Observing Phuong's guerrilla squad moving down his right flank and correctly predicting its intent, the task force commander ordered his trail company, the 174th, into the woodline, thus forcing the PLAF soldiers back to the north. Shortly thereafter, he also ordered his left flank company, the 892nd, to move forward and attack into the treeline north of the 842nd. After moving a short distance, it, too, came under heavy fire and ground to a halt. Even with its senior two officers down, the 842nd rallied twice more to assault C1/261's positions to its front with little effect. With little cover or concealment, TF A remained pinned under the effective guerrilla fire, unable to maneuver itself to safety.[53] Meanwhile, back at Tan Hiep, Dam had absolutely no idea that his southern wing was under attack and believed his operation was going according to plan.

To the west, TF B continued on its northward movement, completely ignorant of TF A's ongoing action. Unlike the 352nd Ranger Company, Lieutenant Thi's unit traveled slightly more than three kilometers in an hour and a half, in large part as a result of moving in a column along the trails leading through the villages instead of through the rice paddies. By 0815, the CG units in the west had occupied their first two march objectives for the operation and began searching for enemy troops and weapons. While conducting the search, the 839th Company engaged what was most likely a forward security element of the PLAF's 514th Battalion, an exchange that resulted in one dead guerrilla and one prisoner. Admitting that he was a member of the 514th, the captured insurgent also told his captors that his unit had been in the area for three days, tangible pieces of information that may or may not have found their way to the division CP.[54]

After remaining airborne for better than two hours, Vann's aircraft required fuel, and the senior division advisor headed back to Tan Hiep. Landing at around 0900, he met with Dam and briefed him on the 2nd Company's progress. Having just received a report from Captain Good that his unit still had not made contact, neither the division commander nor his advisor was aware of the difficulties TF A faced in the south. Now that the fog had cleared sufficiently, the second serial of 2/11 IN, this time the 1st Company, left Tan Hiep for the LZ. To compensate for the 2nd Company's movement toward Ap Tan Thoi, Vann, with Dam's approval, shifted the LZ some 750 meters to the south. Like its predecessor, the second serial landed without incident. About half an hour later, the 3rd Company, the last and final serial, landed at the LZ at 0935.[55] After an interminable two hours, from about 0730 to 0930, 2/11 IN now had all its combat strength on the ground.

Shortly after the third serial landed, the 3rd Company took two or three rounds of fire from the treeline to its west. Reacting to and closing with the contact, the ARVN soldiers fanned out and moved toward the woodline and crossed a canal. Failing to receive further fire, the company commander ordered his soldiers to search the surrounding area and houses thoroughly. After some 40 minutes, the 3rd Company soldiers found two guerrillas armed with a French rifle and two grenades near the canal. Taking them prisoner, the company moved south and met up with the battalion's other two companies around 1100.[56] That 2/11 IN landed three serials without incident should not be surprising, as the PLAF defenses of C1/514 around Ap Tan Thoi were about 1,500 meters away from the LZ and oriented to the southwest, away from the landing site. With a treeline between 2/11 IN and C1/514, it would have been difficult for the guerrillas to mass their fires effectively on the landing helicopters.[57] Perhaps more importantly, Hoang's focus was likely upon the ongoing engagements in the south. By the time of the 3rd Company's landing, C1/261 and TF A had already been engaged for two hours, and the PLAF commander had been issuing orders and repositioning forces to best support his southern units.

Up to this point in the battle, no one at Tan Hiep, either South Vietnamese or American, had the slightest inkling that *DUC THANG* 1 was not proceeding as planned. The minor difficulties caused earlier by the ground fog shrunk to insignificance when, at 0945, the division CP received word that TF A had been in contact for better than two hours and was now pinned down by PLAF fire. Calling from his CP located along Highway 4, Major Tho requested that Dam commit the division reserve. Acting on the province chief's request, the division commander directed that the 1st Company, 1st Battalion, 11th Infantry Regiment (1/1/11 IN), move by helicopter to an area north of the woodline where the guerillas were located. He then turned to Captain Richard Ziegler, the operations advisor who was with the 7th Division's CP at Tan Hiep, to relay his instructions to Vann. Since the division's senior advisor was orbiting near the area Dam envisioned inserting the reserve, the division commander also specified that Vann reconnoiter two possible LZs in the general vicinity of Ap Bac, one located approximately one kilometer north of TF A, the other some 1500 meters to the north-northeast of the beleaguered task force. For the next ten minutes, Vann circled the potential LZs in his L-19 to determine which one would better suit the reserve's landing. After examining the eastern area, Vann rejected it as too small and selected the LZ to the west of Ap Bac.[58]

Turning the L-19 to the west, Captain O'Neill, a pilot from the 93rd Transportation Company who was acting as his company's liaison officer, brought Vann over the second potential LZ. Looking closely for enemy activity, the advisor could not detect any PLAF guerrillas in the vicinity of Ap Bac. He was cautious, however, because Ap Bac "looked suspicious" from where he was, especially since it was the largest built-up area in the general vicinity. With no visible PLAF forces in the area and TF A having been in contact for more than two hours, Vann made the fateful recommendation to insert the reserve to the west of Ap Bac. Continuing his reconnaissance, Vann advised O'Neill that he wanted the reserve placed some 300 meters west of the north-south woodline near Ap Bac to ensure that it landed outside of small arms range. Making yet another low pass over the LZ, the advisor then went on to recommend to the helicopter liaison a flight route out of the landing site. Concurring with Vann's observations, O'Neill then passed along the advisor's instructions to the pilot guiding the inbound H-21s.[59]

While Vann determined the reserve's LZ, the situation for TF A was growing increasingly tense. By 1000, the task force had sustained numerous casualties, among them Captain Tri, the recipient of a wound to the left leg. Tho, besides asking for the division reserve, also initially sought to use his own assets to assist Captain Tri. The province chief issued orders for TF B to change direction and orient its movement toward TF A. By moving his other task force in that direction, Tho hoped to envelop the guerrillas from the west. Thi, acting almost immediately, directed his two strongest companies, the 171st and 172nd, to the east.[60] Despite TF A's difficulties, the situation for the ARVN operation was far from bleak. 2/11 IN had yet to make serious contact, and three companies, the reserve and two CG companies, were now threatening to strike the guerrillas along their western and southern flank.

Shortly after O'Neill relayed the location of the LZ, 1/1/11 IN lifted off from Tan Hiep at 1000 with 102 officers and soldiers and one American advisor, Sergeant First Class Arnold Bowers. Unaware of the presence of C1/261, the company did not expect the greeting it received on the LZ, nor did the pilots, Vann, Dam, or anyone else. Whether good luck on the part of the PLAF, poor judgment on the part of the pilots, or a combination of both, the reserve company landed in a hornet's nest. Oriented to the west and southwest, a fair portion of C1/261's defensive positions faced directly into the LZ. Instead of landing 300 meters to the west of the treeline, as Vann had directed, the helicopters set down only about 200 meters from the trees, well within small arms range of the PLAF positions.[61] As the H-21s touched down, several of the pilots immediately reported that they were taking fire. As one pilot claimed later, "The tree line seemed to explode with machine-gun fire. It was pure hell."[62] The UH-1s began firing into the eastern and southern treelines, but the guerrillas' fire did not slacken. Nine H-21s lifted off, leaving one on the ground.

As the Shawnees left for Tan Hiep, one circled the LZ to make another approach and pick up the downed crew. Instead of putting the downed aircraft between him and the treeline, for some reason the pilot landed his craft to the east side of the damaged helicopter, closer to the guerrillas. Not surprisingly, it, too, was damaged and could not again lift off. Since the five UH-1s were still circling the LZ and firing suppression, one left the formation and circled the two downed H-21s at a low altitude. Coming around for another pass, the Huey approached to land to the west of the Shawnees. Prior to touching down, the Huey lost its tail rotor to PLAF fire, flipped on its right side, and crashed about 30 meters from the grounded transports.[63]

Although two of its ten H-21s were down, the 93rd Transportation Company was not finished suffering losses. As the UH-1 attempted to rescue the downed aircrews, another H-21 landed some two kilometers to the northeast of Ap Bac, forced down by damage sustained at the LZ. A second H-21 landed beside the first, picked up its crew, and proceeded to Tan Hiep (see Fig. 3.4). In a span of approximately ten minutes, the Americans had lost better than 25% of the rotary wing aircraft committed to the operation.[64] Without question, the guerrillas' training efforts through the fall of 1962 had paid dividends and effectively demonstrated the insurgents' newfound skill at countering the Americans' technological superiority.

While the transports struggled to escape further damage and the gunships sought to find the insurgents with their machine gun and rocket fire, the reserve was having serious difficulties on the LZ. After exiting the Shawnees, the ARVN soldiers also received a withering fire from the C1/261 guerrillas. Moving only about 15 meters from where they landed, the reserve's soldiers were pinned down in the rice paddy, unable to move forward or back. One squad

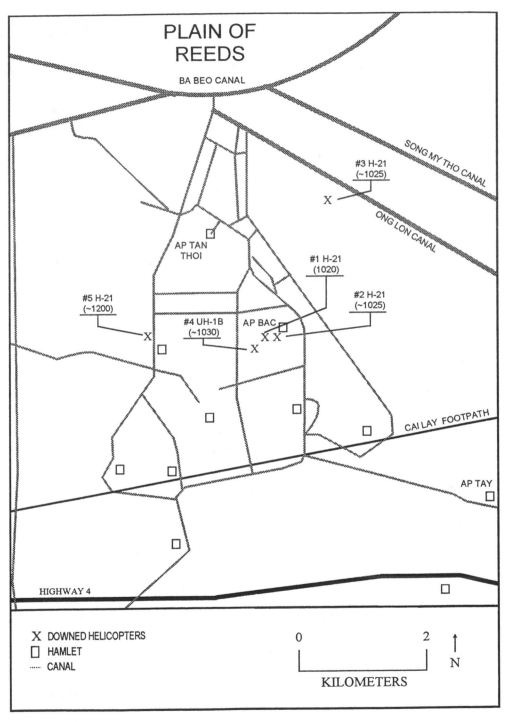

Figure 3.4
Downed Helicopter Locations

somehow managed to escape this fate and found itself almost 150 meters to the south. Instead of continuing to the south and engaging the enemy in the woodline, the squad leader returned to the vicinity of the downed helicopters after receiving orders to do so. Bolstered by his apparent success but concerned that his company was now fighting in two directions (south against TF A and west against 1/1/11 IN), Bay ordered the 60mm mortar crew to fire three rounds at the helicopters, causing little physical damage but further discouraging the shaken 1st Company.[65] Originally intended to assist TF A in the south, it now seemed that the reserve required additional assistance to extricate itself.

Still circling above the battlefield in an L-19, Vann grimly surveyed the damaged helicopters and pinned down reserve company. Off to the northwest about 2,500 meters away, the senior advisor saw Ba's company near Ap Tan Thoi. Although several canals lay between the mechanized company and the reserve, given its proximity and its potential for rapid movement, Ba's company seemed Vann's best hope to assist the reserve. Calling to Tan Hiep on the radio, he requested that Colonel Dam direct 4/2 ACR to the LZ to assist 1/1/11 IN and to secure the downed helicopters. According to Captain Ziegler, who was relaying the information to Vann, the division commander agreed to issue the order. Not content to wait for word to pass along the South Vietnamese chain of command, Vann also contacted the American advisors located with the mechanized company, Captain James B. Scanlon, the senior advisor for 2nd ACR, and Captain Robert Mays, his deputy. Briefly sketching the situation for them, Vann directed the advisors to move quickly to Ap Bac to remedy the situation there.[66]

By the time Scanlon received word of the reserve's difficulties at the LZ at 1030, 4/2 ACR had already had a busy morning. After the company took almost an hour to cross the large canal that it encountered shortly after beginning the operation, the lead platoon under the command of Lieutenant Chou sighted guerrillas approximately 1,500 meters to its front. Engaging them with his vehicle's .50 caliber machine gun, the lieutenant gave chase to the enemy, with the remainder of his platoon's vehicles following closely behind. Quickly traveling the distance, the platoon soon found itself faced with yet another large canal, and the platoon leader dismounted to find a suitable ford. After reporting that he had located a place to cross, Chou received orders from Ba to stay on the near side of the canal and continue to the north toward Ap Tan Thoi. Despite hearing an ongoing firefight to the east that was TF A's engagement, the lead platoon leader dutifully headed north, away from Captain Tri's unit.[67]

As 4/2 ACR changed directions and headed north, Ba's American advisor, Lieutenant William Streeter, was medically evacuated, leaving Scanlon and Mays with the company. Riding on top of an M114 APC that had accompanied 4/2 ACR, Streeter had received a deep cut on his arm when the vehicle jumped a canal, the resulting shock of which threw him into a protruding piece of metal.[68] While a helicopter arrived to pick up Streeter, the carriers proceeded north with the canal to their immediate right. After a short time, the company approached an infantry unit wearing red scarves, the habitual trademark for 2/11 IN.

Continuing farther north, the company soon stopped at a large canal, and it was at this time that Vann called for the carriers to move to Ap Bac (see Fig. 3.5).[69]

What transpired over the next three hours, from approximately 1030 to 1330, was a clear demonstration of the advisory system's limitations. When the Americans with Ba passed along Vann's request to the ARVN commander, he responded with the question, "Why don't they send the infantry?" a clear reference to the elements of 2/11 IN and not his own dismounted soldiers. When Scanlon radioed the company commander's response to Vann, the division advisor said that the mechanized company was the only element that could quickly close on the reserve's LZ. Ba, unimpressed with Vann's explanation, again reiterated his reluctance to move and pointed out that he didn't "take orders from Americans." Changing his radio's frequencies, Vann confirmed with Dam his orders concerning the mechanized company. Coming back on Ba's radio net, the division advisor directed Scanlon to tell the ARVN captain that 4/2 ACR's movement to relieve the reserve was an order. This time, the company commander not only responded that the elements from 2/11 IN would be better for the mission, but he also pointed out that the canal to his company's north precluded his movement to the LZ.[70]

Scanlon simply could not understand Ba's intransigence, particularly since the ARVN officer had become increasingly aggressive through the fall of 1962, almost to the point of recklessness. Scanlon, Mays, and Ba could all clearly see the smoke rising above the reserve's LZ. With Vann circling overhead and sending increasingly threatening radio transmissions, the two American advisors increased their verbal assault against Ba, who still refused to assist the reserve. Seeing that he was getting nowhere, Mays dismounted and moved forward to the canals by himself to find a suitable crossing point, leaving Scanlon to continue with Ba. Changing tactics, the regimental advisor now chastised Ba by suggesting that he was scared to act, hoping to goad the company commander into action. His new approach failed to generate the desired outcome and seemed to solidify Ba in his resolve to stand fast. Despite the relatively short distance to the reserve, the verbal assault by Scanlon, and the ever-increasing pitch of the senior advisor's voice, Captain Ba refused to move.[71]

While still arguing with Ba, Vann observed artillery landing in and around Ap Bac. Receiving word from the frustrated senior advisor that the rounds were falling wide of the probable PLAF positions, the division CP responded that an RVNAF L-19 was observing and adjusting the rounds. Satisfied that someone was controlling the artillery, Vann headed south to locate the CG units while continuing his attempts to spur the mechanized company into action. From the air, TF A appeared to be no longer in contact, and TF B in the west was now just short of the east-west treeline south of the reserve and Ap Bac. Concerned by the possibility of the guerrillas overrunning the helicopters and the reserve, Vann directed Ziegler to impress upon Dam the urgency of closing all available units on the reserve's position.[72]

Even though Vann focused his efforts on getting Ba to move, 4/2 ACR was not the only unit participating in the operation that was in a position to envelop the guerrillas but failed to do so. In the east, Captain Tri's TF A was no longer

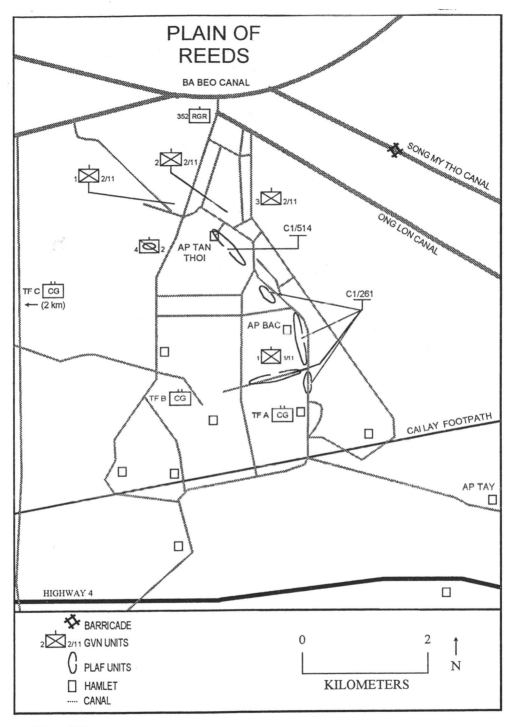

Figure 3.5
Unit Locations, 1030 Hours

taking fire, but neither was it moving north to close with the guerrillas in the woodline. Observing enemy soldiers withdrawing from the treeline along the task force's eastern flank, Lieutenant Bloch believed that they were repositioning to the north to engage the helicopters that were only about 500 meters away. Seeing the possibility of enveloping the insurgents from the south, he recommended to Tri that the task force maneuver to the east and north, using the vegetation and dikes for cover. Instead of taking advantage of the opportunity that presented itself, the task force commander refused, informing the American advisor that his commander, Major Tho, had ordered TF A into a static blocking position. Just as Scanlon and Mays unsuccessfully argued with Ba, so did Bloch fail to convince Tri of the potential gains of his recommended plan. While the reserve's casualties mounted, TF A remained hunkered down less than a half-kilometer away.[73]

Given the urgency of the situation, Ba's and Tri's recalcitrance and unwillingness to act might seem to border upon the inexplicable, but one must keep in mind the political realities of the ARVN officer corps. Although Colonel Dam was the senior ARVN officer in the area, Tri answered to Major Tho, the province chief and the Dinh Tuong Regiment commander. Likewise, Tho, as 2nd ACR commander, was Ba's direct superior. Without question, Tho was a man who was attuned to the political subtleties of the South Vietnamese command structure. Aware of Diem's guidance concerning excessive casualties, Tho most likely did not want to put himself at risk for participating in an operation that resulted in heavy losses. As soon as he became aware that TF A was in heavy contact, he immediately radioed Dam to request the reserve while at the same time directing TF B to the east in order to relieve the pressure on his pinned down task force. Once things went from bad to worse with the loss of the four helicopters, Tho ordered TF A into a static blocking position and allowed TF B to continue its leisurely movement to the northeast.[74] Clearly, as far as the province chief was concerned, the situation on the LZ was Dam's problem and not his own.

Ba was also in a difficult position. Although the 7th Division commander was in his chain of command for the operation, Ba knew well enough that he would have to answer to Tho in case he made a decision that the province chief did not like. As a Buddhist, Ba already had one strike against him as far as Diem was concerned, and the ARVN officer could not afford to get in serious trouble with his superior and still expect to receive a promotion at some point.[75] Whatever the reason for his hesitancy, Ba held firm to his conviction that 2/11 IN was in a better position to help 1/1/11 IN. Having returned with Mays from their reconnaissance and confirming that there was not one but two canals to their front, Ba pointed out that his company would never make it to the LZ in time. Desiring nothing more than to get the company moving again, the advisors reminded Ba of the crossing site Chou had found earlier that morning. Weakening, Ba told Scanlon that if the American thought he could find it again, he could take a carrier back to the south. Not wasting a moment, Scanlon hopped on the vehicle of Lieutenant Chinh, another platoon leader, and headed south at about 1100, some 30 minutes after first receiving word to move to the LZ.[76]

As Scanlon moved south to locate the crossing site and expedite Ba's movement, Vann received a report that there were two seriously wounded Americans on the LZ. As he was to find out later, both were helicopter crewmen who had received wounds upon landing. When Sergeant Bowers, the American advisor traveling with 1/1/11 IN, saw the Huey crash, he immediately ran to it to ensure that all the crew members were out. After assisting one of the pilots out of the wreckage, Bowers returned to find Sergeant William Deal, the crew chief, dangling from his harness inside the helicopter. Fearing that the aircraft's fuel tanks might explode, Bowers kicked out the Huey's front windshield to make it easier to remove the injured soldier. After disconnecting the crew chief's helmet, Bowers realized that the NCO was dead, the victim of a head wound. Grabbing Deal's flight suit, Bowers dragged him clear of the aircraft anyway.[77] Leaving Deal, Bowers then went to the downed Shawnee nearest the treeline and found Specialist Fourth Class (SP/4) Donald Braman, the crew chief, still inside. The young specialist had received a shoulder wound that to Bowers did not appear serious. To ensure that the paddy water did not infect the wound, the sergeant recommended that Braman stay in the helicopter. Not wishing to make his injury worse, the wounded American agreed to await medevac inside the aircraft.[78]

Unable to make contact with Bowers and unsure of the situation near the downed helicopters, Vann continued to berate Ba, Scanlon, and Mays, while at the same time coordinating a medevac mission. Requesting both transport and gunship assets, the senior division advisor received the support in the form of two H-21s and three UH-1s. While he failed to receive any ground fire during the three low-level passes he made over the LZ, Vann was still leery of the possibility of a repeat of the earlier landings. Hedging his bets, the advisor recommended to the flight leader that only one H-21 set down on the LZ while the UH-1s fired suppression to reduce the chances of losing both Shawnees. Acting on his recommendation, the Hueys fired into the woodlines south of Ap Bac, followed by the one H-21 that landed to the west of the downed helicopters. Immediately receiving fire, the H-21 took off again, without Deal or Braman. Barely able to maintain control of his craft, the pilot, following guidance from Captain O'Neill in the L-19, set down on the far side of the north/south canal amidst Ba's company. The Americans had lost yet another helicopter, bringing their total losses for the battle to five (see fig. 3.4). Following the accepted procedure of immediately evacuating downed crews, which so far had resulted in the loss of one transport and one gunship, the second H-21 landed next to the first. Evacuating the recently downed crew, the remaining Shawnee returned to Tan Hiep with its escorting UH-1s. Vann, witnessing the effective PLAF fire, informed Colonel Dam that further medevac attempts were futile until the M113s secured the LZ, making it even more important for the carriers to close on the reserve.[79]

As Vann supervised the abortive medevac attempt, Scanlon and Mays had begun to convince Ba to follow Dam's order to close on the reserve. Finding the crossing site that Chou had located earlier, Scanlon had Chinh radio his commander that they were at a suitable place to cross the large north-south canal. Whether weary of Mays's, Scanlon's, and Vann's challenges, or relieved that his company now had a place to cross the canal, Ba moved his unit south to link up with Scanlon and Chinh. As the company's lead carriers arrived and began their crossing procedures, Scanlon witnessed the Shawnees and Hueys attempting to conduct their medevac mission. About one hour after Vann made his initial request for 4/2 ACR to assist 1/1/11 IN, the lead carriers of the mechanized company began crossing the large north-south canal. At this point, the APCs were only two kilometers from the LZ.[80]

Farther south, another American advisor was also finding himself powerless to bring about a solution to the problems at Ap Bac. Major Jack A. Macslarrow, Tho's advisor, had been counseling aggressive action since he first heard of TF A's engagement. Located in the province chief's CP along Highway 4, Macslarrow considered Tho's request for Dam to commit the reserve "timely." The American was not, however, pleased with what his counterpart chose to do (or not to do) for the remainder of the morning. Hearing from Bloch that an attack through the woodline along TF A's right flank would endanger the guerrillas engaging the reserve, Macslarrow recommended that Tho order the task force out of its static position, a suggestion that the province chief refused to accept. In the South Vietnamese officer's mind, an attack by Tri's task force was impossible because the 7th Division had not ordered him to attack. Worse, the unit was pinned down and incapable of conducting an attack due to the casualties among the leadership, specifically the commanders of the lead company and the task force. To reinforce his position, Tho ordered the 17th CG Battalion's commander to the field to take charge of TF A, but this was a hollow gesture. Even after his arrival at Tho's CP, the CG battalion commander made no attempt over the following six hours to join Tri's task force. In an near-perfect example of foot-dragging, Tho refused to attack with TF A because it lacked a "seasoned, experienced and capable commander," while at the same time not dispatching the 17th CG Battalion commander to the scene only a few kilometers away. Frustrated with Tho's intransigence, Macslarrow attempted to influence the situation through the advisory chain and radioed Ziegler at Tan Hiep, requesting that Dam order Tho into action, an order that may never have arrived.[81]

Despite all that was going wrong with *DUC THANG* 1, the GVN forces were not alone in their difficulties. Subjected to increasingly intense artillery fire and CAS, the platoon of guerrillas in the woodline north of TF A were reaching their limit of tolerance. With one of his unit's automatic rifles inoperative and still not hearing from his commander about the request for reinforcements from the 514th to the north, the platoon leader requested permission from Bay to withdraw from the woodline and move to Ap Bac. Concurring, the C1/261 commander issued orders for the element to move north and assist its sister platoon in assaulting the H-21s on the LZ. Subject to the same laws of chance that had already militated against the GVN forces, the platoon "somehow received the wrong orders," and, instead of moving north along the canal, actually moved to the east and found itself in the open. Immediately spotted by the circling RVNAF L-19 that was directing the artillery and CAS, the platoon received blistering machine gun and rocket fire from the aircraft circling overhead. Shaken and ducking back into the canal, the platoon worked its way north and eventually positioned itself to the rear of C1/261.[82] With the PLAF platoon's departure, the southern approach into Ap Bac was now wide open, but, lacking the authority to advance, Captain Tri held his ground, thus once more missing an opportunity to envelop the insurgents' positions from the south.

As Ba's carriers struggled to cross the large north-south canal and the PLAF guerrillas suffered at the hands of the circling AD-6 Skyraiders, 2/11 IN's three companies continued south toward Ap Tan Thoi. After his units converged at around 1100, the battalion commander arrayed his units in a rough line, with the 1st Company to the west, the 2nd Company in the center and slightly ahead, and the 3rd Company to the east (see Fig. 3.6). As the companies moved toward their objectives, Captain Edward Smith, an advisor traveling with the 3rd Company, spied the eastern-most downed H-21 about one kilometer off to his east. Assured by his counterpart that another element from the 11th Regiment would secure the damaged helicopter, Smith and the ARVN soldiers kept marching toward the C1/514 guerrillas who were waiting for them.[83]

The PLAF battalion commander had not been idle while 2/11 IN made its way toward his CP. Concerned by the number of ARVN troops approaching from the north, Hoang denied Bay's request for reinforcements and simply ordered his southern company to "stand firm." Advising C1/514 to prepare for the rapidly approaching fight with the closing enemy force, he was also keenly aware of the number of untried guerrillas in C1/514 and sought to bolster their morale by advising them of the successes of C1/261. Bich, acting on his higher commander's advice, dispatched a reconnaissance force and soon received word from local civilians that the ARVN soldiers were approaching. Thus warned, the C1/514 commander dispatched four cells from one platoon and a squad from another platoon to the north side of Ap Tan Thoi to hinder the enemy battalion's approach. Waiting until the lead company of 2/11 IN had closed to within 20 meters of its positions, C1/514 opened fire, catching the 2nd Company soldiers almost completely by surprise.[84]

Although the guerrillas' firing was sporadic at first, the ARVN company in contact made little forward progress. The difficulties in slogging through the swampy rice field north of the village coupled with the surprise of the insurgents' fire served to mire the 2nd Company. Not wanting to allow Captain Chin to lose what little momentum he had, the 2/11 IN commander sought to gain the upper hand in the engagement and called forward his 60mm mortars and two machine guns. With his units spread between the woodlines, canals, and smaller rice paddies, he was unable to generate enough fire to suppress the guerrillas who faced his battalion. With his soldiers hunkered down, the fighting around Ap Tan Thoi quickly degenerated into a stalemate. While the ARVN commander brought up his heavier weapons, Bich, the C1/514 commander, felt that he was getting the better of the exchange. Seeking to reinforce his initial success, the PLAF officer faced about another platoon and set it against the

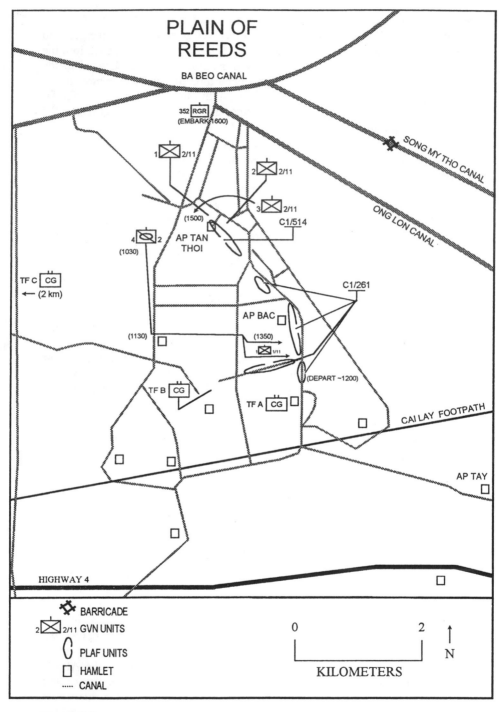

Figure 3.6
Unit Movements, 1030–1600 Hours

almost immobile 2nd Company.[85]

While 2/11 IN struggled with the PLAF north of Ap Tan Thoi, Ba's company was making slow progress crossing the large north-south canal. In keeping with his aggressive spirit, Lieutenant Chou was the first to cross the canal, followed by two more of his carriers. Eager to get to the helicopters, Captain Mays grabbed a radio off Ba's APC and jumped aboard Chou's vehicle. With the advisor loaded up, they pressed on to the east and the reserve, but their way was not yet clear. Three more canals still lay between them and the LZ, the last of which was only about 500 meters from the helicopters but would require at least a half-hour to cross. Upon arriving at the last canal, Ba reverted to his earlier hesitancy. Taking his time, he finally located what he considered a suitable crossing point. Following Ba's example, neither the company officers nor the soldiers showed any inclination to hurry across the last canal. Many were sitting in and around the carriers; others watched the ongoing air strikes. When the first carrier to attempt a crossing became mired in the far bank, requiring another carrier to pull it back out, Scanlon approached Captain Trong, the regimental operations officer, and asked that he direct the nearest M113 crew to attempt to cross at another point. Returning to the original site, the advisor saw the crews half-heartedly chopping brush to fill the canal in order to facilitate the crossing. He simply could not understand why Ba, when his company was so close to its objective, was once again purposefully taking his time.[86]

This lackadaisical attitude may have resulted from the cumulative effect of several factors. Ba's unwillingness to get involved in something he might later regret clearly reflected in his exchanges with the American advisors. This certainly must have made an impression on the nearby vehicle crews and infantryman, especially when taken in conjunction with the strong possibility that the crews had monitored the ongoing radio traffic on and around the LZ. Another factor influencing their lack of urgency may simply have been what they saw TF B doing to their southeast. When Lieutenant Thi received the order to wait for the APCs, his task force had moved to a point just short of the treeline that had previously concealed the southern PLAF platoon. As the carriers moved to the east, TF B remained on the mechanized company's southern flank, waiting for the APCs to come abreast of the task force's lead two companies. Since by this time it was close to lunch, the CG soldiers began to build cooking fires and to prepare their midday meals. Not taking fire, the task forces soldiers casually sat or stood around, presenting an idyllic scene for the soldiers of 4/2 ACR to the north.[87]

To the PLAF units in and around Ap Bac and Ap Tan Thoi, it appeared that the 7th Division was slowly massing a coordinated assault. The 2/11 IN, although not making much progress against C1/514, was pressing firmly enough to keep the northern PLAF company fixed in place. South of Ap Bac, the two CG task forces stood a short distance away from completely enveloping C1/261. Worse, the mechanized company was crossing its last obstacle and would soon close with the insurgents who were dug into the sides of the dikes. Not only did C1/261 have to face the coming onslaught by itself, but it would also have to conduct the defense without its best platoon. Still missing after its withdrawal from the southern woodline, the platoon had not yet found its way to the company CP. Concerned about his precarious position, Bay informed Hoang of his situation and requested orders, perhaps hoping to get the word to withdraw. Offering little more than moral support, the battalion commander instructed his southern company "to hold its front . . . and not to leave the battle." Passing along word of C1/514's success in the north, Hoang also assured the company that he would dispatch personnel to locate the lost platoon and return it to the positions at Ap Bac. Steeling themselves for the coming assault, the company cadre visited the men in their positions and echoed the motivational statement, *"It is better to die at one's post"* (emphasis in the original). Ordering his cadre to build the guerrillas' waning morale, Bay could do little except make minor changes to his unit's positions and wait for the APCs to arrive.[88]

Working slowly but steadily, the 4/2 ACR soldiers successfully crossed their first carrier after filling the canal with brush, but the second was not so lucky and became stuck in the far bank. Repeating the process as they had so many times already, the APC crew members on the far side of the obstacle pulled the mired vehicle across, a process each successive crew had to repeat for the following carrier. Once again, Chou managed to get his vehicle across first, and, pairing up with the next vehicle to cross, set out for the helicopters that lay less than 500 meters away. Not wanting to be left behind, Captain Mays, who had been traveling with Captain Ba, jumped across the canal to board Chou's carrier. Ba was next to cross and, just like the lieutenant before him, waited for another carrier before charging off to the south and east. Scanlon, whose vehicle had not yet crossed, impatiently moved forward and mounted one of the two vehicles that formed a third pair. Shortly before two in the afternoon, almost three and a half hours after receiving word that it was to move to the LZ, 4/2 ACR, with 6 of its 13 carriers, was finally closing with the guerrillas who continued to stymie the reserve.[89]

Aggressive as always, Chou moved to the south side of the helicopters and then turned to the east. Following his lead platoon leader's path, Ba and his accompanying carrier were a short distance behind. Once Scanlon's two APCs crossed, they moved a shorter distance to the south and turned early to the east, forming a second prong of the attack while at the same time widening the mechanized company's front. Moving rapidly forward in pairs instead of slowing to coordinate their attack, the lead APCs' crews were relying upon shock, and not mass, to break the guerrillas' resistance, just as they had done with such success in the previous months. The ease with which they advanced may also have been related to the absence of direct fire from the woodline beyond Ap Bac. As he rode forward, Scanlon was astonished at how quiet it had become. Later describing the scene before him as "like a picnic," he believed that the guerrillas had withdrawn and the engagement on the LZ already resolved.[90] As the carriers drew up abreast of the aircraft, the moment had arrived for C1/261 to demonstrate its mettle. Having maintained strict fire discipline as the hulking machines bore down on their positions, the insurgents opened fire with a fusillade from their dug in positions, catching the six carriers completely by surprise. Unable to locate the origin of the enemy fire, neither the

South Vietnamese officers nor the American advisors knew which way to direct the carriers or their heavy machine guns' rounds.[91]

Reverting to what they had been trained to do under fire, the vehicle commanders dropped their APCs' rear ramps and allowed the infantry to dismount. In every engagement with the guerrillas up to this point of the war, this tactic of dismounting the infantrymen well short of the enemy had brought success to the mechanized company. As a result, the troops who left the carriers were not mentally prepared for what happened next. As they cleared the ramps and spread out to assault, they faced a hailstorm of small arms fire, and several infantrymen fell within minutes of dismounting. Either unwilling or unable to move, the mechanized soldiers went to ground and sought what little cover they could find in the rice paddy. Unable to locate the guerrillas' positions, they could not return effective fire against the C1/261 positions. The carriers' .50 caliber machine guns possessed the potential to suppress the enemy in the woodline, but many of the vehicle commanders failed to aim their weapons because to do so would require them to expose themselves to the incoming fire. As a result, a fair portion of the heavy machine gun rounds flew harmlessly into and over the treetops instead of against the insurgent positions. Still mounted, Scanlon continuously prodded his vehicle's gunners to maintain their positions in the cupola ring to ensure that the weapon stayed on target. Having sited machine guns at opposite corners of the north/south woodline, Bay had caught Ba's company in a deadly crossfire with telling effect.[92]

The dismounted 4/2 ACR soldiers were not the only members of the company to take casualties, as the drivers and vehicle commanders began to suffer a heavy number of killed and wounded from the well-aimed PLAF fire. The drivers' habits and the exposed positions of the vehicle commanders tended to contribute to the guerrillas' success. Most of the M113 drivers elevated their seats and exposed their heads above their vision ports for better observation, even though their stations were equipped with periscopes that allowed them to remain inside the APCs while driving. With their heads fully exposed to the small arms fire, several drivers in Ba's company suffered head wounds. Along the same lines, the vehicle commanders also lacked protection for their upper torsos while manning the .50 caliber machine guns. Not only did this result in many chest wounds, but it also severely reduced the effectiveness of the vehicles' heavy machine guns. Staying low in the cupola rings to minimize their exposure and consequently unable to identify the PLAF positions in the treeline, the APC commanders achieved ever-decreasing success in returning effective fire and suppressing the guerrillas.[93] As Scanlon related after the battle, "After the third guy came down with a bullet through the head, it was darn difficult to get the fourth guy up there" to continue firing.[94] Surprised by the guerrillas' fierce fire and unable to silence the enemy in the woodline, the attack on the north side of the helicopters ground to a halt.

In the midst of this fracas, both Scanlon and Mays went into action to assist the wounded South Vietnamese and Americans. As the carrier he was on began to back up, Scanlon saw that the other vehicle intended to leave one of its wounded behind. Jumping off his vehicle, he managed to halt the other carrier and, with another ARVN soldier, dragged the wounded man aboard. During this action, two other soldiers also received wounds, and despite Scanlon's exhortations to continue the attack, the two carriers began to move behind the helicopters to take cover from the incoming small arms fire. Disgusted, Scanlon jumped down and watched the two carriers beat a hasty retreat. At roughly the same time, Mays had also been busy. Having ridden forward with Chou, he arrived at the helicopters just prior to the guerillas' opening fire. Wanting to locate the wounded Americans, the advisor had the platoon leader stop the carrier near the downed Shawnee and Huey pilots. As Mays unsuccessfully attempted to ascertain from the pilots where the wounded were, the insurgents began to take them under fire. Struggling to ignore the lashing fire, the captain found Sergeant Bowers, who stated he knew of the two injured crewmen. Rushing to one of the Shawnees, they entered Specialist Braman's helicopter and found that the young crew chief was dead, the second American to die at Ap Bac. Exiting the aircraft, Mays left Bowers, remounted on Chou's vehicle, and continued off to the east.[95]

As Chou's two carriers moved out, Ba and his accompanying carrier came up behind them. Taking particularly heavy fire from a PLAF machine gun located in the southeast corner of the LZ, the APCs moved toward it in an attempt to close with it and knock it out. Mays, realizing that they were not receiving fire from their right flank, radioed Ba and recommended that he attempt to envelop the machine gun from the south. Either not receiving the American's transmission or ignoring him, Ba did not respond, and when a PLAF round clipped Mays's radio antenna, the American lost contact with the company commander. Unable to communicate with anyone outside his vehicle, Mays watched helplessly as the attack of the four carriers rapidly degenerated into a series of individual APC actions.[96]

While watching his two carriers retire, Scanlon spotted Bowers and moved over to him. Bowers quickly pointed out the guerrilla positions, and the two Americans ran over to where the pilots were taking cover. The advisors saw Chou's carriers assault, briefly stop, and then begin to back up. Scanlon's decreasing confidence in bringing the engagement to a close soared when he saw the approach of the company's flame thrower–equipped M113. Expecting the thrower's napalm to burn out the guerrillas in the woodline and end the resistance, the advisor turned to one of the pilots next to him and began to brag, "This will do it." Scanlon's optimism was short-lived. Pulling up, the vehicle loosed a "a large ball of flame . . . to a range of 23-30 meters," causing the overly confident captain to describe it as having all "the force and effect of a Zippo lighter."[97] Having bounced over several canals en route to the LZ, the compressed air tanks had lost pressure, rendering yet another technological advance ineffective against the determined guerrillas.[98]

As some of the remaining carriers came up from the crossing site, they attacked individually and in small groups against the well-sited machine gun in the southeastern corner of the LZ with no success. Seeing the carriers moving toward the enemy positions, Lieutenant Thi began to move his companies into position. Pushing the 172nd Company forward, the TF B commander held both the 171st and 839th in anticipation of maneuvering through the woodline and enveloping the PLAF units from the south. Calling Major Tho for permission to attack into the woodline with his entire task force, the lieutenant received the directive to stand fast. Purportedly concerned about incurring casualties from the incoming artillery and CAS in and around Ap Bac, Tho told his subordinate to wait until the firing ceased. Knowing full well his potentially advantageous tactical position, Thi called several times throughout the afternoon to attack but never received authority to do so, depriving Ba of sorely needed reinforcements.[99] Even without the assistance of TF B, the beleaguered Ba did manage to mass seven or eight carriers into a semicoordinated attack, and for a brief time it seemed that perhaps the APCs would bring about a decision.[100]

Forming for another assault, the lead carriers once again closed with the woodline, and this time the guerrillas were faced with a seemingly desperate situation. Having withstood several assaults already and running low on ammunition, the insurgents steeled themselves in anticipation of the collision. When Ba's lead carriers closed to within 20 or 30 meters of the woodline, the moment of truth arrived for the PLAF soldiers. Charged with adrenaline, two guerrillas fired rifle grenades and several others jumped out of their holes and tossed hand grenades at the vehicles. Although at least one grenade landed on top of the carriers, and three guerrillas "were sacrificed," this attack failed to inflict any casualties among the ARVN soldiers on the vehicles. Despite the lack of casualties, the carriers broke off the attack and once again moved away from the woodline. Although a few APCs tried again in individual actions against the treeline later in the day, the company commander was unable to generate another sizable, coordinated attack. Whether the mechanized soldiers lost their will because they could not destroy the troublesome machine gun in the southeast, the shock of the hand grenades was too much for them, or Ba could no longer communicate with them because of the rising casualties among the vehicle commanders, 4/2 ACR's attack on C1/261 came to a halt. Withdrawing behind the helicopters, Ba's company hunkered down and fired its machine guns from a distance, and the mechanized portion of the assault into the LZ ended with little to show for it except the ARVN killed and wounded.[101]

As the powerless Vann watched the M113s withdraw and hold their positions to the west of the downed helicopters, he realized that the 7th Division was not going to close on Ap Bac before nightfall. With the afternoon waning and less than four hours of daylight left, Vann recommended to Colonel Dam that he request the 8th Airborne Battalion (8th ABN), a JGS reserve unit, to drop to the east of Ap Bac, effectively closing the cordon. If the ARVN forces could not take Ap Bac, Vann reasoned, they could at least hold the PLAF in position until they could mass enough forces and firepower to close with and destroy the insurgents the following morning.[102]

Responding to Vann's recommendation, Dam radioed him that the airborne battalion would drop to the *west* of Ap Bac, thus facilitating link-up with the friendly units in the area. Incredulous, Vann returned to the division CP at Tan Hiep. On arrival, he found Brigadier General Tran Thien Kheim, the chief of staff of the JGS, General Huynh Van Cao, the IV Corps commander, and

Colonel Daniel Porter, the senior American advisor for IV Corps, in the CP with Colonel Dam. A Diem appointee, Cao had previously commanded the 7th Division and believed himself a model of Napoleonic generalship. Always carrying a swagger stick, Cao demonstrated his vanity by writing a novel he entitled *He Grows under Fire*, a thinly veiled tribute to his martial capabilities.[103] Earlier the previous year, Cao expressed his confidence in both his prowess and the abilities of the 7th Division in an interview with the *Pacific Stars and Stripes*, stating, "The more [PLAF] that come the more we kill."[104]

Yet for all his expressed self-confidence, Cao was a man who hated combat: "He lacked the nerves of a soldier. During one operation when nervous strain undid him he ran out of the command tent, vomited, and ordered the artillery to stop firing a barrage in support of an infantry unit engaged with the guerrillas. The noise upset him too much, he said."[105] The IV Corps commander was also of a political nature and wished to remain in Diem's good graces, and after the loss of the ranger platoon the previous October, he did everything within his power to avoid casualties.[106] Not surprisingly, Cao repeatedly resisted American attempts to seek out and destroy the PLAF units, and this reluctance manifested itself again, this time in the 7th Division's command post. Against the virulent protestations of both Vann and Porter, Cao decided at 1430 to employ the airborne battalion to the west. With the memory of Diem's warnings about excessive casualties weighing upon him, the corps commander left open an avenue of egress for the PLAF once dusk fell.[107] With Cao's decision, the opportunity for the ARVN to turn defeat into victory passed. There would be nothing to stand in the way of a PLAF retreat to the west with the coming of night and its protection from the CAS and artillery.

As 4/2 ACR struggled inconclusively on the LZ, 2/11 IN was still locked in sporadic combat with the guerrillas in and around Ap Tan Thoi. Achieving little success by attempting to push into the village with the 2nd Company in the center, the 2/11 IN commander sent for the 3rd Company's commander to break the deadlock. Located on the battalion's eastern flank, the company commander moved quickly to find his superior and receive his orders. Believing that an envelopment from the west might dislocate his opposition, the battalion commander issued orders for the 3rd Company to move through the rear of the 2nd Company and attack through the 1st Company, which was on the battalion's western flank. Conducting a quick reconnaissance, the 3rd Company's commander returned and briefed his NCOs on the route of movement. Personally leading his unit, the commander set off at a rapid pace in an effort to reinvigorate the battalion's stalled attack.[108]

Captain Smith, who was still with the 3rd Company, found it difficult to keep up with the rapidly moving commander. In an effort to find a shorter route to the directed attack position, Smith cut around a bush and prepared to drop into a canal when he noticed Captain Good lying flat on his back with his shirt off and a bandage around his neck and shoulder. Asking for water to rinse his mouth and wash his face, the injured American told Smith that he did not know how long he had been lying on the ground, nor did he know if Vann knew of his wounded condition. Concerned, Smith set off to find a radio to coordinate for a medevac for Good. As he moved out, he heard firing off to the west, which signaled that the 1st and 3rd Companies were again in contact.[109]

With the increased firing, the 1st Company sent forward a machine gun to engage the enemy, and traveling with it was another American advisor, Captain George Feliciano. Apparently just missing Smith, he, too, found Good wrapped in a field dressing. Like Smith, Feliciano set off to find a means to contact higher, and he soon located Captain Chin, the 2nd Company commander. Feliciano requested to use his radio to inform Vann, but the ARVN commander refused, apparently believing that Good's wound was not serious. Infuriated, Feliciano carried Good farther to the rear, away from the firing, where a short time later Smith joined them. Having contacted Vann and requested a Huey to pick up Good, the two Americans carefully moved him a short distance to the pickup zone (PZ). Quickly responding to Vann's request, the aircraft arrived at approximately 1530 and evacuated Good and six other Vietnamese wounded. Although arriving a short time later at Tan Hiep, the young American captain perished from a loss of blood.[110] The death toll for the Americans now stood at three for the Battle of Ap Bac; the ARVN were to lose many more.

While 2/11 IN sought to press its way into Ap Tan Thoi, the situation on the reserve's LZ was beginning to quiet down. Now that Ba's company had assumed defensive positions and showed no indication of continuing the attack, C1/261's fire slackened in an effort to conserve ammunition. As Scanlon moved about the battlefield, he happened upon a lieutenant from 1/1/11 IN. Addressing the lieutenant in English, the advisor requested that the ARVN officer follow him into the southern woodline in an effort to find and silence the machine gun that had caused so many difficulties. The lieutenant rewarded Scanlon's query with a confused look and responded that he did not understand what the advisor was suggesting. Once again the American attempted to get his point across, this time in Vietnamese, but the South Vietnamese officer still replied that he did not comprehend the American's request. Any defense the officer might have offered in not understanding English disappeared when he then proceeded to ask several unrelated questions and told Scanlon of the inbound airborne forces. After fruitlessly attempting several more times to convince the lieutenant to coordinate his efforts with Ba's attacks, the American began to look for the mechanized company commander in the hopes of somehow influencing the action. Once again frustrated in his efforts to bring about an offensive movement, he took advantage of the ongoing CAS and moved on toward Ba's vehicle.[111]

As the action between the carriers and the guerrillas became an exchange of desultory long-range small arms fire, Major Prevost arrived overhead in an L-19 to assist in directing the B-26 that was on station over the battlefield. Scheduled to depart the 7th Division's advisory detachment that very day, the ALO had gotten wind of what had been happening near Ap Bac and rushed to the airstrip at Tan Hiep. Receiving guidance from Cao that he wanted the ALO airborne, Prevost took off with an RVNAF observer and headed to the LZ. Arriving approximately ten minutes before the bomber, the Vietnamese observer with Prevost dropped smoke and began to direct the B-26 to the intended targets. Under the guidance of the Vietnamese observer, the aircraft dropped both napalm and high explosive bombs with little effect, as they straddled the guerrilla positions. Seeing that the APCs were still under sporadic fire, the bomber crew asked to use both machine guns and rockets on subsequent passes. Receiving approval, the bomber came around for another pass and met with success. This time with Prevost relaying the observer's instructions, the B-26 clearly struck the location of the troublesome machine gun in the southeastern corner of the woodline. Reporting that they still had ordnance aboard, the bomber's crew began another pass. Claiming that an artillery mission was inbound, the observer flying with Prevost abruptly directed the bomber to "[g]o home" and then asked to return to Tan Hiep. Upon landing, the ALO's information concerning the suspension of the airstrikes both surprised and angered Dam, who ordered their resumption.[112] Like most everything else for the 7th Division commander during the battle, even the most simple of tasks, like that of guiding a single ship CAS sortie, had become extremely complex.

Although there were additional airstrikes later in the afternoon, the B-26 runs under Prevost's guidance appeared to have the most effect against the guerrillas. After their completion shortly before 1600, the advisors on the LZ reported that once again the PLAF was firing toward the carriers but not on the same scale as before.[113] As the afternoon progressed toward evening, it seemed to Scanlon that the insurgents were withdrawing, but he was only partially correct in his estimation. The action against Ba's company for Bay was, in a word, "tense." The platoon that had withdrawn from the company's southern flank, when found by a scout dispatched by Hoang, refused his orders to return and left the company to fight the carriers shorthanded. In the midst of the fight, two squads, ordered by the company commander to withdraw, became disoriented by the airstrikes and did not reach their new positions. Two other squads, also ordered to withdraw, similarly failed to find their way to their new positions because of poor navigation. Despite the loss of those units, the remainder of C1/261 weathered the airstrikes and final assaults by the APCs and held its ground. Realizing that engaging the carriers after their movement behind the helicopters was tantamount to wasting precious ammunition, Bay allowed his soldiers to cease their fire and to await his orders.[114]

Content to wait for the incoming 8th ABN, the GVN forces in the south generally held their positions, while 2/11 IN in the north continued to trade small arms fire with the guerrillas in Ap Tan Thoi. Yet despite this loss of momentum, not all the RVNAF commanders were willing to stand by and wait. Having delivered the 352nd Ranger Company to the 11th Infantry Regiment CP, the naval task force commander from the 21st RAG decided at about 1730 to put his engineers and their 4,000 pounds of demolitions to work. Having bypassed the large obstacle in the Song My Tho Canal earlier that morning, the commander issued orders for the engineers to clear the barricade. Leaving the CP shortly thereafter, the engineer detachment proceeded up the canal and planted the demolitions under the watchful eye of Captain Garland Reid, the accompanying advisor. Taking their time, the engineers thoroughly wired the barricade, and, in a sheet of white flame, the obstruction blocking the Song My Tho Canal ceased to exist at 2030, provoking a small arms barrage from the western side of the canal. Lasting about 20 minutes, the exchange of small arms fire eventually petered out, and the detachment returned to the 11th's CP, accomplishing what was arguably the GVN's only successful action of the day.[115]

With dusk imminent, seven C-123 aircraft carrying their 300 or so paratroopers from the 8th ABN arrived over Ap Bac. Following an L-19, they made one pass over the drop zone without releasing any troops. As the aircraft came around for another pass, several advisors saw the spotter aircraft mark the drop zone with white phosphorus smoke. This time, the C-123s disgorged their human cargo between Ap Bac and Ap Tan Thoi shortly after 1800 into a location that Colonel Dam had not designated beforehand (see Fig. 3.7). Although 2/11 IN was heartened by the airborne assault to the point of blowing bugles and cheering, that was the extent of their contribution. Despite now facing two full battalions, C1/514 engaged the dropping soldiers in the air and on the ground, inflicting several casualties.[116]

Outside of small arms range from Ap Tan Thoi, the airborne troopers along the southern portion of the drop zone were not under fire, and they reacted far differently from their peers to the north. Instead of moving quickly to the firefight, they strolled around the drop zone, walked along the dikes, and took their time assembling while their compatriots engaged in fierce hand-to-hand combat in and among the hedges of Ap Tan Thoi. The lack of motivation at the far end of the drop zone may well have resulted from a lack of supervision, as the battalion commander, like most other senior ARVN commanders at Ap Bac, chose not to jump in with his battalion.[117] For all its problems, however, the 8th ABN was not alone in suffering hardships in the rapidly dwindling daylight. C1/514 was also having its share of difficulties, particularly among its recent recruits. Some of the newer guerrillas, having never seen paratroopers before, "were afraid and hid in the ditch and getting wet, [sic] their weapons did not work." Despite some terrified guerrillas and waterlogged weapons, the PLAF got the better of the exchange and cut the paratroopers' formation into two smaller groups.[118]

With darkness now around him, Hoang was unsure of how many GVN forces he faced and where they were located. Guessing that he did not have sufficient strength to hold off the increasingly numerous enemy units, he decided that he could not withstand the assault that was sure to occur the next morning. His men's condition also weighed heavily in his mind. Fighting all day and running short of ammunition, the "cadre and soldiers were hungry, thirsty, and tired." The wounded also required evacuation. Worse, C1/261 was still missing one of its platoons, as well as a few smaller elements. Conferring with Bich, Hoang examined his few available options. In the PLAF commander's estimate, a delaying action around Ap Bac and Ap Tan Thoi was "unnecessary" since the villages themselves were of no particular importance. Believing that he had dealt the GVN forces a significant blow, Hoang ordered his units to move to Ap Tan Thoi proper to prepare for a withdrawal to the east "at any cost."[119]

As the PLAF units consolidated for their withdrawal, Scanlon received word from Vann that helicopters were en route to drop off ammunition and evacuate

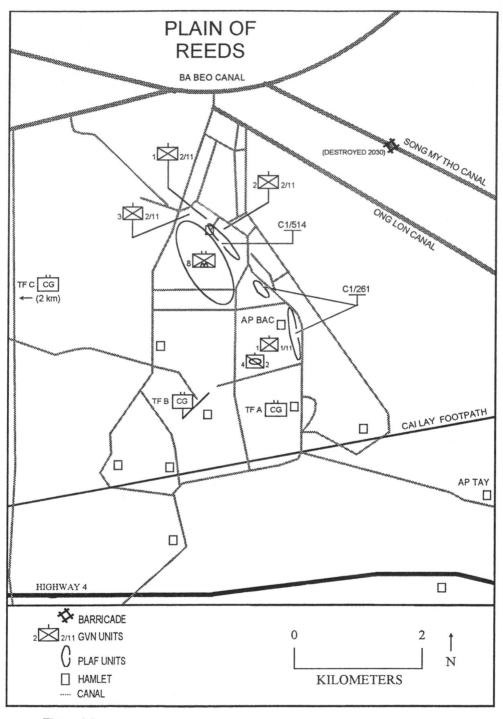

Figure 3.7
Unit Locations, 1805 Hours

the wounded. Not wanting to lose any more aircraft, the senior advisor directed that they land some 500 meters to the west of the downed helicopters, adjacent to where 4/2 ACR had conducted its final canal crossing earlier in the afternoon. Receiving permission from Ba to use two carriers to transport the wounded, Scanlon and another advisor, Captain Parker, gathered what casualties they could and moved them to the PZ. After getting the wounded to the canal, Scanlon returned to the mechanized company's CP and learned from Mays that Vann was concerned about the security of the ammunition left by the helicopters. According to the senior advisor, no one was attempting to locate and gain control of it. Despite Ba's orders to one of his lieutenants to find the ordnance, Vann once again called Scanlon to inform him that the ammunition was still missing. Frustrated and worried that the PLAF might capture the munitions and use them in a later engagement, Vann ordered the advisors to find them. Setting off with the regimental operations officer's M114, Scanlon, Parker, and Bowers returned to the PZ, where they found several of the wounded still awaiting evacuation. After failing to secure any volunteers to help locate the ammunition, Scanlon asked Captain Trong, the operations officer, to order his soldiers in the area to begin a search. Complaining that they had not yet eaten, the soldiers refused, and the Americans were left to their own devices to carry out Vann's wishes. At about this same time, the last helicopter of the night took off, leaving the bodies of Sergeant Deal and SP/4 Braman. Because of the number of Vietnamese wounded, there was not enough room to evacuate the two dead Americans, and their remains spent the night on the battlefield.[120]

After crossing the canal and finding the ammunition, Scanlon began to carry it himself to the other side, and it was only after this gesture that the South Vietnamese soldiers began to help. Securing the last of the ammunition crates, the Americans then moved off to clear out the downed Shawnees of any remaining items of value. Once the rations, extra ammunition, and machine guns from the helicopters were aboard the carrier, Scanlon returned to Ba's CP to finish out the night, thus ending an extremely long and frustrating day.[121] Scanlon's experiences during the battle illustrated one of the most critical weaknesses in the American advisory system. When he felt that a task needed to be accomplished, and the ARVN officers or soldiers failed to do it after his suggestions, he did it himself, just as almost every other American officer or NCO would have. While American professionalism and impatience tended to pay short-term dividends by getting the immediate job done, they also undermined the development of the ARVN's officer corps in the long run by reinforcing unacceptable behavior. As was demonstrated throughout day, if the mission was important enough and the ARVN officers or soldiers waited long enough, the Americans would grow impatient and most likely do it themselves. If defeating the insurgency were truly the GVN's fight, continuous American attempts to influence the fighting should have been the least, and not the most, likely pattern of the advisory effort.

Despite the last resupply helicopter's departure and the increasing darkness, the paratroopers and elements of 2/11 IN to the north continued to slug it out with the guerrillas among the hedges and canals surrounding Ap Tan Thoi. In one of the day's final miscues, a T-28, while attempting to assist its friendly elements on the ground, conducted at least two strafing runs either on or near the ARVN units. After seeing the yellow smoke thrown by the 2nd Company, the pilot ceased firing, leaving an unknown number of casualties, another testament to the lack of RVNAF air-ground coordination.[122]

With complete darkness now covering the battlefield, the fire began to diminish in and around Ap Tan Thoi, and, by 1930, it was almost completely silent.[123] Recommending that Dam request a C-47 flare ship, Prevost intended to keep aircraft on station throughout the night in case the PLAF attempted to withdraw to the Plain of Reeds. Receiving approval, he forwarded the request, and, by 2000, a flare ship was on station, ready to illuminate the area. Once again, Dam found himself helpless in the face of a convoluted and political chain of command. When asked by the ALO to begin the illumination, the division commander stated he could not authorize it because the 8th ABN did not wish the flares. Suffering through yet another outburst from Vann, Dam either would not or could not authorize the pyrotechnics. With Cao's approval, the C-47 harmlessly orbited without illuminating the area.[124]

As 4/2 ACR and the CG task forces crept into the woodline south of Ap Bac for the night, the PLAF units began their withdrawal, taking advantage of the darkness and the opening Cao gave them by dropping the 8th ABN to the west. After receiving reports from the scouts dispatched to reconnoiter the area, Hoang conferred with his two company commanders. With 2/11 IN to the north and the naval task force farther down the main canal to the south, the guerrillas chose a route that threaded northeast between the GVN units. Giving his subordinates time to inform their soldiers, the PLAF commander fixed the departure time at 2200. Withdrawing by platoons with elements of C1/261 leading, the guerrillas headed northeast to live and to fight another day.[125] With the last platoon of C1/514 departing from Ap Tan Thoi, the Battle of Ap Bac was essentially over, but events would continue to play themselves out over the next few days.

As 3 January 1963 dawned, helicopters began to fly into Ap Bac to evacuate the dead and wounded, resupply the GVN forces, and drop off several advisors and observers. Among those arriving early on 3 January was Brigadier General Robert York, commander of the Combat Development and Test Center, a detachment charged with evaluating Army weapons and tactics. Originally interested in inspecting the downed UH-1B, the general and his aide proceeded to examine the PLAF fighting positions along the woodline east of Ap Bac.[126] When asked for his opinion about what he believed had happened, the general replied simply: "They [the guerrillas] got away—that's what happened."[127]

Believing that perhaps somehow the PLAF might still be in force near Ap Bac, the 7th Division coordinated the arrival of several additional units to participate in an another attempt to surround the hamlet. Having received a new division order at 0720 that morning, the 11th Infantry Regiment ordered 2/11 IN and the 8th ABN to a position just north of Ap Bac. Although the division intended for these two battalions to attack the village at 1000, the attack did not occur as planned because the airborne commander complained of the high number of casualties sustained and his ongoing police of parachutes. By 1125, 2/11 IN was on its way to Ap Bac with the 8th ABN following in reserve.[128]

At the same time 2/11 IN was moving to its new objective, three other ARVN units were gathering near Ap Tay, a village four kilometers to the southeast of the previous day's battlefield. To assist the 352nd Ranger Company, the 349th Ranger Company received orders to move toward Ap Tay and to link up with its sister company, a task that it accomplished later that afternoon. Another mechanized company, 5th Mechanized Squadron, 1st Armored Cavalry Regiment (5/1 ACR), was also on its way. Receiving its mission at the division CP at Tan Hiep, the newly formed company, having only graduated from its training course the previous week, proceeded to the area of Ap Bac as well. Charged with moving directly across the rice paddies from Highway 4, the company made little progress across the canals and dikes. Traveling just over a kilometer, 5/1 ACR received orders to establish a blocking position and remained static near the village of Ap Tay for the remainder of the day.[129] The third unit moving toward Ap Bac, 1st Battalion, 10th Infantry Regiment (1/10 IN), was clearly the most unlucky of the three newly arrived units. Another battalion of the 7th Division, it closed on Ap Bac from the south with the mission of assisting 2/11 IN. As it moved into Ap Bac at about 1145, preparatory fires of 4.2-inch mortar rounds rained down around the hapless battalion. Suffering 5 KIA and 14 WIA, the battalion was the victim of yet another example of Tho's negligence, this time an artillery mission that he had not cleared with the 7th Division. General York and his aide, both of whom had been nearby, miraculously escaped unscathed.[130]

Shaking off the unfortunate fratricide incident, 2/11 IN and 1/10 IN conducted a search of Ap Bac, what Vann later called "just a walk-thru," while 4/2 ACR remained near the helicopters to protect them. Exceedingly frustrated with the apparent escape of the guerrillas, the American advisors continued to press their counterparts to find the enemy and engage him. About two hours after the "attack" into Ap Bac, the 7th Division's advisors pieced together several intelligence reports that indicated that the PLAF was gathering in strength in Ap Tay, quite near 5/1 ACR's blocking position. Seizing upon the chance to rectify the previous day's oversights, Vann recommended to Dam that the division converge its units on Ap Tay, thus encircling the insurgents. Amenable to the senior division advisor's suggestion, the South Vietnamese commander issued orders for 2/11 IN and the 8th ABN to proceed south toward the village.[131]

Having conducted a thorough search of Ap Bac and finding no trace of the guerrillas' presence in the village except for several blood stains left by the wounded, 2/11 IN started south for Ap Tay at about 1300. Soon meeting up with the airborne battalion, the two units began their movement to the south. Now possessing four line companies with the attachment of 1/1/11 IN, 2/11 IN walked for some two hours before breaking for a meal. After an hour break, the battalion once again moved toward its objective and established its ordered blocking positions along the Cai Lay footpath at roughly eight in the evening. Passing through 2/11 IN's positions, the 8th ABN continued to the south side of the path and established its own assembly area. To their east, the 349th and 352nd

Ranger Companies had established a screen between 5/1 ACR's carriers and the footpath.[132] With two battalions, two ranger companies, and a mechanized company arrayed near Ap Tay, it seemed to the advisors that the GVN units might redeem themselves (see Fig. 3.8).

The problems of coordination with the Dinh Tuong Regiment, however, continued to plague the unfortunate Dam. Both TF A and TF B participated during the search operations near Ap Bac, and when the division issued orders for the 11th Infantry's units to move south, Major Tho ordered his two task forces to the southeast as well. Shortly after issuing his orders, however, Tho informed his advisor, Major Macslarrow, that the two task forces now fell under the command of the 11th and began to dismantle his CP. By 1700, the province chief had left the radio net and moved his CP back to its headquarters building at My Tho. Within an hour and a half of the Dinh Tuong Regiment commander's yielding of command over his task forces, both purportedly received orders to move to Highway 4 and return to My Tho, which they accomplished within a few hours. Contrary to Dam's belief that he had a presence along Highway 4, the southern approaches to Ap Tay remained unguarded throughout the night.[133]

The 7th Division commander did have some indication that all was not right with the CG units when he received word from Macslarrow at 2100 that the task forces had returned to My Tho. Calling Tho, Dam directed him to redeploy his units along Highway 4, and the division commander later received the false report that they were moving to their assigned blocking positions. By the following morning, 4 January, Macslarrow still was not confident that the CG blocking forces were in place, and, leaving some 40 minutes before the scheduled attack at 0730, the sector advisor departed with Captain James Drummond, the 7th Division's intelligence advisor, to verify that the CG units were in position. Much to their consternation, they found no blocking force at all. Leaving Macslarrow, Drummond proceeded to Tho's headquarters to "strongly recommend" that he deploy at least a company to the blocking positions along Highway 4.[134]

As the intelligence advisor petitioned Tho for forces, the situation along the highway became worse for the little force that had now coalesced around the sector advisor. By 0930, Macslarrow reported some 200 to 300 PLAF stragglers moving south, out of Ap Tay, toward his position along Highway 4. Vann, who had been monitoring the radio, directed the advisor to stay put with the 18 SDC soldiers and two Malayan scout cars that had met him on the road. Not having any other troops at his disposal, the division advisor ordered the only personnel he could lawfully command to help: the remaining advisory detachment personnel at My Tho. Arriving at about the same time as Tho and the 839th CG Company, some 60 American personnel had moved to the blocking position in about 20 minutes. Trading sporadic small arms fire with the insurgents, the Americans captured between 17 and 32 PLAF guerrillas along the highway, while the 839th cowered in the ditches and Tho stood idly by without making any attempt to influence the action.[135] Although Vann claimed that his "sole reason" for moving the Americans to the blocking position "was to protect that major [Macslarrow]," one cannot help but wonder if it was actually an act of

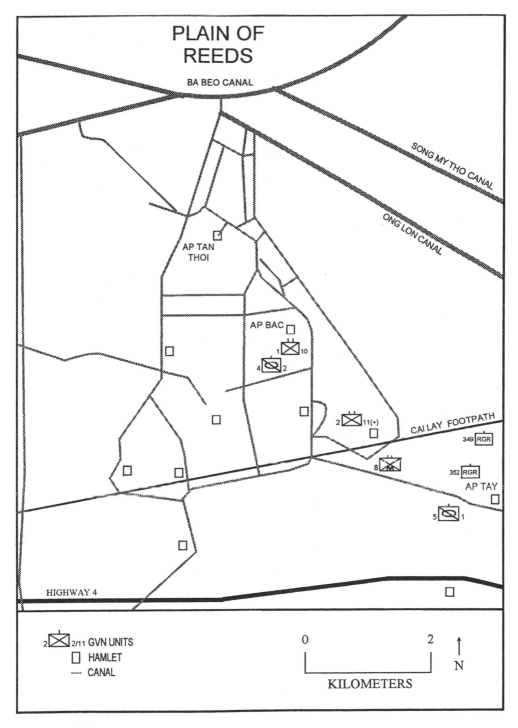

Figure 3.8
GVN Unit Locations, 1900 Hours, 3 January 1963

desperation after the unbelievable frustration of the previous two days.[136]

The 7th Division had better success controlling the movements of the units north of Highway 4. Having received orders to continue south toward Ap Tay shortly before 0630, 2/11 IN left its positions north of the Cai Lay footpath and traveled east approximately two kilometers before turning south. Moving steadily, the battalion did not make contact with any guerrillas during its march. Gun-shy after their experiences in and around Ap Tan Thoi and unwilling to take any chances, the lead companies often fired into the villages before physically arriving, a technique known as "reconnaissance by fire," to ensure that the huts were clear of the enemy. Passing through 5/1 ACR, which was still holding its positions near Ap Tay, and halting short of Highway 4, 2/11 IN occupied blocking positions shortly before noon when its soldiers heard firing in front of the ranger companies located farther to the east (see Fig. 3.9). Within half an hour, the battalion received orders to move to the highway, board trucks, and return to My Tho, thus bringing 2/11 IN's participation in the operation to an end. The 8th ABN, despite still being in the vicinity and under the command of the 11th Infantry, seemed no longer a part of the day's operation. Often meandering through 2/11 IN's columns, the airborne soldiers did not appear to have a mission or a purpose, another indication that they were JGS, and not 7th Division, assets.[137]

With the return of the units near Ap Tay to their respective bases, Vann considered Operation *DUC THANG* 1 officially over as of 1500 on 4 January, but there was still the matter of policing the remains of the downed helicopters. Of the four damaged H-21s, maintenance personnel repaired two relatively quickly, and they returned uneventfully to Tan Hiep. The third Shawnee received PLAF ground fire during its return trip and limped back to the LZ, where the mechanics once again repaired it. After its second attempt, it managed to rejoin its company. The Huey, having lost its tail rotor, returned to American control, slung under the belly of another helicopter.

The last cargo helicopter caused the most problems by crashing during its test flight on the afternoon of 5 January. Believing it beyond repair, the maintenance team decided that salvaging the aircraft, and not repairing it, was the best course. Although the 7th Division's operation was over by the afternoon of 4 January, two days earlier, the lone H-21 still remained on the LZ with both 4/2 ACR and 1/10 IN providing security. Wanting to assess the situation on the LZ himself, Vann arrived on the afternoon of 6 January and had yet another verbal exchange with Ba. Not satisfied that Ba's carriers were in a position to prevent the guerrillas from occupying their former positions and firing into the salvage efforts, the senior advisor directed the 4/2 ACR commander to push his vehicles farther to the north, away from the LZ. Responding that he was responsible for the LZ and would be the one to "go to jail" if his defense failed, Ba refused to reposition his APCs. Fuming, Vann retorted that "he would personnaly [sic] see to it that he [Ba] would be relieved and that he would go to jail." As if to spite the division advisor, Ba waited a short time before moving three of his carriers out a short distance, but did little else to increase his security around the maintenance team.[138]

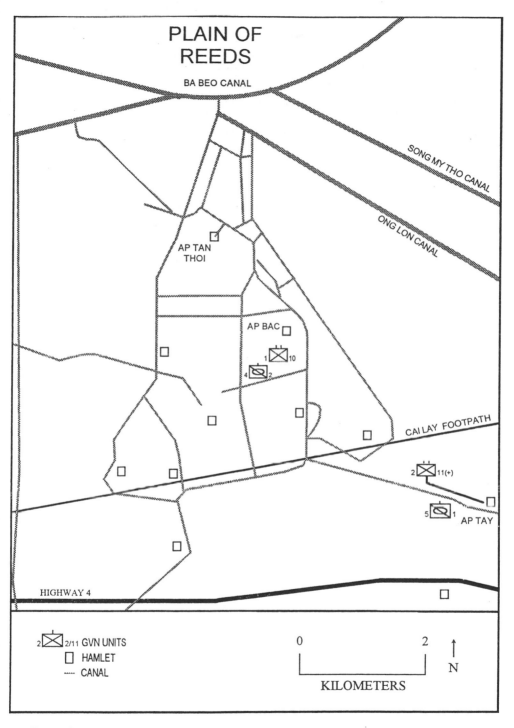

Figure 3.9
GVN Unit Locations, 1100 Hours, 4 January 1963

Some two hours later, Scanlon noticed a commotion on Ba's vehicle. Gesturing to the woodline, the 4/2 ACR commander told the advisor that he believed that some guerrillas had reoccupied the fighting positions along the canals. Shouting to the maintenance crewmen to return to Tan Hiep, Scanlon then received word from Vann to carry out the remaining helicopter pieces in the carriers to preclude the PLAF from recycling the metal for weapons and munitions. Quickly picking up the remaining fragments, the mechanized company moved south toward My Tho and away from the suspected enemy. As they crossed the canals, Scanlon noted that the crews were taking only about 15 minutes to ford the obstacles, unlike the 30 minutes to an hour that they had taken on the day of the battle. Wondering what would explain the significantly quicker fording times, the advisor surmised that the soldiers were "worried about the VC attacking their moving column of 14 armored vehicles." With the company's return to My Tho at approximately 2230 hours on 6 January, the ARVN soldiers were able to breathe a sigh of relief that they did not make contact again.[139]

With the PLAF already gone from the field, the GVN forces licking their wounds safely in their base camps, and all the American helicopters removed from the area, the Battle of Ap Bac truly came to an end. The lull after the battle, however, did not last long at all. In fact, another battle had already begun, but this time between different belligerents: the U.S. government and the press.

NOTES

1. Emphasis in the original; U.S. Military Assistance Command, Vietnam, *Ap Bac Battle, 2 January 1963; Translation of VC Document, 20 April 1963*, C0043021, 18 (hereafter *Ap Bac*) (Vietnam Archive).

2. George Marshall, ed., *Infantry in Battle*, rev. ed. (Washington, D.C.: *The Infantry Journal*, 1939), 69.

3. The following analysis relies upon the 1:50,000 map sheet that encompasses the Ap Bac area. 29th Engineer Battalion, *Cai Lay* (map) (Fort Belvoir, VA: U.S. Army Corps of Engineers Army Map Service, 1955) (sheet 6242III, 1:50,000) (folder 3, box 39, Vann-Sheehan Vietnam War Collection, Library of Congress Manuscript Division [hereafter VSVWC]).

4. Department of the Army, *Mounted Combat in Vietnam* by Donn Starry, Vietnam Studies (Washington, D.C.: U.S. Government Printing Office, 1978), 41; Lieutenant Colonel James B. Scanlon, U.S. Army (Retired), interview by Neil Sheehan, 2 March 1977, 1–2, 4, 7 (folder 10, box 76, VSVWC).

5. Senior Advisor, 7th Infantry Division, After Action Report for the Battle of Ap Bac, 9 January 1963, 4 (U.S. Army Center of Military History Historians' Working Files [hereafter AAR and CMH]). This document is a transcription of the original report and contains numerous errors, and it does not include any of the annexes or appendices. A complete carbon of the original report in its entirety, though blurry, is in folder 11, box 38, VSVWC.

6. Lieutenant General Nguyen Dinh Uoc, People's Army of Vietnam, interview by author, 16 April 1999, Lubbock, TX; *Ap Bac*, 3, 7.

7. *Ap Bac*, 10; Major Pham Van Gong, People's Liberation Armed Forces, interview by author, 17 July 2000, Ap Bac, Vietnam. Burchett's account identifies the senior PLAF commander as "Duyen," which was most likely a pseudonym. Wilfred Burchett,

Vietnam: Inside Story of the Guerrilla War (New York: International Publishers, 1965), 86.

8. *Ap Bac* lists four separate engagements but states "our 3 successful counter mopping-up operations." *Ap Bac*, 2 and *passim*.

9. Dr. Nguyen Huu Nguyen, Social Sciences and Humanities Center of Ho Chi Minh City, interview by author, 16 July 2000, Ho Chi Minh City, Vietnam.

10. *Ap Bac*, 4.

11. Dr. Nguyen Huu Nguyen, Social Sciences and Humanities Center of Ho Chi Minh City, interview by author, 16 July 2000, Ho Chi Minh City, Vietnam; *Ap Bac*, 10. The recollections of Major Gong, an assistant platoon leader in the 514th Provincial Battalion, tend to support this interpretation. In describing the battle, he admitted that the guerrillas near Ap Bac were surprised by the appearance of the M113s on the landing zone. When asked why they did not withdraw to the east, he replied that by that point in the day (approximately 1300), withdrawal was impossible because of the proximity of the ARVN forces and the ongoing airstrikes. If this is truly the case, then the guerrillas' stand at Ap Bac was more the result of a poor decision than a deliberate effort on the part of the PLAF to fight it out against an overwhelming enemy force. Major Pham Van Gong, People's Liberation Armed Forces, interview by author, 17 July 2000, Ap Bac, Vietnam.

12. James McCoy, *Secrets of the Viet Cong* (New York: Hippocrene Books, 1992), 45; *Ap Bac*, sketch 1; Major Pham Van Gong, People's Liberation Armed Forces, interview by author, 17 July 2000, Ap Bac, Vietnam.

13. *Ap Bac*, 8, lists two regular companies (100 each), a support unit (30), two squads of C5/261 (7 each), one regional platoon (30), one provincial platoon (30), 30 local guerrillas, and two cells (6) (parenthetical numbers are author's estimates). Palmer places PLAF strength at 500. Sheehan estimates "about 320 Main Force and Regional guerrillas." Burchett reports "about 230 men." Dave R. Palmer, *Summons of the Trumpet*, rev. ed. (New York: Ballantine Books, 1984), 44; Neil Sheehan, *A Bright Shining Lie* (New York: Random House, 1988), 206; Burchett, *Vietnam*, 86.

14. *Ap Bac*, 4, 8; Major Pham Van Gong, People's Liberation Armed Forces, interview by author, 17 July 2000, Ap Bac, Vietnam.

15. Major Pham Van Gong, People's Liberation Armed Forces, interview by author, 17 July 2000, Ap Bac, Vietnam; *Ap Bac*, 8; David Halberstam, *The Making of a Quagmire* (New York: Random House, 1965), 148; AAR, 4. *Ap Bac* specifies that the 13th Support Unit brought "1 MG and 1 – 60mm Mortar"; Halberstam states that there were least 12 BARs and three machine guns; the AAR identifies at least four .30 caliber machine guns. With BARs as a platoon asset and light machine guns (.30 caliber) as a company asset, 12 and four are not unreasonable estimates. Department of the Army, *The Communist Insurgent Infrastructure in South Vietnam: A Study of Organization and Strategy* by Michael Conley, Pamphlet 550-106 (Washington, D.C.: U.S. Government Printing Office, 1967), 146.

16. *Ap Bac*, 10; Thomas J. Lewis, "Year of the Hare: Bureaucratic Distortion in the U.S. Military View of the Vietnam War in 1963" (M.A. diss., George Washington University, 1972), 27.

17. Palmer, *Summons of the Trumpet*, 41.

18. Halberstam, *The Making of a Quagmire*, 146.

19. Sheehan, *A Bright Shining Lie*, 203.

20. To reduce the chance of a security leak, Dam directed that the planning cell consist of only eight members: the division commander, the deputy chief of staff, the intelligence officer, the division artillery commander, the American senior division advisor (Lieutenant Colonel John P. Vann), the intelligence advisor (Captain James Drummond), the operations advisor (Captain Richard Ziegler), and the supporting

helicopter company liaison officer. Interestingly, the division operations officer and the American air liaison officer (ALO) were not included. AAR, 4, 15; Annex B. (All referenced annexes and their appendices are attachments to Vann's main after action report and come from folder 11, box 38, VSVWC.)

21. Some commentators, particularly William Kennedy, take issue with the development of the operation around sketchy intelligence reports. In one sense, experiences from 1962 tend to support this view; in one "Lessons Learned," the message was clear: "In this sub-limited war, only when intelligence is accurate, detailed and timely can operations of any description be successful." Taken in context, however, the warning of the "Lessons Learned" was more concerned with the possibility of conducting an operation and not finding the enemy than the enemy mustering enough strength to inflict heavy ARVN casualties. While the lack of a clear picture of the PLAF's dispositions and strength had rather serious implications, one cannot blame the staff for not fully developing the intelligence picture, nor can one blame the American advisors for recommending the operation. As had happened so many times through 1962, the longer the ARVN waited, the greater the probability that the PLAF units would disappear before the South Vietnamese troops could engage them. The guerrillas' previous tendency to break contact, the 7th Division's overwhelming superiority in combat power, and Vann's inability to generate any meaningful operations through the fall and winter of 1962 most certainly must have weighed more heavily in the division advisor's mind than the possibility of the PLAF digging in. William V. Kennedy, *The Military and the Media: Why the Press Cannot Be Trusted to Cover a War* (Westport, CT: Praeger, 1993), 96; Memo, H. K. Eggleston, CHUSASEC, to Distribution "B," subject: Lessons Learned Number 5, 11 April 1962 (U.S. Army Military History Institute Digital Library [hereafter USAMHIDL]).

22. Annex B; AAR, 15–16.

23. AAR, 16, 5; Annex C, appendix 1. Although designated to act as a reserve element, Support Company, 12th Infantry Regiment (SPT CO/12 IN), did not see action during Ap Bac. AAR, 1.

24. AAR, 1, 18; Annex E, appendices 1 and 2; Annex C, appendix 1.

25. Ba's unit remained a company-sized element despite its optimistic "mechanized rifle squadron" designation. Department of the Army, *Mounted Combat in Vietnam*, 24; *Ap Bac*, 1.

26. Department of the Army, *Mounted Combat in Vietnam*, 22, 24; Lieutenant Colonel James B. Scanlon, U.S. Army (Retired), interview by Neil Sheehan, 2 March 1977, 1–2.

27. 1st Company, 1st Battalion, 11th Infantry Regiment (1/1/11 IN) and SPT CO/12 IN were also organic units, but they were to participate only if the division commander had to commit his reserve. AAR, 15.

28. Department of the Air Force, *The Advisory Years to 1965* by Robert Futrell, U.S Air Force in Southeast Asia (Washington, D.C.: Office of Air Force History, 1981), 157. The exact type of the five UH-1s is unclear, although at least one was most likely a B model. Futrell cites four UH-1As and one UH-1B; the AAR lists five UH-1Bs in support. Ziegler's memorandum for record, written the morning after the battle, states that "[f]our of the five HU1B were hit." In the very next sentence, Ziegler wrote that "one HU1A was shot down," an indicator that even the G3 advisor was not keeping exact count of which type of aircraft they were. In the ALO's annex, Prevost credited the Hueys with firing "8400 rounds of .30 Cal and 7.62 MM Machine Gun Ammunition." Since the A models carried .30 caliber machine guns and the B models 7.62mm, it is likely that there was at least one UH-1B at Ap Bac. AAR, 2; Memo for record, Richard G. Ziegler, subject:

Record of Events of *DUC THANG* 1, 7th Infantry Division Operation From 020630 Jan to Present Situation, 3 January 1963 (folder 3, box 83, VSVWC); Annex B.

29. AAR, 2.

30. Department of the Air Force, *Advisory Years to 1965*, 157–158; AAR, 16.

31. In some cases, the ARVN units had more advisors present than the advisory TOE provided. For example, 2/11 IN had three captains and one lieutenant present during the battle instead of the authorized captain, lieutenant, and NCO. AAR, 3–4.

32. Annex E, appendix 2.

33. Annex E, appendix 1. The difficulties in moving to the attack positions did not merit commentary by the advisor for TF B, Major William J. Hart, Jr. It is possible that perhaps Bloch misunderstood the order of movement or that such difficulties occurred with such frequency that Hart did not feel it necessary to describe them.

34. AAR, 2. The LCM and the LCVPs were landing craft that had proven themselves in the amphibious operations of World War II; the STCAN/FOMs (the acronym for *Services Technique des Constructions et Armes Navales/France Outre Mer*) were, in the words of a former American naval advisor, "gutless, river patrol boat[s . . . that] were nearly totally useless, slow, weakly armed, with one .50 cal[iber machine gun], and had too deep draft for effective riverine operations." Dr. James R. Reckner, Lubbock, TX, letters to author, West Point, NY, 26 and 28 August 1999.

35. Interestingly enough, the designated location along the canal was only about 1,000 meters northeast of the 11th Infantry Regiment's CP. Annex E, appendix 11.

36. *Ap Bac*, 10–11 Inexplicably, almost none of the times cited in the captured PLAF AAR match those of the American reports. In this case, the guerrillas reported that the rangers landed between 0300 and 0400; the 352nd Ranger Company's advisor, Captain James E. Torrence, logged their departure from My Tho at 0530. Annex E, appendix 9.

37. AAR, 5. American experiences with airmobile operations over the previous months led to the practice of using a fixed wing aircraft like the L-19 to act as an airborne CP until the commander on the ground had assumed control of the operation. Memo, H. K. Eggleston, CHUSASEC, to Special Distribution, subject: Lessons Learned Number 22, 8 September 1962 (USAMHIDL). With Dam remaining at Tan Hiep, Vann was the senior ranking officer (either American or South Vietnamese) to observe the battle.

38. Sheehan's account exhaustingly retells Vann's life. Sheehan, *A Bright Shining Lie*, 430–431.

39. Ibid., 468.

40. Halberstam, *The Making of a Quagmire*, 164.

41. Terence Maitland et al., *Raising the Stakes*, the Vietnam Experience (Boston: Boston Publishing Company, 1982), 62.

42. Dr. Don Walker, Texas Tech University, interview by author, 11 September 1997, Lubbock, TX.

43. Palmer, *Summons of the Trumpet*, 39.

44. Sheehan, *A Bright Shining Lie*, 107-108.

45. Halberstam, *The Making of a Quagmire*, 167; Vann also echoed these sentiments in his later briefings. Vann, briefing notes, n.d., 3; Lieutenant Colonel John Vann, cancelled JCS brief, 8 July 1963, 4 (folder 3, box 39, VSVWC). To suggest that Vann was alone in these beliefs, however, would be misleading. Most of his contemporaries shared these views, and the USASEC had described these same thoughts the previous summer in a "Lessons Learned." Memo, H. K. Eggleston, CHUSASEC, to Special Distribution, subject: Lessons Learned Number 20, 27 August 1962 (USAMHIDL).

46. General William B. Rosson, U.S. Army (Retired), interview by author, 15 April 1997, Lubbock, TX.

47. Annex E, appendices 1 and 2.

48. Annex E, appendix 3.

49. AAR, 5–6; Annex E, appendices 5 and 6.

50. AAR, 5; Annex C, appendix 2; Annex E, appendix 9.

51. AAR, 6; Annex E, appendix 2; *Ap Bac*, 13.

52. *Ap Bac*, 13.

53. Ibid.; Annex E, appendix 2.

54. *Ap Bac*, 11; Annex E, appendix 1.

55. AAR, 6; Annex E, appendices 5 and 6.

56. AAR, 6; Annex E, appendix 5.

57. *Ap Bac*, sketch 1.

58. AAR, 6; Annex C, appendix 1.

59. AAR, 6–7.

60. Ibid., 7; Annex C, appendix 1; Annex E, appendix 1.

61. Annex E, appendix 8; Vann, cancelled JCS brief, 7; AAR, 7.

62. "The Helicopter War Runs into Trouble," *Time* LXXXI (11 January 1963): 29.

63. Message, COMUSMACV to CINCPAC, 021447ZJAN63 (Frame 169, reel 4, *The John F. Kennedy National Security Files, 1961–1963* [hereafter *JFK*]); AAR, 7; Annex E, appendix 8.

64. AAR, 7. Interestingly, the Vietnam Studies monograph concerning airmobility downplays this loss of one of the newest helicopter models in the Army's inventory: "[F]rom 16 October 1962 through 15 March 1963 . . . [w]hile no armed helicopter was shot down, one UH-1B was seriously damaged as a result of ground fire." If one narrowly defines "shot down" as having resulted from air to air combat, then this statement is technically correct. The MACV was more direct in its spot report to CINCPAC: "1 UH-1B destroyed on impact after having tail rotor shot away." Department of the Army, *Airmobility, 1961–1971* by John Tolson, Vietnam Studies (Washington, D.C.: U.S. Government Printing Office, 1973), 31; Message, COMUSMACV to CINCPAC, 021447ZJAN63.

65. Annex E, appendix 8; *Ap Bac*, 14; Sheehan, *A Bright Shining Lie*, 222.

66. AAR, 7–8; Annex E, appendix 3; Lieutenant Colonel James B. Scanlon, U.S. Army (Retired), interview by Neil Sheehan, 2 March 1977, 25.

67. Annex E, appendices 3 and 4; Lieutenant Colonel James B. Scanlon, U.S. Army (Retired), interview by Neil Sheehan, 2 March 1977, 6. Scanlon, in his appendix, spelled the aggressive platoon leader's name "Chou." Mays' appendix and Sheehan's transcription of his interview with Scanlon dropped the "u."

68. AAR, 8; Annex E, appendix 3. On the day of the battle, 4/2 ACR fielded 13 M113s. The M114 present that day belonged to the regimental operations officer, Captain Trong. Mays' primary duty during the operation was to evaluate the effectiveness of the M114, although he also accompanied 4/2 ACR because, according to Scanlon, none of the American advisors liked "staying in." Lieutenant Colonel James B. Scanlon, U.S. Army (Retired), interview by Neil Sheehan, 2 March 1977, 25.

69. Scanlon's appendix places the northern-most position of 4/2 ACR 300 meters south of where Vann reported them in his AAR. Both Mays and Scanlon described an east-west canal as the reason the company did not continue north. Such a canal existed almost one kilometer north of where Scanlon reported his location, and it is possible that the carriers continued north at a much faster rate than Scanlon believed, which would also explain why Ba's company ran into elements of 2/11 IN. AAR, 8; Annex E, appendix 3; Lieutenant Colonel James B. Scanlon, U.S. Army (Retired), interview by Neil Sheehan, 2 March 1977, 1, 6.

70. Lieutenant Colonel James B. Scanlon, U.S. Army (Retired), interview by Neil Sheehan, 2 March 1977, 2–3.

71. Ibid., 1, 3; Annex E, appendix 3; AAR, 8.

72. AAR, 8; Lieutenant Colonel James B. Scanlon, U.S. Army (Retired), interview by Neil Sheehan, 2 March 1977, 1, 3.

73. Annex E, appendix 2.

74. Annex E, appendices 1 and 2; Sheehan, *A Bright Shining Lie*, 213, 234–235.

75. Scanlon later admitted that Ba's actions still remained a mystery to him 14 years after the battle. He could not confirm whether Ba's claims of not having communications with the division were true, nor could he deny that Ba was in contact with Tho in order to seek guidance. Since Ba's radio did not have an external speaker, Scanlon could only hear the mechanized commander's transmissions and not the traffic he was receiving. Lieutenant Colonel James B. Scanlon, U.S. Army (Retired), interview by Neil Sheehan, 2 March 1977, 3–4, 6; Sheehan, *A Bright Shining Lie*, 233.

76. Lieutenant Colonel James B. Scanlon, U.S. Army (Retired), interview by Neil Sheehan, 2 March 1977, 3. Both Mays and Scanlon took credit for suggesting the move south in their reports. Annex E, appendices 3 and 4.

77. AAR, 8; Annex E, appendix 8; Department of Defense Press Release, 3 January 1963 (frame 185, reel 4, *JFK*); Sheehan, *A Bright Shining Lie*, 216, 221–222.

78. Department of Defense Press Release, 3 January 1963; Sheehan, *A Bright Shining Lie*, 222–223.

79. AAR, 8–9. Despite firing 8400 rounds of .30 caliber and 7.62 mm machine gun ammunition and 100 2.75-inch rockets in and around Ap Bac, the gunships failed throughout the day to inflict significant casualties upon the insurgents. Annex B.

80. Annex E, appendix 3; Lieutenant Colonel James B. Scanlon, U.S. Army (Retired), interview by Neil Sheehan, 2 March 1977, 4.

81. Annex C, Appendix 1; Major Jack Macslarrow, U.S. Army, My Tho, letter to Major Lam Quang Tho, Army of the Republic of Vietnam, My Tho, 3 January 1963 (folder 11, box 38, VSVWC). The theme of not receiving orders appears throughout the battle and its aftermath. Macslarrow reported in his annex that Tho received an order to attack from Dam at approximately 1600 hours. In an addendum to his annex, the advisor reported that Tho later told him that he never received an order from the division to attack. In the AAR, Ziegler reported that Tho "refused at least three orders by the 7th Division Commander to move his units to attack." Just as in Ba's case, there is no way to verify which, if any, orders Tho received from Dam. In fairness to the TF A commander, a Vietnamese working in Tho's CP later told Macslarrow that Tri requested permission to attack, but the deputy for military operations, in Tho's presence, denied the request. Annex C, appendix 1; AAR, 17.

82. *Ap Bac*, 16–17.

83. Annex E, appendix 5.

84. *Ap Bac*, 15–16.

85. Annex E, appendices 5 and 6; *Ap Bac*, 16.

86. Annex E, appendices 3 and 4; Lieutenant Colonel James B. Scanlon, U.S. Army (Retired), interview by Neil Sheehan, 2 March 1977, 7.

87. Lieutenant Colonel James B. Scanlon, U.S. Army (Retired), interview by Neil Sheehan, 2 March 1977, 7; Annex E, appendix 1; Lewis, "Year of the Hare," 30.

88. *Ap Bac*, 17.

89. Annex E, appendices 3 and 4; Lieutenant Colonel James B. Scanlon, U.S. Army (Retired), interview by Neil Sheehan, 2 March 1977, 10.

90. Lieutenant Colonel James B. Scanlon, U.S. Army (Retired), interview by Neil Sheehan, 2 March 1977, 8, 13; Lewis, "Year of the Hare," 30.

91. Annex E, appendices 3 and 4.

92. Ibid.; Lieutenant Colonel James B. Scanlon, U.S. Army (Retired), interview by Neil Sheehan, 2 March 1977, 8–9.

93. Sheehan, *A Bright Shining Lie*, 251; Department of the Army, *Mounted Combat in Vietnam*, 27; Annex E, appendix 3.

94. Lewis, "Year of the Hare," 31.

95. Annex E, appendices 3 and 4; Sheehan, *A Bright Shining Lie*, 247–248.

96. Annex E, appendix 4.

97. AAR, 15; Lieutenant Colonel James B. Scanlon, U.S. Army (Retired), interview by Neil Sheehan, 2 March 1977, 16.

98. Lieutenant Colonel James B. Scanlon, U.S. Army (Retired), interview by Neil Sheehan, 2 March 1977, 16; Annex E, appendix 3.

99. Annex E, appendix 1.

100. Lieutenant Colonel James B. Scanlon, U.S. Army (Retired), interview by Neil Sheehan, 2 March 1977, 14.

101. *Ap Bac*, 19; Annex E, appendices 4 and 8; Lieutenant Colonel James B. Scanlon, U.S. Army (Retired), interview by Neil Sheehan, 2 March 1977, 15–16.

102. AAR, 9. For some reason, no one issued orders for the two CG companies from TF C to move from their western blocking position.

103. Palmer, *Summons of the Trumpet*, 42; Sheehan, *A Bright Shining Lie*, 76.

104. "Vietnamese Colonel Unworried," *Pacific Stars and Stripes* (24 April 1962) (folder 9, box 2, unit 1, Douglas Pike Collection, Vietnam Archive).

105. Sheehan, *A Bright Shining Lie*, 76.

106. Palmer, *Summons of the Trumpet*, 42; Sheehan, *A Bright Shining Lie*, 78, 120–121; Halberstam, *The Making of a Quagmire*, 95. See also p. 41, n. 99.

107. AAR, 9; Stanley Karnow, *Vietnam: A History* (New York: Viking Press, 1983), 261–262; Sheehan, *A Bright Shining Lie*, 258–259.

108. Annex E, appendix 5.

109. Ibid.

110. Annex E, appendices 5 and 6; AAR, 9. Although Chin's actions may appear inexcusable, one must keep in mind the circumstances surrounding this incident. As described earlier, South Vietnamese soldiers could expect medevac only if an American was also wounded. This fact must certainly have bred a fair amount of resentment in the ARVN officers, a sentiment that may have been at the heart of Chin's seemingly negligent action.

111. Annex E, appendix 3; Lieutenant Colonel James B. Scanlon, U.S. Army (Retired), interview by Neil Sheehan, 2 March 1977, 14.

112. Annex B.

113. Prevost reported that the "main VC resistance facing the M-113's had ceased after the B-26 strike." Scanlon wrote that following the airstrike "there seemed to be a slacking [sic] off in VC fire." Bowers, while corroborating Scanlon's observation, also qualified this lessening of fire with the comment that "as soon as the plane passed over the VC opened fire again." Given the persistence in PLAF fire, it seems apparent that Futrell's claim that the B-26's "repeated runs with napalm, bombs, rockets, and guns broke the Viet Cong defensive position near the village" is overstated. Annex B; Annex E, appendices 3 and 8; Department of the Air Force, *Advisory Years to 1965*, 158.

114. Annex E, appendix 3; *Ap Bac*, 19–20.

115. Annex E, appendix 11.

116. AAR, 10; Annex B; Annex E, appendices 3, 5, and 6; *Ap Bac*, 20–21.

117. AAR, 10, 18. The airborne battalion commander, a captain, joined his unit the following day by helicopter.

118. *Ap Bac*, 21.

119. Ibid., 22, 24.

120. Annex E, appendix 3; Lieutenant Colonel James B. Scanlon, U.S. Army (Retired), interview by Neil Sheehan, 2 March 1977, 21.

121. Lieutenant Colonel James B. Scanlon, U.S. Army (Retired), interview by Neil Sheehan, 2 March 1977, 21; Annex E, appendix 3; AAR, 10.

122. AAR, 10; Annex E, appendices 5 and 6. Both Smith and Feliciano suggested that the strafing runs caused casualties, but after querying both the battalion commander and executive officer, Prevost came to the conclusion that the runs failed to cause any friendly losses. Annex B.

123. Annex E, appendix 5.

124. AAR, 10; Annex B.

125. Traveling a distance of approximately 14 kilometers, the guerrillas "arrived safely at their bases at 0700 hours" the next morning. Annex E, appendix 4; *Ap Bac*, 25; Major Pham Van Gong, People's Liberation Armed Forces, interview by author, 17 July 2000, Ap Bac, Vietnam.

126. William P. Brooks, Jr., "Vietnam: A Different Perspective" (unpublished manuscript, 1998), 102 (folder 1, box 1, William P. Brooks, Jr., Papers, U.S. Army Military History Institute).

127. Halberstam, *The Making of a Quagmire*, 155.

128. Annex C, appendix 2; AAR, 18.

129. Annex C, appendix 2; Annex E, appendix 10.

130. Annex B; AAR, 10; Halberstam, *The Making of a Quagmire*, 155.

131. AAR, 11; Annex E, appendix 3.

132. AAR, 11; Annex C, appendix 2; Annex E, appendices 1 and 5.

133. Annex C, appendix 1; Annex E, appendix 1. Neither Macslarrow nor Hart was able to identify the originating headquarters for the orders to return to My Tho. Major Harold Dill, the advisor for the 11th Infantry, did not list the CG task forces as attached units in his appendix, an indication that the regiment did not believe the task forces were attached units. Annex C, appendix 2.

134. AAR, 11–12; Annex B; Annex C, appendix 1.

135. Annex C, appendix 1.

136. "GIs Take 17 Viet Reds Without Firing a Shot," *Washington Post* (5 January 1963). Arnett reported 17 prisoners; Halberstam and Macslarrow, 32. "Motley U.S. Force Blocks Vietcong," *New York Times* (5 January 1963); Annex C, appendix 1.

137. Annex C, appendix 2; Annex E, appendix 5.

138. AAR, 12; Annex E, appendix 3.

139. Annex E, appendix 3; AAR, 12.

Brigadier General Francis Brink, the first CHMAAG. Photo P20205, National Archives Still Picture Branch, College Park, Maryland.

Major General Thomas Trapnell, the second CHMAAG and a firm believer in using the "Korea model" for training the VNA (shown here as a lieutenant general and commander of Third Army). National Infantry Museum, Fort Benning, Georgia.

Major General John O'Daniel, Trapnell's replacement as the CHMAAG. National Infantry Museum, Fort Benning, Georgia.

Lieutenant General Samuel T. Williams, the longest serving CHMAAG (shown here as a major general and the deputy commander of Eighth Army). Photo C9717, National Archives Still Picture Branch, College Park, Maryland.

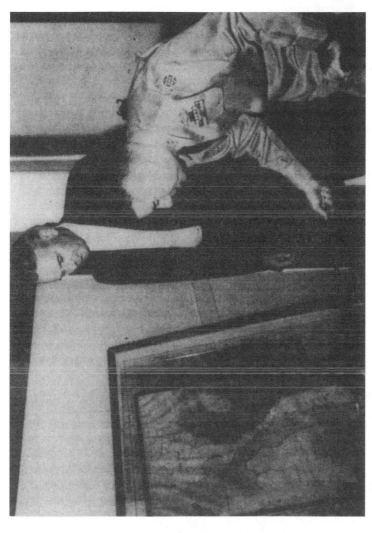

CHMAAG Lieutenant General Lionel McGarr briefing General Maxwell Taylor during the latter's trip to Vietnam, October 1961. Department of the Army, *Images of a Lengthy War* by Joel D. Meyerson, U.S. Army in Vietnam (Washington, D.C.: U.S. Army Center of Military History, 1986), 78.

Tangible results of Taylor's November 1961 report: Helicopters and armored personnel carriers in South Vietnam. Above, H-21s from the 93rd Transportation Company with UH-1s in overwatch return from an aerial operation in the Mekong Delta. Below, M113s move through a rice paddy in 1962. Photos 604550 and 600278, National Archives Still Picture Branch, College Park, Maryland.

Major General Charles Timmes, the last CHMAAG. Photo PCC133250, National Archives Still Picture Branch, College Park, Maryland.

Lieutenant Colonel John P. Vann (left) confers with Major Nguyen Duy Bach, 11th Infantry Regiment commander, while Major Harold Dill (right), Bach's senior advisor, looks on. Photo 600276, National Archives Still Picture Branch, College Park, Maryland.

What Vann saw from above: An overhead view of the reserve's LZ. Note the three downed helicopters and the M113 tracks. Photo 600623, National Archives Still Picture Branch, College Park, Maryland.

Picking up the pieces: Another Huey lifts out the wreckage. Photo 600626, National Archives Still Picture Branch, College Park, Maryland.

Generals Earle Wheeler, U.S. Army chief of staff, and Paul Harkins, COMUSMACV, confer during the former's January 1963 visit to Vietnam. Photo 610231, National Archives Still Picture Branch, College Park, Maryland.

The Ap Bac memorial commemorates the three guerrillas who were "sacrificed" during 4/2 ACR's final organized assault against C1/261. Author's collection, West Point, New York.

4

The Aftermath

The fight was rough at the outset, and the Government forces had
more casualties than usual, but I don't understand how anyone can
call the Ap Bac battle a defeat. The Government forces had an
objective, they took that objective, the VC left and their casualties
were greater than those of the Government forces—what more do
you want?[1]

General Paul D. Harkins
30 January 1963

The fight at Ap Bac was not the most costly battle of the Second Indochina War,
but it was certainly the most significant up to that point in the conflict. The
ARVN had suffered many minor defeats at the hands of the PLAF before; the
loss of the ranger platoon in October 1962 near Ap My Luong demonstrated the
PLAF's growing tactical competence against the ARVN's air assaults. At that
time, the PLAF engaged the rangers and surprised them, but the guerrillas
withdrew shortly thereafter, choosing to break contact. At Ap Bac, whether by
design or accident, for the first time the PLAF successfully stood its ground
against an air assault, artillery and CAS, and APCs. Outnumbered and
outgunned, the insurgents inflicted numerous casualties upon the South
Vietnamese and withdrew under pressure in good order, one of the most difficult
of all military operations.

In terms of human and materiel loss at Ap Bac, the belligerents offered
wildly different appraisals of the fighting. In their initial report, the guerrillas
proudly claimed 370 ARVN KIA or WIA; ten American KIA (among them
Vann) and 9 WIA; three APCs; and eight helicopters at the expense of 18 KIA,
33 WIA, and three captured. A later interview with one of the commanders at
Ap Bac recorded 400 ARVN casualties, 13 PLAF killed and 15 wounded.
Reports by the Americans also varied; Vann claimed three American KIA and
six WIA; 63 ARVN KIA and 109 WIA, and five helicopters to an estimated 100
PLAF KIA, while U.S. Army, Pacific (USARPAC), placed the losses at three
American KIA and six WIA; 25 ARVN KIA and 100 WIA; and five helicopters,
but did not offer any estimates of PLAF losses.[2] One thing that both the PLAF

and the American advisors agreed upon was that Ap Bac was a military defeat for the ARVN, a belief echoed by the press but contested by Harkins and Felt. How each group reacted to Ap Bac illustrated, to a certain extent, the level of its understanding of the situation in Vietnam.

THE INITIAL REACTIONS

The PLAF believed itself the victor of Ap Bac both politically and militarily. On the political front, the PLAF noted the reactions among the civilians in the area, particularly the family members of those ARVN, CG, and SDC soldiers engaged at Ap Bac. Possibly influenced by PLAF cadres, by noon on the day of the battle, some 200 civilians demonstrated in the Cai Lay District capital. Wanting to see their spouses, the demonstrators ignored the district chief's orders to disperse and did not leave the capital until nightfall. This manifestation of civil discontent was not limited to Cai Lay District; at the same time, 300 family members demonstrated in front of the My Tho city hospital "against the death [sic] of their husbands." Both the police and the CG intervened to disperse the crowd forcibly, "thus causing much anger and hatred among the victims."[3]

The following day, 3 January, did not bring a reduction in emotions among the ARVN, CG, and SDC families. In Go Cong, spouses "poured" into the hospital to look for their relatives and bypassed the police barricade surrounding the morgue. Once again, the police sought to quell the disturbance, and the district chief, concerned for his safety, drove to Saigon, "because he did not dare to stay home."[4] The loss of a husband or brother at Ap Bac was devastating enough for many families; the repressive measures taken by the local government in dispelling the crowds only served to heighten their outrage. In keeping with the political-military framework of *dau tranh*, the insurgents successfully tied their military operations in the field to their political activities designed to undermine the Diem regime.

The NLF, the PLAF's front organization, also capitalized upon the propaganda opportunity the battle presented. The *Liberation Press*, the front's news agency, devoted an entire issue to the events at Ap Bac. Proclaiming a great victory, the magazine praised the fighting qualities of the guerrillas, attributing their success to their "heroism, calmness, self confidence and strong unity." Despite superior weapons and numbers, the ARVN demonstrated its inability to defeat the insurgents in the field. In the *Press*'s estimate, the PLAF was destined for success because "violence cannot triumph over the just cause." Playing up the idea that Diem was only an American puppet, the article went on to predict what lay in store for the Vietnamese: "[T]he US imperialists also aim at justifying an eventual intensification of their armed intervention in South Vietnam, exerting higher pressure on Ngo [D]inh Diem so as to grasp the full command of the South Vietnam army."[5] Ap Bac not only provided the NLF with the opportunity to denigrate the GVN and Diem, but also to portray the Americans as the equivalent of the French, an analogy that would strike home with any Vietnamese, communist or nationalist.

Not only did the PLAF believe it had won political gains at the local level, but it also saw success at the international level. Citing radio news reports, it noted "confusion among the imperialists." Radio stations from the U.S., France, Britain, and Australia broadcast reports of the battle and credited the guerrillas with a victory. Even Beijing and Moscow admitted that the insurgents were making progress against the GVN. The PLAF viewed these political gains in hopeful terms. Ap Bac had the "effect of encouraging our people in their struggle and of urging them to obtain more and more successes until Final Victory. . . . The AP BAC victory was considered . . . as a great one which would encourage all Vietnamese people."[6]

The insurgents recognized Ap Bac's more tangible military results. The recently developed counter mopping-up tactics were successful against the ARVN's overwhelming superiority of personnel and equipment. Calling the battle a "victorious counter mopping-up operation . . . [and] a great victory of our Armed Forces," the insurgents believed that "although the enemy employed a large strength of Air, Navy, Artillery, Armor and Infantry forces . . . the enemy was bitterly defeated and suffered substantial losses," a claim based rightfully upon the ARVN's casualties. The guerrillas were also successful in organizing an integrated command of three separate types of forces, a sign that the PLAF leadership had developed command and control procedures to incorporate effectively the main force, regional, and local forces.[7]

The PLAF was not the only group to consider Ap Bac an ARVN defeat. The American advisors, most noticeably Vann and Colonel Porter, the senior advisor for IV Corps, believed the battle a failure for the ARVN. When asked by David Halberstam, then reporting for the *New York Times*, what had happened the day before, Vann became visibly upset and "spilled his gut." Red in the face, Vann kicked the dirt and blurted out, "A miserable damn performance, just like always." The 7th Division's senior advisor was not alone in his immediate reaction. Captain Ziegler, the division's G3 advisor, penned this brief assessment in his operations journal: "It's [*DUC THANG* 1] a real disgrace."[8]

Putting it just as bluntly in his after action report, Vann wrote his superiors: "Because of the psychological and propaganda advantage gained from the publicity given (and exaggerated) by the US Press in discussing US helicopter and personnel losses, the known friendly casualties of 172, plus the failure of friendly forces to ever make [an] effective coordinated attack against the VC, this operation must be considered a *failure*."[9] Porter agreed with Vann's assessment. Before forwarding Vann's report to his superiors, the IV Corps advisor attached his endorsement, calling it "possibly the best documented, most comprehensive, most valuable, and most revealing of any of the reports submitted by III or IV Corps during the past 12 months."[10] Despite suggestions to the contrary, Vann was not alone in his harsh assessment of *DUC THANG* 1. American advisors both superior and subordinate to him firmly believed that Ap Bac was not an ARVN victory.

The American reporters in Vietnam, whether believing that the PLAF had won a stunning victory or seizing on the advisors' frustrations, portrayed the battle in rather foreboding terms. Halberstam's first article concerning the battle on 3 January 1963 called it "a major defeat," prompting the JCS to request of CINCPAC an "immediate report as to the veracity and full particulars if story authentic." Portraying the battle in imagery-laden terms, his article the following day described Tho's mistaken shelling of Ap Bac and General York as a "nightmarish end to a nightmarish two days."[11]

To Halberstam, the battle was not simply a defeat for the ARVN but also a warning signal to the U.S. His article of 4 January addressed a topic that reverberated throughout the American press: the ARVN's willingness (or unwillingness) to prosecute the war. He asserted that "[t]he Vietnamese regulars . . . lost the initiative from the first moment and never showed much aggressive instinct and consequently suffered heavier casualties." Halberstam was not alone in his analysis; Neil Sheehan, writing for United Press International, submitted an article the same day that claimed "Americans criticized what they termed the 'lack of aggressiveness' of the Vietnamese commanders."[12]

What the reporters in Vietnam were writing about Ap Bac and the ARVN did not go unnoticed by General Harkins. He had been present at Tan Hiep on the morning of 3 January and had formed his own opinion of the situation. During his visit to the 7th Division's CP, he received a briefing from Vann concerning the previous day's action. When approached by Halberstam and Peter Arnett concerning his impression of the battle, Harkins responded: "We've got them in a trap and we're going to spring it in half an hour." A short time later, he left for Saigon, seemingly unconcerned about the events of the previous day.[13] Two days after the battle, he summarized the reporters' articles by writing in a confidential cable that "[a]s usual with press releases, some of the facts are correct—some are not." After discussing the conduct of the battle, Harkins addressed the heart of the articles' criticisms: The efficacy of the ARVN and the advisory system. Regarding Vann's "miserable damn performance" remark, COMUSMACV admitted that it "can be taken either way. In some cases they [the ARVN] could have done better, and I think they should have."[14]

Harkins then went on to concede a more telling point: "Our advisors were with the Vietnamese during the operation and in some cases their advice was heeded and in some cases it was not—*but it was par for the course*" (emphasis added), an intimation that even COMUSMACV was at least dimly aware of the advisory system's shortcomings. Yet to him, Ap Bac was just another battle against the PLAF, and, despite the analysis of the advisors present and the press, it was one that was relatively successful. In summing up, he wrote that "[l]ike any engagements in war, there are days—and there are days. This day they [the ARVN] got a bear by the tail and they didn't let go of it. *At least they got most of it*. Though some of the tail slipped away" (emphasis added).[15] While admitting that some of the guerrillas withdrew, he understated the true nature of Ap Bac's result, a trend that Harkins would continue to follow throughout the following weeks.

The American reporters in Vietnam continued the "lack of aggressiveness" theme during the following week. Halberstam reported that American advisors questioned their role in Vietnam because they felt "that what happened at Ap Bac goes far deeper than one battle and is directly tied to the question—whether the Vietnamese are really interested in having American advisors and listening to them."[16] Sheehan was even more direct in his indictment of the ARVN by attributing the death of Captain Good, the senior advisor for 2/11 IN, to the timidity of the South Vietnamese soldiers: "Vietnamese infantrymen refused direct orders to advance during Wednesday's battle at Ap Bac and . . . an American Army captain was killed while out front pleading with them to attack. . . . One U.S. advisor said bitterly, 'These people (the Vietnamese) won't listen—they make the same mistakes over and over again in the same way.'"[17] For the reporters in Vietnam, the burden of this specific defeat lay on the ARVN and not the American advisors present at Ap Bac. Indirectly, however, these reports questioned the validity of American policies in Vietnam since the ARVN had been under the tutelage of the U.S. Army since 1955.

Editorials in the U.S. echoed the field reporters' views and more directly called for an assessment of South Vietnamese military capabilities. One of the earliest analyses appeared on 5 January. Concerned mainly with the tactical conduct of Ap Bac, the editorial excused the advisors for the outcome of the battle, claiming that it was "through no fault of the participating Americans." After describing the operation's faults, the article turned to what it believed the most serious deficiency: "And most important of all, the South Vietnamese troops displayed some of the same basic faults they had demonstrated in other operations; they showed . . . little desire to attack." In closing, the article called for a reassessment of American willingness to rely on technological advances to tip the scales in Vietnam. Indirectly criticizing the ARVN, it concluded that "machines—no matter how good—can help and supplement, but cannot replace . . . the man on the ground."[18]

The *New York Times* again addressed ARVN effectiveness on 15 January. Reminding readers that "losses in one battle, or even a dozen battles, do not portend loss of the war in South Vietnam," the editorial attacked not the American government but the South Vietnamese government. The trouble in Vietnam was not poor American policy but a "suspicious, dictatorial [South Vietnamese] government." Preoccupied with "preserving itself in power," the GVN "seriously hamper[ed] the spirit and effectiveness of the South Vietnamese military forces." Instead of calling upon the Kennedy administration to reevaluate its policies in Vietnam, the editorial put the onus on the GVN, calling for the "need for stronger efforts in this direction [of democratic reforms]."[19]

The printed word was not the only medium to criticize the Vietnamese. Known for his biting commentary through Willie and Joe of World War II fame, Bill Mauldin offered his own perspective. The cartoon that appeared on 14 January portrayed an ARVN soldier eye-deep in a foxhole with an American advisor kneeling next to it, arms upraised in a beseeching pose. The caption neatly expressed the feelings of Vann and his compatriots: "When I say attack, don't just lean forward."[20] When viewed in a larger perspective, however, the cartoon spoke more about the GVN's leadership than the individual soldier, since the label on the Vietnamese soldier's helmet was "Vietnam," not "ARVN." Regardless of the interpretation, the cartoon spoke volumes about the emerging American opinion of Diem's government and its prosecution of the war.

Other editorials, while criticizing the ARVN's conduct at Ap Bac, also called for American introspection. On 8 January, a *Times* editorial challenged the Kennedy administration's policies in Vietnam. Pointing out that former senator Kennedy had opposed assisting the French in 1954 because such an action was "doomed to failure," the article argued that the Vietnamese timidity at Ap Bac "confronts President Kennedy with the 1954 thesis of Senator Kennedy." Despite the critical tone of his article, the author conceded the difficulties facing the administration: "It will be very difficult for the President to find an alternative to the U.S. policy that has proved ineffectual and trends to deeper and deeper military involvement in Southeast Asia."[21]

Foreign observers also questioned the roles of the U.S. and Republic of Vietnam, and some suggested that the Americans were almost committed past the point of making a policy change. Richard Hughes, writing from Hong Kong for the *London Sunday Times*, claimed that the result of a meeting between Harkins and Felt shortly after Ap Bac was a recommendation to increase American involvement. He opened his article with the pronouncement that "American officers must now begin to assert combat command over South Vietnamese troops in the field." Although this represented a major change in policy, he did not expect a public announcement of it because of "the Washington fiction that no American troops are involved in combat and that U.S. officers and 'trainers' are on the scene merely to 'advise, observe, support and assist.'" Citing the ARVN's "recent series of reverses," Hughes suggested that this proposed increase in American involvement was inevitable. Conjuring up an image that was sure to strike a nerve among Americans, he claimed that "[t]he current crisis in South Viet-Nam indeed is alarmingly reminiscent of the lost cause which confronted Gen. George Marshall in China at the end of World War II." As far as he was concerned, "[t]he deepening combat commitment has long since passed the point at which active and more effective U.S. direction could or should be shelved." To Hughes, Ap Bac illustrated the only two options open to the U.S.: Complete withdrawal and neutralization of Vietnam, just as the Americans had done the year before in Laos, or "at least a 10-year local war to uphold a reactionary, isolated and unpopular regime." Given Hughes' tone, the choice was clear.[22]

The *Wall Street Journal* chose to challenge not the decision to fight in Vietnam, but a basic component of American culture: the "can-do spirit." Agreeing that the setbacks in Southeast Asia did not argue "against the strategic reasons for trying to keep the Communists from conquering South Vietnam," the editorial astutely proposed that the U.S needed to reassess its ability to develop the GVN and to recognize the limits of American influence: "And perhaps we should all realize that there are certain things the U.S., for all its military power, cannot do. One is to reshape the nature of peoples of radically different traditions and values," a warning that is as relevant today as it was to the Kennedy administration almost forty years ago.[23]

While the press questioned American policies and South Vietnamese efficacy, Harkins and Admiral Felt, CINCPAC, offered their own assessments of the ARVN soldier and the war in Vietnam. By 10 January, Harkins had had his fill of the media's portrayal of the ARVN and released an official statement to the press. In it, he expressed concern "over recent allegations critical of the valor and courage of the Vietnamese soldier." Harkins cited the deaths of "approximately ten thousand Vietnamese" throughout 1962 as proof of their willingness to prosecute the war. Coming to the ARVN's defense, COMUSMACV accused those who were critical of "the fighting qualities of the Armed Forces of the Republic of Vietnam" of doing a "disservice to the thousands of gallant and courageous men who are fighting so well in defense of their country." Regarding the American advisors, Harkins was laudatory as well, proclaiming "them among the best ever assembled." Excerpts from this statement soon found their way into the *New York Herald Tribune* and the *New York Times.*[24]

However, Harkins's statement missed the thrust of the press's criticisms. While critical of the Vietnamese soldiers' unwillingness to attack, the American reporters in Vietnam believed that the deeper problem lay with the ARVN leadership. Harkins tacitly acknowledged a leadership problem within TF A by writing in his confidential cable on 4 January that the CG unit "had lost . . . [its] commander due to wounds and no one seemed to want to take over," but he did not address this significant shortcoming in his press release. He chose instead to focus on the more emotional topic of ARVN unwillingness to engage in hand-to-hand combat with the PLAF, perhaps a more easily defended issue.[25]

Halberstam's next article, appearing on 11 January, seized on Harkins's omission. The reporter readily asserted that "the Vietnamese soldier is just as good as the people want him to be." Instead, the issue in Vietnam was that the American advisors considered the ARVN soldier "to be poorly led and feel that the greatest gap at present is in field leaders and NCOs." The advisors and the press did not doubt the fighting abilities of the soldiers but rather the officers, since Americans in Vietnam "feel real affection and respect for the Vietnamese private," a sentiment that many advisors clearly held.[26]

Admiral Felt also lent his support to Harkins's confidence in the GVN. Arriving in Vietnam a week after Ap Bac to confer with COMUSMACV, Felt offered his view of the battle to reporters who met him on his arrival. Responding to Sheehan's request that he offer his assessment, the admiral replied that he did not believe what he had read in the papers. Contrary to the news reports, Ap Bac "was a Vietnamese victory—not a defeat as the papers say."[27]

CINCPAC was not only sure of a Vietnamese victory at Ap Bac, but he also believed in total GVN victory, proclaiming that "I am confident the Vietnamese are going to win their war." Despite the "recent casualties suffered by Vietnamese forces at Ap Bac [which were] . . . a bad accident," the war in Vietnam was "taking a generally favorable course." En route to Honolulu, Felt told reporters at a Taipei press conference that the PLAF were "getting licked."[28] Given their public statements, COMUSMACV and CINCPAC certainly did not share the lower-level advisors' and the press' belief that Ap Bac held special significance, but all, whether they admitted it or not, shared a desire to explain Ap Bac's outcome. The larger issues of policy and strategy aside, they needed to look no farther than the tactical level, since what happened on the ground and in the air above the battlefield was a microcosm of the greater problems in the ARVN and American advisory efforts.

TACTICAL ANALYSIS

Ap Bac demonstrated once again that outnumbering an opponent does not necessarily ensure success against a determined enemy. Despite the 7th Division's overwhelming numerical superiority, Colonel Dam was unable to mass his forces in a coordinated attack, allowing the guerrillas to face each unit separately. While lack of aircraft and the ground fog at Tan Hiep prevented 2/11 IN from landing all of its units simultaneously and slowed the 352nd Ranger Company's southern movement, these factors did not contribute significantly to the South Vietnamese defeat. While there was a delay in the second and third serials, 2/11 IN did not make contact until after all its units had landed north of Ap Tan Thoi and thus was not subject to defeat in detail at that point.

What did prevent the 7th Division from bringing its forces together at the decisive place and time was the commander's inability to coordinate his subordinate units' actions. Although converging on Ap Bac along three separate axes (north—2/11 IN, west—4/2 ACR, and south—TFs A and B), Dam's division and its supporting units did not come together in a timely manner. The disjointed actions of the ARVN units, particularly 4/2 ACR in the west and TFs A and B in the south, allowed the PLAF to take advantage of its central position and move its forces to meet each individual threat as it developed. Not pressed in the north initially, commander Hai Hoang shifted units south to frustrate TF A's advance. Later that morning when the southern task forces had gone to ground and the APCs had not yet arrived, the PLAF commander relocated some of his guerrillas farther north, thus frustrating 2/11 IN's efforts to cross the canal and enter Ap Tan Thoi, a process that continued throughout the day. Worse, three separate companies, almost an entire battalion's worth of South Vietnamese soldiers, did not fight at Ap Bac. Even after the ground fog lifted, the 352nd Ranger Company remained in position until ordered to guard the 11th Infantry Regiment's CP despite being only about 1,700 meters away from the action. Although farther away, TF C, the 173rd and 175th CG Companies, also failed to move from its blocking position throughout the day. Regardless of the 7th Division's overwhelming troop strength, the uncoordinated efforts of its subordinate units did not allow the division commander to mass his forces against the smaller PLAF foe.

Although most commentators generally accept this inability to converge on the PLAF as a primary reason for the ARVN defeat, not all believe the blame lies with Colonel Dam. Others have suggested that the American advisors, and not the Vietnamese, bear the responsibility for the outcome of Ap Bac. As the argument goes, the operation, involving many different units that were unaccustomed to working together, was too complex given the Vietnamese level of training. The American officers' expectations were simply too high, and they should not have been surprised by the outcome. One commentator in particular has suggested that even American National Guard and Reserve units would have reacted in the same fashion had they been "committed to action with no more experience in combined arms training and operations than" the ARVN units at Ap Bac. In the final analysis, "it would have been all but impossible for any unit, South Viet Namese, American or whatever to do much better than the ARVN did at Ap Bac given their state of individual and unit training."[29]

While possessing some merit, this argument overlooks two telling points. First, *DUC THANG* 1 was not in any way a complex operation. Although there were three battalion-sized and three company-sized elements in the battle (2/11 IN, TF A, TF B; and 4/2 ACR, 1/1/11 IN, and the 352nd Ranger Company, respectively), closer inspection reveals that the 7th Division had only two subordinate commands, the 11th Infantry Regiment (2/11 IN, 1/1/11 IN, and the 352nd Ranger Company) and the Dinh Tuong Regiment (TF A, TF B, and 4/2 ACR). From Dam's perspective, Ap Bac was no more than two separate commands moving toward one another. The distances separating them were five kilometers, at most, which was not an excessively long distance to traverse. All but 4/2 ACR had only to move in a straight line from their jump-off points to their objectives, requiring little, if any, navigation. Even with such a straightforward operation, it is true that units lacking training might have difficulties executing any plan, particularly when faced with a determined enemy. This lack of training does not, however, answer why certain ARVN officers repeatedly refused orders from their higher commanders, which leads to the second point. The failure to close the ring south and west of Ap Bac seemed more a result of Tho's and Ba's refusals, not an inability or lack of training, to move their units forward, particularly when one takes into account the advantageous movements by Tri and Thi in the south. While some American units may experience difficulties in coordinating and executing complex operations early in their training periods, it is doubtful that any of their officers would refuse orders as Major Tho and Captain Ba did at Ap Bac.

Coordination problems also prevented the 7th Division from effectively using the firepower assets available to it. Despite the number of artillery pieces and aircraft in support, the ARVN never integrated the available fire support into the operation. Throughout the fight, mortar and artillery fires and CAS rained into and around Ap Bac with little effect on the PLAF. A portion of this inefficacy stemmed from the lack of artillery forward observers (FOs) and the training deficiencies of both FOs and forward air controllers (FACs). Both task forces in the south failed to bring their FOs with them, resulting in artillery fires that were not properly directed. The RVNAF FOs and FACs that were present were unable to coordinate or control the assets at their disposal properly, resulting in ineffective artillery and airstrikes.[30]

The South Vietnamese forces also failed to use the flare ship that was available to illuminate the battlefield, thereby allowing the PLAF to withdraw unobserved and unmolested into the darkness. To counter the ARVN's inability to fire observed artillery against the withdrawing insurgents, Vann recommended that the artillery fire approximately 500 rounds of high explosive into the darkness in the hope that at least some casualties would result. Not following the advisor's suggestion, Dam decided to fire only 100 during the hours of darkness, but by the next morning, only some 45 rounds actually had impacted around Ap Bac.[31] Worse yet, in at least two cases, possibly on the evening of 2 January and definitely on the morning of 3 January, uncoordinated fires resulted in fratricide and numerous ARVN casualties. Unable to synchronize its supporting fires, the 7th Division suffered considerably from a lack of coordinated mortar and artillery fires and CAS.

The ARVN at Ap Bac also suffered from not ensuring the surprise of the impending operation. Despite Dam's precautions of allowing only a small cell plan the operation and issuing his order the night before the operation, the PLAF had already divined the ARVN's intentions.[32] With Diem's birthday on 3 January, the guerrillas reportedly predicted a large operation in honor of the South Vietnamese president. The PLAF also observed the massing of ARVN forces over a two-day period beginning on 1 January. The 7th Division had not been subtle in preparing for *DUC THANG* 1 and did little to camouflage its movements, particularly the amount of noise generated by the vehicular and vessel movements prior to the operation's start.[33] Through their inability to disguise their intentions, the South Vietnamese commanders lost an important psychological advantage by allowing the guerrillas to prepare themselves mentally for the fight. With this mental preparation, the PLAF perhaps developed a resolve to stand and fight at Ap Bac that it might not have enjoyed had it been surprised.

DUC THANG 1, both in concept and execution, violated several principles, but most grievous was the failure to ensure that all the South Vietnamese units at Ap Bac fell under Dam's control. The Dinh Tuong Regiment, although composed of GVN assets, was not under the direct command of Colonel Dam because of Major Tho's status as a province chief. A sizeable portion of combat assets committed to Ap Bac, therefore, was not truly under the division commander's direct control. Dam's most mobile and lethal asset, 4/2 ACR, also did not respond quickly to his directives to assist the reserve company near Ap Bac because Ba, knowing that he would have to answer to Tho after the operation, chose to act in his own personal interest instead of the interests of the division. Along the same lines and contrary to Dam's orders, TF B, located on the flank of the PLAF positions and situated perfectly to clear the east-west woodline and relieve TF A, did not attack because Major Tho would not order it. Even within the 7th Division itself, particularly in the reserve company, some leaders did not respond to the division commander's orders. This tendency was not restricted to the fighting on 2 January, as the units participating in the operations on 3 and 4 January also failed to respond to Dam's directives. Instead of establishing blocking positions on the evening of 3 January, Tho's CG companies redeployed to My Tho, leaving Major Macslarrow, Captain Drummond, and the few SDC soldiers they had with them to hold off the guerrillas moving south out of Ap Tay the following day. In summing up Dam's inability to unify his units' actions, the American advisors attributed part of the ARVN defeat to "[a] complete lack of discipline in battle that permits commanders at all levels, and even private soldiers, to refuse to obey any orders they personally find distasteful."[34]

Although the lack of discipline contributed to the GVN's failure at Ap Bac, the root cause was that of poor leadership. One of the most glaring shortcomings during the conduct of the battle was the troubling absence of senior leadership. Vann, as a lieutenant colonel, was the most senior of all officers in and around the battlefield. The highest-ranking ARVN officers present were captains; none of the senior ARVN commanders, including the division commander, the Dinh Tuong Regiment commander, and the 11th Infantry Regiment commander, was within five kilometers of the fighting. Although the 8th ABN commander did join up with his unit, he did so by helicopter the following day instead of jumping in with his soldiers. Acting solely on reports from their subordinates, these South Vietnamese leaders made their decisions in the safety and comfort of their CPs without directly observing the battlefield either on the ground or above it. After the battle, Vann indicted the "system of command that never places a Vietnamese Officer above the rank of Captain either on or over the battlefield." Despite Ba's personal leadership of 4/2 ACR's attack at Ap Bac, Vann was not impressed with the mechanized commander's performance. The American was so incensed over the actions of Tho and Ba that he recommended that "a Board of Inquiry . . . determine their fitness to retain their commands."[35] One wonders how Ba might have acted had Tho been pinned down with TF A.

Another disturbing facet of the ARVN leaders' performance was their apparent lack of aggressiveness in taking the fight to the enemy. Agreeing with the American reporters concerning the South Vietnamese officers, Vann discussed the "reluctance of ARVN Commanders at all levels . . . to close with and destroy the enemy," citing the drop of the 8th ABN to the west as proof of his assertion.[36] Vann was not the only American advisor present at Ap Bac to make this observation. Major Macslarrow, Tho's advisor, also wrote that a "seven-hour period elapsed during which no attack was initiated, despite my continual advice to do so. . . . The American Advisor who accompanied Task Force 'ALPHA', later informed me that an attack by his unit could have readily been accomplished after the Division Reserve . . . had been committed."[37] It seemed that the reporters were not the only Americans in Vietnam who doubted the ARVN officers' abilities to prosecute the war.

More damning was Colonel Porter's evaluation of the ARVN leadership at Ap Bac. Of the 15 ARVN weaknesses he noted in his endorsement of Vann's report, 14 were related to functions of command. Echoing Vann's remarks, Porter condemned the "[f]ailure of the Corps, Division, Regimental and Sector commanders to go to the battlefield to direct, supervise and observe the actions of subordinate commanders and participating units." Porter not only indicted the senior South Vietnamese leadership for its absence from Ap Bac, but also ARVN leaders at all levels for their failure to mass combat power in accordance with doctrine. He cited the "[f]ailure of commanders at all echelons to act decisively, to control and direct their available firepower, and to employ the principles of fire and maneuver to assault or outflank enemy positions." Worse, the ARVN officers did not provide one of the most basic functions of command: Motivation in combat. Porter described the deficiencies as a "[f]ailure . . . to instill in their subordinates . . . a will to win, a fighting spirit and dedication to duty, by bold, daring, courageous, [and] aggressive action."[38]

One of the greatest shortcomings Porter noted concerned the ARVN's inability "to pin-point offenders and to fix responsibilities for ineffective and irresponsible leadership, and failure to take action to eliminate such individuals." Yet what made the senior corps advisor's memorandum so troubling was not so much the long list of ARVN failures but the fact that the deficiencies were recurring problems. These were not one-time faults that the advisors expected to correct before the next large operation; to the contrary, Porter prefaced his comments by noting that the weaknesses occurred "in the bulk of other operations in the old III Corps as well as in the new IV Corps."[39] Porter identified one of the root problems the Americans faced in Vietnam: How to prevent the ARVN from suffering from the same mistakes again and again. In the wake of the tremors at Ap Bac, one would expect the belligerents to examine closely their conduct of the war and make changes accordingly. In some instances, tactics and procedures changed, but neither the Vietnamese nor the Americans altered the larger issues of doctrine or policy.

CHANGES IN TACTICS, DOCTRINE, AND POLICY

For the PLAF, Ap Bac provided an opportunity to proclaim its strength and ability to stand up to the ARVN. Party historians wrote that the battle "marked the maturity of the South Vietnamese Liberation Army in organization, tactics, [and] political work." The guerrillas were not the "raggedy-ass little bastards" that some American advisors believed them to be; to the contrary, the PLAF ably demonstrated its combat abilities against a larger and technologically advanced foe.[40]

The battle also allowed the cadres to assess the effectiveness of their counter mopping-up tactics. Not surprisingly, the guerrillas thought their tactics to be the antidote to the ARVN sweeps, but they also believed that they could not abandon guerrilla warfare, particularly since the GVN continued to possess such superiority in numbers and technologically advanced weapons. Consequently, the PLAF leadership directed after Ap Bac that "the main concept of friendly counter mop up tactic[s] . . . continue[s] to be *'Counter mop-up guerrilla warfare.'*" Ap Bac confirmed in the guerrillas' minds that this tactical method provided them with a sound solution to the ARVN's technological and numerical superiority. A guerrilla commander later acknowledged that the battle "was of great importance to us . . . because it showed we could defeat the helicopter tactics. And it showed that even when we employ a small force we can defend ourselves against vastly superior enemy forces." Capitalizing on its victory at Ap Bac, the PLAF also instituted the "Apbac [*sic*] emulation drive in killing enemy troops and performing feats of arms," an effort to inspire other guerrilla units to inflict defeats upon the GVN.[41]

By emphasizing the guerrilla nature of the coming battles against the GVN, the PLAF also continued to embrace the protracted nature of its struggle. Despite the hope Ap Bac brought the PLAF, the Lao Dong cautioned its southern brethren not to forget the potential long-term struggle ahead: "Although the revolutionary movement in South Vietnam is still developing strongly in the political, economic, and military fields, the path of the South Vietnamese revolution is still a circuitous, tortuous, long, and arduous path."[42] In short, Ap Bac increased the PLAF's confidence in its tactics and confirmed its beliefs in a protracted struggle. Otherwise, the battle brought little else to the guerrillas, particularly in the way of policy changes or direct intervention on the part of the DRV.

Like their opponents, the Americans and South Vietnamese also evaluated, at least to some degree, the tactics used at Ap Bac. One of the most troubling facets of the battle was the PLAF effectiveness against the M113s' crews. The high number of vehicle crew casualties and the unwillingness of the soldiers to expose themselves fully while firing the carriers' machine guns spurred numerous comments in after action reports. Vann recommended that a "metal shield must be placed on the M-113 and M-114 around the Cal 50 machine gun to give protection to the gunner, otherwise the weapons will not be used in critical situations."[43]

Shortly thereafter, 2nd ACR, 4/2 ACR's higher headquarters, fabricated gun shields for the carriers' cupolas using soft steel plating. The crewmen soon found out that the shields, made from a sunken ship's hull, could be penetrated rather easily. Faced with this unfortunate discovery, the 80th Ordnance Depot fashioned 46 new shields from salvaged vehicles. Throughout the remainder of 1963, ordnance technicians fitted shields for the rest of the carriers in Vietnam. By early 1964, soldiers received M113s with gun shields already mounted, a legacy of the PLAF's victory at Ap Bac.[44]

Another area of concern for the Americans involved the difficulties that the M113s and their crews experienced while attempting to cross the many irrigation canals. Although Ba's intransigence explained a fair portion of 4/2 ACR's slow movement to the reserve's LZ, fording the many canals on the way to the helicopters certainly slowed the APCs' movement and nullified their potential shock effect against the guerrillas. Two weeks after Ap Bac, whether by accident or design, the USASEC issued "Lessons Learned Number 26—M113 Operations," a twenty-five-page document outlining employment considerations for the carriers that directly addressed the mobility issue. While the memorandum briefly discussed tactical considerations for the APCs, the majority of its text involved terrain concerns and fording techniques. Replete with diagrams of towing techniques, crossing methods, and the use of demolitions to assist in the reduction of the irrigation dikes, the document was clearly focused upon addressing the perceived mobility problems of the M113s in the Mekong Delta region. Admitting that "much remains to be learned as mechanized units come into wider use" and seeking to hone its employment of American technology, the USASEC asked that the memorandum's readers "inform this headquarters . . . of other problem areas and suggested solutions."[45]

For all its technological advances, the U.S. Army continued to struggle with adapting its weapon systems for the guerrilla war in South Vietnam.

The growing tensions between MACV and the press increased as a result of the battle. Although bad feelings between the two had gained momentum throughout the latter portion of 1962, Ap Bac brought matters to a head. The lower echelon advisors' comments about the ARVN's performance, Harkins's belief that the battle was an ARVN victory, and Felt's parting shot at a reporter to "[g]et on the team" all served to aggravate an already strained relationship.[46] Despite MACV's establishment of military information officers at the four corps tactical zone headquarters "to serve as the eyes and ears" of its Office of Information, improved communications to supplement the usually terse operational summaries with additional information, and weekly press conferences, the damage had been done. Where before Ap Bac reporters were "relatively agreeable," after the fight they became convinced that MACV was lying to them, a feeling that became more emotional with time.[47]

The press was not the only party to harbor bad feelings about Ap Bac. Despite later accounts that portrayed Vann as quite friendly with the press, the 7th Division's senior advisor seemed to resent the reporters' portrayal of what occurred at Ap Bac. As he wrote his superiors, the reporters were a "perplexing problem." Not only did they arrive in fatigues, but they "got invited into the CP area thru their previous acquaintanceships with US personnel who were too polite to order them out." Most damaging was their skewed reports of the fighting. Relying on accounts from aircrews who had "limited knowledge" of the engagements, the reporters "exaggerated the friendly failures, [and] maximized the enemy's favorable actions." Disgusted, he recommended that "control and/or censorship be imposed for all correspondents."[48] Quite astutely, John Mecklin, the embassy's chief of public affairs, observed that "[a] man from Mars . . . could have been excused if he got the impression that the newsmen, as well as the VC, were the enemy."[49]

How the U.S. Army and the ARVN planned to use the helicopter in battle came under examination, which resulted in some procedural changes. Prior to and during Ap Bac, the rules of engagement (ROE) for American gunships was quite restrictive, requiring them to possess American crews and a GVN crewmember or observer, and only to deliver fire "considered defensive in nature." This latter restriction, as interpreted by CINCPAC and COMUSMACV, meant that an "aircraft must be fired upon before [it] may engage a target, even when an enemy target is clearly identified." To make better use of the gunships' capabilities, a JCS evaluation team recommended upon its return from Vietnam in late January that CINCPAC reevaluate its interpretation of the ROE. The JCS was concerned that CINCPAC's interpretation of the ROE was "more restrictive" than it intended, particularly in the wake of the aircraft losses at Ap Bac. Consequently, it overrode Felt's interpretation by authorizing him "to permit all helicopters to fire on clearly identified Viet Cong elements which are considered to be a threat to the safety of the helicopters and their passengers," a move that caught the State Department completely by surprise.[50] This new ROE now allowed the crews to engage the guerrillas before taking fire, a signal that the Americans were more willing to take the lead in combat operations.

Another area that the Americans scrutinized concerned the procedures for downed aircrews. Over the previous year, the helicopter companies had informally adopted a "buddy" system that ensured timely extraction of downed aircrews by employing the rotary wing aircraft in pairs. Stating that a "pair of aircraft [can] protect one another and pick up survivors," a "Lessons Learned" memorandum suggested in the fall of 1962 that the "system has paid off in SVN and both passengers and crew are confident that immediate rescue operations will be initiated if an aircraft is downed."[51] Since three of the five helicopters lost at Ap Bac were the direct result of attempting to retrieve already downed helicopter crews, Vann was unsure of the system's merits and recommended that the 45th Transportation Battalion (the 93rd Transportation Company's higher headquarters) review its procedures. Porter, while recognizing these rescue attempts as "courageous," also recommended that the transportation battalion evaluate the effectiveness of its evacuation techniques.[52] Even General Harkins initially believed that "[i]t took a lot of guts" for the pilots to attempt an evacuation, but MACV needed to "review whether we are on the right track in going in after downed helicopters particularly when it is in the middle of a battle area." Despite pressure by the press and the White House, MACV's stated policy on evacuation procedures remained unaltered. When asked in late January whether any procedural changes were in the making, Harkins denied any such activity, claiming that "nothing indicates the need for such a change of tactics."[53]

Privately, the Army Concept Team in Vietnam (ACTIV), an organization headed by Brigadier General Edward L. Rowny and charged with testing counterinsurgency concepts, modified the standing operating procedures (SOP) governing aircrew recovery. Instead of immediately dispatching other helicopters to the site of downed aircraft, the SOP now dictated that the helicopter support company commander possessed the authority to determine the method of recovery. This new procedure allowed the commander a broader view of the situation and precluded the automatic dispatch of helicopters to an area that might not yet be secure.[54] Despite the realization that endangering aircraft for individuals was an expensive method of retrieving service members and ACTIV's changes to the recovery SOP, Americans became firmly entrenched in a "culture of rescue." As the Second Indochina War progressed, an ever-increasing number of crewmen risked their lives and aircraft to extract downed American airmen or wounded soldiers and marines, a tradition that continues to the present day. Whether as a result of increased sensitivity to casualties or simply because the helicopter permitted such operations, extractions under fire in South Vietnam would become a common occurrence for almost all American helicopter crews.

The Americans also wrestled with how best to command and control (C^2) air assault operations. Scarcity of doctrinal guidance was one reason for ACTIV's presence in Vietnam, but the team had not yet translated its findings into a manual. The 1962 version of *Operations* devoted two sections to airmobile operations but did not address in depth how to command, control, or execute such missions.[55] As yet, there was no firm guidance for how best to control an air assault, and there was no set requirement for the helicopter units to provide a C^2 aircraft for the ground commander during the execution phase. Shortly after assuming command of the 7th Advisory Detachment, Vann circulated a helicopter SOP for his advisors and the division. The SOP addressed various air assault–related issues but did not discuss C^2 requirements. Given his frustration with the L-19 that he had to use during the battle, Vann recommended in his after action report that for all future regimental or larger-sized operations, the ground commander should receive a UH-1 for C^2 and medevac purposes. Two months after the battle, Vann issued a revised helicopter SOP that required a UH-1B for C^2 purposes; in the case of unavailability, two H-21s would suffice.[56] In response to Ap Bac, the U.S. Army was honing the air assault tactics that proved so devastating to the PAVN and PLAF forces later in the war.

Aside from the mounting of gun shields, an increased attempt by MACV to mend its fences with the press, and the changes to the ROE and helicopter procedures, the Americans and South Vietnamese changed little in response to Ap Bac. One area requiring improvement yet receiving little attention involved medical treatment for ARVN battle casualties. Vann highlighted the shortcomings in the ARVN medical procedures, noting that "there had been little planning or preparation" for this eventuality. Despite the number of South Vietnamese medical personnel, "[e]ven the barest of first aid . . . was not administered" to the ARVN wounded. Offering his observation that "[i]t is evident the medical personnel require much training," Vann identified a problem that was to plague the South Vietnamese soldiers for the duration of the war.[57]

Despite the advisors' public and private criticisms of the advisory system, the MAAG's role and relationship to the ARVN (and, later, MACV's when it absorbed the MAAG in 1964) remained unchanged. Although MACV studies offered possible solutions to the Americans' authority problems over the South Vietnamese, including a combined command structure, U.S. advisors remained just that, advisors. Despite Vann's warning "that *too much* pressure is placed on the US Officer to 'get along' and *not enough* on the Vietnamese Officer," American advisors continued to lack any authority beyond their own skills of persuasion.[58] Shortly after Vann's departure from South Vietnam, the USASEC issued a "Lessons Learned" that once again proscribed command authority for advisors. In clear terms, the memorandum cautioned its reader to "always remember that you are an advisor and have no command jurisdiction."[59] After assuming MACV's command in 1964, General William C. Westmoreland reaffirmed this belief by observing that advisors were "to appraise the situation and . . . give sound advice." The command emphasis on upbeat reports was also clear, since COMUSMACV directed his field advisors to "accentuate the positive, and . . . work out solutions to [their] problems in [a] dynamic way."[60] Even the advisors' training remained weak. As late as 1969, training consisted only of the MATA Course, and it still did not include extensive Vietnamese language or cultural instruction. Learning about and communicating with the Vietnamese was clearly secondary to being positive and making progress.[61]

COMUSMACV's command relationship with CINCPAC also came under Washington's scrutiny, but the examination bore no fruit. For some reason, it was the State Department that was more concerned with Harkins's reporting chain than the JCS, perhaps because the State Department's civilians felt less bound by military convention. Visiting Vietnam at about the same time as Ap Bac, Roger Hilsman engaged in a conversation with General Rowny to determine the latter's impressions of the situation there. Rowny described Admiral Felt's meddlesome attitude toward MACV, stating that Harkins made "no protest when Felt move[d] squads around on the map generally feeling that if it will make Felt happy, okay. . . . CINCPAC is still trying to run the war even in practical detail."[62] In Rowny's view, Admiral Felt was far too involved in Vietnam, effectively undercutting Harkins's efforts.

Michael Forrestal, an NSC staffer who had also spoken with Rowny during the same visit, passed along his concern with this issue to the president at least twice. Shortly after returning from Vietnam, he sent a note to the president addressing a scheduled briefing that concerned General Earle G. Wheeler's report to the president concerning the general's own recent trip to Vietnam. In listing points that Kennedy needed to "keep . . .in mind for discussion and action," Forrestal listed five issues concerning Wheeler's trip, the second of which dealt with "review[ing] the command relationship between CinCPac [sic] and Harkins. Ideally, Harkins should report to the JCS directly." The NSC staffer followed up two days later with an even more detailed list than that of 28 January. Of the now seven points listed, the first question cut directly to the issue of the chain of command: "Should General Harkins report directly to the JCS instead of CinCPac?" Forrestal's attempt to broach the topic through the president came to naught; three days later he characterized the meeting as a "complete waste of . . . time." After apologizing to Kennedy, he went on to recommend "a quiet campaign" to, among other things, "get General Harkins a direct line of communication to the JCS."[63]

Forrestal was not alone in his attempts to put Harkins directly under JCS control. A week after Forrestal's note to the president, W. Averell Harriman, the assistant secretary of state for Far Eastern affairs, wrote to General Maxwell D. Taylor, CJCS, "that there would be a substantial benefit if General Harkins . . . report directly to the Chiefs of Staff. . . . We have too much at stake to permit the sensitivity of command procedures to interfere with the most direct and effective channels."[64] Taylor responded five days later that he had initiated a JCS study that would focus on Harriman's chain of command concerns.

After the staff completed its study some two months later, Taylor and Harriman discussed its findings in the CJCS's office. The chairman pointed out that the directive governing Harkins's mission in Vietnam "gave Harkins adequate authority to deal with local incidents and to conduct the campaign as he saw fit without further specific guidance from higher headquarters." According to the chairman, there was no reason to remove Pacific Command (PACOM) and Admiral Felt from MACV's reporting chain. Despite Harriman's appearance of being "reasonably well satisfied," he "reserved the right to reopen the matter if . . . in his judgment," the relationship no longer supported MACV's needs.[65] With that, the question of MACV's reporting chain died a silent death, and for the duration of the American involvement in Vietnam, MACV remained a PACOM subordinate command.

The ARVN officers' weaknesses in training and aggressiveness also continued to plague American efforts to make the South Vietnamese officer corps successful in prosecuting the war. Before his departure from Vietnam, Colonel Porter offered his commentary on the problems facing the ARVN leadership. Acknowledging that "[t]remendous progress has been made . . . in the fields of leadership and command since 1 January 1962," the departing senior advisor for IV Corps identified profound deficiencies in the South Vietnamese application of American doctrine, both in tactics and aggressiveness. He cautioned his superiors that "[t]here seems to be an almost universal lack of understanding . . . on the principles of fire and movement, and in the principles of fire and maneuver. . . . This matter is constantly stressed and emphasized throughout the entire advisory organization, but little or no progress has been noted. . . . One of the greatest weaknesses in GVN commanders . . . is the failure to pursue the VC as they withdraw."[66]

Not surprisingly, Vann also offered critical commentary on the ARVN leadership as he rotated back to the U.S. Concerned about the South Vietnamese officers' unwillingness to respond to American advice, he enclosed a sample written critique for Vietnamese counterparts with his final report. He suggested to his superiors that "[i]t has been my experience that oral critiques to counterparts are largely ignored or forgotten," an intimation of the difficulties in bringing about ARVN change, and observed that "it appears both ridiculous and wasteful to have advisors here and not have them utilized."[67]

Problems with the political nature of the ARVN leadership did not lessen after Porter's and Vann's departures. In an effort to explore his options concerning the senior South Vietnamese leadership, General Westmoreland commissioned a MACV study in early 1965 to suggest recommendations to improve the professionalism of the officer corps. The study's findings were bleak and described the "power appetite and irresponsibility of several of the VN senior officers." Despite the South Vietnamese armed forces' organizational structure, the military juntas were the "focal point of power within the RVNAF," not the JGS. One later study went so far as to suggest establishing a "coup inhibitor": Each general officer would receive a trust account of between $5,000 and $20,000. For each month the officer did not involve himself in political plotting, MACV would deposit another $250 to $1,000 in the account. While the plan did not receive much serious attention, it illustrates the desperation MACV was approaching in transforming the ARVN officer corps into a professional organization. In the end, perhaps this transformation was beyond the Americans' reach. As one group of ARVN officers observed after the war, "there was one thing that this [advisory] effort seemed never to achieve: The inculcation of motivation and effective leadership. This was, after all, neither the fault of US advisers nor a shortcoming in the advisory effort, but a basic weakness of our political regime."[68]

Doctrinally, the ARVN remained focused on conventional warfare. Despite MACV's limited attempts at training antiguerrilla tactics and providing counterinsurgency advice, its expectations of a conventional force bringing about victory in South Vietnam not only remained but actually increased as the PLAF fielded larger units. During a proposed expansion of the ARVN in 1966, Westmoreland answered a recommendation from the American embassy to concentrate the new forces on counterinsurgency warfare with the retort: "It takes a conventionally organized military force to fight VC main forces as well as guerrillas."[69] Failing to recognize fully the political dimensions of the Second Indochina War, MACV maintained its focus on a conventional approach in the years immediately following Ap Bac.

The ARVN also sustained its tendency to employ excessive preparatory fires before tactical operations after Ap Bac. Perhaps driven by the desire to avoid casualties and Diem's ire, South Vietnamese commanders continued to pummel potential LZs with artillery and CAS before the troop helicopters arrived. Despite the need for protecting the soldiers upon landing, Colonel Porter characterized heavy preparatory fires as "highly undesirable," since "[s]uch strikes not only kill many innocent women and children, but give the VC ample time to hide, withdraw, or to be prepared to fire on the helicopters as they land."[70] In a sense, the ARVN had become even more conventionally minded in the application of firepower than its American advisors.

Most damaging of all was the fixed nature of American strategy in Vietnam. Over the nine months after Ap Bac, the JCS and the White House received five major and numerous minor reports concerning the situation in Vietnam, all of which generally supported MACV's programs. Michael Forrestal and Roger Hilsman, both present in Vietnam during early January 1963, submitted to the president their conclusions in a memorandum later that month. Despite seeing firsthand the reactions of American personnel in Vietnam, the two officials clearly set the tone of their assessment by their first sentence: "The war in South Vietnam is clearly going better than it was a year ago." Describing the previous year's activities, the opening paragraphs of the report noted several gains, particularly with regard to the number of people under GVN control and the increasing ARVN effectiveness in the field. While concluding that "we are probably winning," they also admitted in their report that "the negative side of the ledger is still awesome," and cited Ap Bac as an example of the guerrillas' potency. Of pressing concern to them was the lack of an integrated plan to join the political aspects of the Strategic Hamlet Program with the military aspects of the ARVN combat operations in the field, particularly since the "the strategic concept has never been spelled out in any one document." Despite this glaring shortcoming and the challenges faced by the GVN, the two officials felt "that the basis [sic] strategic concept developed last year is still valid," a belief echoed by every successive team from Washington, D.C, over the following eight months.[71]

In the flurry of activity that immediately followed Ap Bac, the JCS decided on 7 January to dispatch a team to conduct "an assessment of the situation in South Vietnam." Since Army Chief of Staff Earle G. Wheeler had twice postponed earlier visits to the region, the JCS selected him to head the team of 12 other military officers to "form a military judgment as to the prospects for a successful conclusion of the conflict in a reasonable period of time." After visiting 12 different locations in Vietnam, the team offered eight recommendations, none of which seriously challenged American policy and strategy in Vietnam. In its conclusions, the team expressed its confidence in the course chosen by the administration and MACV:

The situation in South Vietnam has been reoriented . . . from a circumstance of near desperation to a condition where victory is now a hopeful prospect. This leads to the conclusion that the current support program in Vietnam is adequate, and should be retained. . . . [W]e are slowly winning in the present thrust, and . . . *there is no compelling reason to change.* . . . [U]nless the Viet Cong chooses to escalate the conflict, *the principal ingredients for eventual success have been assembled in South Vietnam* [emphasis added].[72]

Like Forrestal and Hilsman, the team found no reason for changing the American course in Vietnam, despite the division and corps advisors' apparent concerns.

Harkins continued his optimistic appraisals after Ap Bac as well. His "Comprehensive Plan for South Vietnam" (CPSVN), forwarded to CINCPAC in late January 1963, was based upon the assumption that the insurgency would be under control within three years, or the end of 1965. COMUSMACV was so confident in the GVN's overall progress against the PLAF that he anticipated reducing the MAAG's strength by one half after fiscal year 1965 (FY 65) and the complete elimination of both MACV and Headquarters, Support Activity, Saigon (HSAS), the major support command headquarters in Vietnam.[73] This extremely positive outlook of South Vietnamese success and projected American withdrawals did not meet with resistance from his higher headquarters. The Wheeler team, having been briefed on the CPSVN during its visit, was supportive and recommended to the JCS that they accept MACV's concept as the "generally sound basis for planning the phase-out of United States support." After reviewing the plan over the next month, the JCS requested on 7 March that Secretary McNamara approve the CPSVN. To the JCS, the situation in South Vietnam was well enough in hand that serious fiscal planning could begin for the withdrawal of American forces in late 1965.[74]

The military was not alone it its optimistic appraisal of the situation in Vietnam. A National Intelligence Estimate dated 17 April echoed the team's conclusions. Boldly stating its assessment, the estimate "believe[d] that Communist progress ha[d] been blunted and that the situation [was] improving." With regard to the GVN's ability to defeat the insurgency, the estimate suggested "that the Viet Cong can be contained militarily and that further progress can be made in expanding the area of government control." Despite its caution that "it is [not] possible at this time to project the future course of the war with any confidence," the estimate's optimistic tenor was clear and certainly in line with the most recent reports from Vietnam.[75]

In early May, McNamara returned to Honolulu for one of his periodic conferences with the ambassador, CINCPAC, and COMUSMACV. At the meeting on 6 May, Harkins characteristically opened the session with a discussion of the "over-all progress that has been made . . . and conveyed the feeling of optimism that all elements of the Country Team now have." Although admitting that the struggle was protracted in nature, he averred that "we are winning the war in Vietnam." While the group discussed various technical aspects of the advisory effort, it did not question the larger policy issues of American involvement or Diem's legitimacy. The tone of the conference was positive enough to encourage the defense secretary to direct CINCPAC and COMUSMACV to develop a plan to withdraw some 1,000 Americans later in the year "if the situation allows." He also directed a reassessment of the CPSVN, the result of which was minor changes to equipment and fiscal requests.[76] Once again, the senior leadership was confident enough in its policies to even suggest American personnel withdrawals later in the year.

Senior American military and civilian officials were not the only ones to bring good news about Vietnam to Washington. In late May, Colonel F. P. Serong of the Australian army expressed to members of the Special Group Counterinsurgency his apparent confidence in ultimate GVN victory in South Vietnam. The Australian was convinced that "we are winning the war in Viet-Nam," given the favorable statistical indicators and the volume of intelligence provided by the rural South Vietnamese. Serong's opinion carried weight, not only because of his extensive counterinsurgency experience in Malaya, but he had also issued a critical analysis of the GVN and ARVN the year before.[77] For such a harsh critic to reverse his opinion of the previous year was not lost on the group.

By the end of June 1963, one of the Wheeler team's members, Major General Victor Krulak, was back in Vietnam. As the JCS's special assistant for counterinsurgency and special activities, Krulak, a marine, was intimately familiar with the situation in Vietnam. Speaking in an earlier Special Group Counterinsurgency meeting about his trip with the Wheeler team, Krulak stated that "real progress . . . [had] been made in the struggle against the Viet Cong." This opinion was not changed during his late June visit. His assessment of the counterinsurgency campaign was extremely positive, noting that it was "moving forward on the military and economic fronts. There is reason for optimism in both of these areas. . . . Military operations are more effective. . . . *[O]ur present course is sound and* that, absolutely pursued, *it will see the job done*" (emphasis added).[78]

Krulak reiterated his positive outlook after his early September visit to Southeast Asia in a contentious meeting with President Kennedy and representatives from the State and Defense Departments on 10 September. He opened the forum with a summary of his trip report and reiterated his position that "[t]he shooting war is still going ahead at an impressive pace." Although the end of the war was not in sight, Krulak believed that the Buddhist crisis and its ensuing political problems for Diem had not appreciably affected the war effort. In his eyes, American policies and strategy in Vietnam were on course. As he had twice earlier, the JCS's counterinsurgency expert returned from Southeast Asia firm in his conviction that MACV's infrastructure and support to the GVN was more than adequate to defeat the insurgency in South Vietnam.[79]

There were, however, those at the meeting who disagreed with Krulak's evaluation. Joseph Mendenhall, a State Department official whom Hilsman had sent along at the last minute with Krulak to Vietnam, did not share Krulak's rosy outlook. To the contrary, observed Mendenhall, all was not well in Vietnam. Building upon his telegram to Hilsman of the previous day, the NSC staffer painted a grim picture of the situation. He reported a "virtual breakdown of the civil government in Saigon," a clear contradiction of Krulak's impressions. Faced with two diametrically opposed viewpoints, the president asked his now famous question: "The two of you did visit the same country, didn't you?" Although no one wished to answer, the general finally broke the silence by suggesting that he had presented a rural viewpoint; Mendenhall, having spent most of his visit in Saigon, offered an urban perspective.[80]

The meeting's atmosphere remained charged for its duration. Rufus Phillips of the Agency for International Development offered to explain this divergence in views. To Phillips, the war in Vietnam was going well in the I, II, and III Corps regions, but was being lost in the IV Corps, or Mekong Delta, region. Such a bold statement did not escape Krulak's response; he accused Phillips of challenging Harkins's assessment, a measure Krulak was not willing to take. In the general's view, the war "was not being lost in a purely military sense," a comment that caused Phillips to remark astutely that "this was not a military war but a political war. It was a war for men's minds more than a battle against the Viet Cong." After State and Defense Department members traded further barbs, the president thanked those who had rendered reports and asked for a meeting the following day.[81] Even in the midst of diverging views, America's policymakers sought to maintain course with no direction changes.

Surprisingly, the meeting on 10 September did not dampen Taylor's desire to answer McNamara's request of 3 September that the chairman "submit a projection of the US military strength in the Republic of Vietnam, by month, for the period September–December 63, inclusive," for the purpose of planning the withdrawal of 1,000 American advisors.[82] The day after the meeting, on 11 September, Taylor reported that American advisor strength would peak at 16,732 in October as a result of U.S. Air Force support personnel whose deployment had already been approved and programmed, but the first increment of 276 Americans would depart in November, assuming "that the withdrawal . . . will be approved." To meet the planned number of 1,000, another 724 advisors would return the following month, leaving 15,732 American military personnel in South Vietnam. Comfortable with these projections, Taylor offered no reservations or commentary concerning the possible adverse effects of the scheduled withdrawal, even in the wake of the previous day's meeting.[83]

The only tangible outcome of the early September meetings with President Kennedy was the inevitable fact-finding mission. On 21 September, the president charged the secretary of defense with conducting "the best possible on-the-spot appraisal of the military and paramilitary effort to defeat the Viet

Cong." Interestingly, Kennedy had dispatched his senior military advisors, McNamara and Taylor, to Vietnam on his behalf, but he did not send with them any senior representation from the State Department, despite acknowledging in the same memorandum that "[i]t is obvious that the overall political situation and the military and paramilitary effort are closely interconnected in all sorts of ways." Perhaps wishing to avoid any unpleasant confrontations similar to what had resulted from the Krulak-Mendenhall mission, the president made the trip a Defense Department matter.[84]

The resulting report from the trip might well have been rendered by Forrestal and Hilsman, the Wheeler team, or Krulak. Despite the PLAF victory at Ap Bac, the reverses in the IV Corps area, the Buddhist crisis, and the ensuing campaign of repression by the Diem government, McNamara and Taylor's first of six conclusions was simply: "The military campaign has made great progress and continues to progress." The other five dealt with the increasing political tensions, the decreasing ARVN loyalty toward their president, and the possible harmful effects of Diem's repression on the war effort. These concerns aside, the team recommended that the U.S. adopt as its stated policy that "[t]he military program in Vietnam has made progress and *is sound in principle*" (emphasis added). Harking back to the May Honolulu conference, the secretary and the chairman also still believed that by the end of 1965 "[i]t should be possible to withdraw the bulk of U.S. personnel by that time" and correspondingly recommended that the Department of Defense "should announce in the very near future . . . plans to withdraw 1,000 U.S. military personnel by the end of 1963." Fully in accordance with the team's recommendations, the NSC subsequently endorsed the report in Record of Action Number 2472, dated 2 October 1963, thus accepting it as a statement of U.S. policy. That same day, with the president's approval, Press Secretary Pierre Salinger issued a White House statement that declared that not only were the American military measures in Vietnam adequate for the situation at hand, but also that "the major part of the U.S. military task can be completed by the end of 1965." Because the American military assistance efforts were so promising, the administration also predicted that "by the end of this year [1963], the U.S. program for training Vietnamese should have progressed to the point where 1,000 U.S. military personnel assigned to South Viet Nam can be withdrawn."[85] Imminent success, and not imminent failure, appeared to be the mainspring of the scheduled U.S. withdrawal.

There were, however, American officials in Washington who did offer some critical analysis of the situation in South Vietnam. As discussed earlier, Forrestal and Hilsman's report, the April National Intelligence Estimate, and Mendenhall's and Phillips' observations all contained some troubling aspects and did not completely square with the prevailing optimism. Even memoranda forwarded by the believer Krulak contained elements of dissent. Beginning in July 1962, the general began collating reports rendered by officers participating in orientation visits to Vietnam and distributing the resulting summaries. Titled "Exchange of Counterinsurgency Lessons Learned," the memorandum on the eve of Ap Bac might well have been a portent of the battle's outcome. Of the visiting officers' 17 listed comments, 15 were critical of the South Vietnamese armed forces' efforts. Some were critical of the ARVN's apathy and lack of aggressiveness; others attacked Diem's reluctance to arm aircraft with anything larger than 20-pound fragmentation bombs. One officer sarcastically summed up his feelings about the military and political situation in South Vietnam with four words: "It is a mess." Others were more direct: "The Vietnamese are quite good at attacking an open rice field with nothing in it and are equally proficient at quickly by-passing any heavily wooded area that might contain a few VC. . . . The attitude of the Army is pervaded by apathy. They just don't seem to possess the will to win."[86] With such august recipients as the U.S. Army chief of staff, the chief of naval operations, the U.S. Air Force chief of staff, and the American military's senior field commander, it is odd that none was concerned by these disturbing observations.

Even more troubling were the assessments of Major General William B. Rosson, the special assistant to the chief of staff for special warfare activities, the U.S. Army Staff's equivalent to General Krulak's position on the JCS. Rosson was no stranger to the situation in South Vietnam, having served on the French staff and in the MAAG during 1954 and 1955. During a trip to Vietnam in May 1962, he visited advisors and conducted office calls in much the same way as most other officials from Washington. What was not similar, however, was his impression of the possibility of an early defeat of the insurgency. In his farewell call with COMUSMACV, Rosson "stated as discreetly as possible that, contrary to the optimism he [Harkins] appeared to entertain," the PLAF was far from defeated. The special assistant went on to recommend that "this subject could profit from a series of future appraisals" and that MACV would do well to temper its prevailing optimism. In typical fashion, Harkins dismissed his concerns, stating that appraisals continued in their importance. Further, he was confident that Rosson would change his mind "with respect to unwarranted optimism . . . by the time of [his] next visit."[87]

Rosson was unmoved by Harkins's stance. After submitting his trip report, he fully expected "much ado" from the U.S. Army and Joint Staffs, given his reservations about the prevailing attitudes in South Vietnam. Much to his disappointment, the U.S. Army Staff processed his findings with no fanfare, commenting that it would serve as "guidance for the Army staff in studying and processing policy, plans, programs and related actions pertaining to Southeast Asia." Despite the findings by the staff's counterinsurgency expert, the attitude of optimism continued in the Pentagon and MACV.[88]

His reservations about American programs remained after a January 1963 visit. In much the same manner as his May 1962 visit, COMUSMACV assured Rosson that the newly drafted CPSVN "would produce timely solutions to the various problems" the staff officer had noted. Once again, Rosson submitted his trip report, expecting some reaction from the U.S. Army Staff, but he was "disappoint[ed]" that his findings were "absorbed routinely . . . on the basis that [they] reflected progress in most areas." At this point, Rosson concluded that the CPSVN "was unrealistic . . . [and] based on day-dreaming as against justifiable optimism."[89] Reservations about American policies in Vietnam were not restricted to the junior American advisors or holdouts in the State Department but within the U.S. Army Staff as well.

Within six months after Ap Bac, the JCS and the White House received numerous reports by senior civilian and military officials from both the State and Defense Departments that confirmed the administration's and MACV's policies as effective. All offered optimistic appraisals and visions of imminent victory in Vietnam. There were those, however, who did not believe the prevailing attitudes in Saigon and Washington. American advisors, some U.S. Army Staff officers, some State Department officials, and reporters generally shared the common belief that all was not well in South Vietnam. In the period following Ap Bac, given all the battle demonstrated about ARVN difficulties and PLAF proficiencies, one cannot help but wonder how American policy remained unchanged.

Despite the growing concerns voiced by those cited earlier, the Kennedy administration little altered its policies in Vietnam as a result of Ap Bac. Even after losing 33% of the committed American air assets in a fight in which the PLAF stood its ground, the consensus among senior American officials was that all was generally well in Vietnam, and the president's early October policy statement reinforced that position. However, this group of highly intelligent, experienced civilian and military leaders did not see the battle as a climactic event, nor did they see it as a portent of difficulties ahead. To the contrary, they proceeded with their plans for Southeast Asia as if nothing significant had happened.

Many factors are involved in this interesting phenomenon, but one of the most important variables was COMUSMACV, General Paul D. Harkins. As the senior military officer in Southeast Asia, his perceptions and beliefs certainly carried the most weight with visitors to Vietnam and decisionmakers in Washington. Harkins was a self-proclaimed optimist, a fact that was not lost on his staff or subordinates. Within a short time of taking command in Vietnam, COMUSMACV was already confident in the GVN's ultimate victory over the PLAF. At the July 1962 Honolulu conference, only five months after assuming command of MACV, Harkins assured Secretary of Defense McNamara that "there is no doubt that we are on the winning side." When the secretary asked Harkins how much longer the GVN required to bring the insurgency under control, the general "estimated about one year from the time . . . [the] RVNAF, CG, and SDC [are] fully operational and really pressing the VC in all areas," clearly a statement not based upon reality.[90]

Harkins did not restrict voicing his optimism to Defense Department officials. In a September 1962 conversation with Diem, the general "said that he was perhaps optimistic—but that he always was. He felt one year would be enough to achieve victory."[91] His willingness to voice a positive outlook extended even to the press. Shortly after taking command of MACV, a *Time* cover story quoted him as saying: "I am an optimist, and I am not going to allow my staff to be pessimistic."[92] Less than two weeks before Ap Bac, he expressed his confusion about the media's penchant for criticizing the GVN's and MACV's policies by stating that he didn't "know why people continue to be pessimistic. I know, since I have been here, things have gotten so much better."[93] For a young staff officer or advisor, such a statement must have had some effect on how he conducted his business.

Junior officers were not alone in feeling pressure from Harkins's stated expectations of their attitudes. The corps advisors, full colonels with better than 20 years' service, divined MACV's guidance and to a certain extent toed the line as well. Colonel Wilbur Wilson, the senior advisor for II Corps, and later III Corps, was known for his outspoken manner and "frankness to the point of brutality."[94] Yet for his willingness to speak his mind, he was not above encouraging a positive outlook in his subordinate advisors. In the III Corps mission folder, Wilson's 1963 guidance was clear: "Every Advisor, no matter what role he may be performing, MUST STRIVE FOR SUCCESS AND NEVER ADMIT DEFEAT OR PESSIMISM IN PURSUANCE OF OUR OBJECTIVES."[95] While encouraging mission focus in Wilson's subordinates, this message clearly put the onus on the advisors to maintain a positive outlook and could easily be mistaken for Westmoreland's guidance of the following year.

For all Harkins's declared optimism, one cannot help but wonder how much of it was genuine and how much of it was directed from above. Optimistic reports about the situation in Vietnam were not new phenomena; despite General Taylor's seemingly direct criticisms of the GVN in his report of November 1961, it, too, possessed the "tendency . . . to put Saigon's weaknesses in the best light." The secretary of defense also served to reinforce this attitude. Experiencing this pressure firsthand, Rosson later observed that "once key officials were on record as being optimistic or were believed to be so, optimism became the official or recognized position."[96] In most organizations, subordinates tend to reflect the attitudes and beliefs of their superiors, and the Defense Department was no exception to this generalization.

Harkins was also a protégé of Taylor, who was soon to assume his role as the CJCS, and to a large extent owed his appointment to the future chairman. Harkins had been Taylor's commandant of cadets during the latter's superintendency at the Military Academy following World War II. He had also been Taylor's chief of staff when Taylor commanded Eighth Army in Korea. COMUSMACV certainly was not known for his intellectual capabilities and had no counterinsurgency experience. In deference to Taylor and his desire for progress, perhaps Harkins was conducting himself in the manner he believed his superiors expected. As Harkins later told another general officer, "I couldn't ignore General Taylor's advice."[97]

Optimism only explains a portion of Harkins's assessment. Expressing his confusion about the lack of faith in the South Vietnamese in late 1962, he perhaps intimated his inability to understand the true situation in Vietnam. His military background certainly did not provide him a body of knowledge from which to draw. Ap Bac was something new to Vietnam, a fact PACOM recognized by characterizing it as "one of the bloodiest and costliest battles of [the] S[outh] Vietnam[ese] War. . . . This is one of [the] first instances where [the] VC have elected to stand and fight."[98] Yet COMUSMACV simply dismissed it as a case of getting "a bear by the tail and [not] let[ting] go of it." Compared to his experiences with much larger engagements and battles during World War II and Korea, this may have been true, but this analogy was not applicable to the insurgency in Vietnam. Focusing on the village of Ap Bac and not the South Vietnamese people as "the objective," he, like his predecessors, manifested his inability to grasp the subtleties of insurgency warfare.

If COMUSMACV failed to understand the war his command was advising how to prosecute, perhaps it was due in part to his isolation from the day-to-day experiences of his advisors. Although perhaps correct in his later recollection that "I don't think that there was a day that I didn't go out if I could get out," he certainly did not stay out for any length of time. When he arrived at the 7th Division's CP at Tan Hiep the morning after Ap Bac, Harkins was immaculately dressed in his khaki uniform, sporting highly shined shoes and his customary cigarette holder. After receiving Vann's short briefing on the previous day's battle, he departed the strip in his twin-engine Beechcraft. Despite his participation in numerous World War II campaigns, there was little in Harkins's previous experience that applied to Vietnam, and this shortcoming was exacerbated by his tendency to gather information by short visits and briefings. Commenting after the war on how COMUSMACV could possibly consider Ap Bac a victory, Lieutenant Colonel James Scanlon, 2nd ACR's advisor at the time of the battle, simply responded: "Well, you see, General Harkins wasn't down there where we were. I don't care how much you know about the war, once you get that far removed, I don't see how you can really have a feeling for it."[99]

Harkins was not the only senior American official to conduct whirlwind visits of Vietnam's countryside. Few, if any, of the inspecting Washington officers or civilians remained in Southeast Asia for more than a week at a time. Many went to Vietnam at the behest of Secretary McNamara with little or no warning aboard a "McNamara Special," a four-engine Boeing 707 equipped to refuel B-52 bombers in flight. Once on the ground, they traveled quickly from area to area, spending only brief periods of time with the advisors or officials who were intimately familiar with the situation. This pattern of observation precluded the visitors from forming a complete picture of the situation, thereby making them more susceptible to the images given them by MACV or the embassy. Many times, the visitors traveled the same routes and so returned to Washington with the same impressions as their predecessors. The itinerary followed by McNamara in late September 1963 was essentially the same as the one Krulak had used some two weeks earlier, and, not surprisingly, the secretary of defense's conclusions closely matched that of the Marine general. Not only did the short duration of the visits degrade their effectiveness, but their frequency had the unfortunate side effect of overtaxing the MAAG. Advisors who gave briefings to distinguished visitors or participated in their question and answer sessions were consequently advisors who were not in the field with the ARVN soldiers, which was their purpose for being in Vietnam in the first place.[100]

Besides optimism and insulation from the war, Harkins's sincere desire to believe South Vietnamese reports colored his view. During one of General

Krulak's many briefings by ARVN officers, a Vietnamese officer listed his division's strategic hamlet status as possessing 123 hamlets in its area of responsibility. When it was his turn to brief, the American advisor to the division, Lieutenant Colonel Fred Ladd, qualified his counterpart's remarks by stating that there were actually only eight hamlets worthy of the title. Instead of supporting one of his subordinates, or querying him in private, Harkins rebuked him in front of the entire group, claiming that Americans had no business doubting the South Vietnamese statistics. To COMUSMACV, it was an inherent responsibility of all Americans to believe and accept their counterparts' reports. This fervent belief to take the Vietnamese at face value lasted well after his retirement. In the general's recollection, "[o]nly in two or three instances, did I find a man, either a military commander, or a province chief, that I didn't think was telling me the truth."[101] Once again, the actions of the senior American military officer in Vietnam spoke volumes to his subordinates about what were acceptable reporting procedures.

While a prime example of the eternal optimist, Harkins was not alone in his desire to paint the situation in Vietnam in the best possible terms. As discussed earlier, senior State and Defense Department officials all echoed COMUSMACV's assessment. To express doubt, particularly in early 1963, directly challenged President Kennedy's proclamation during the State of the Union Address that "[t]he spearpoint of aggression has been blunted in South Vietnam."[102] This optimism, whether stated or inferred, had the effect of "dominating or minimizing contrary views, including intelligence and the judgments of experienced field personnel." Even General Rosson, by no means a Pollyanna, believed that despite his sober analyses, he contributed to the "syndrome. . . through [the] enthusiastic belief that expanded employment of Special Warfare assets offered lucrative counterinsurgency rewards."[103]

This "syndrome," as Rosson termed it, included restricting information that might be detrimental to Washington's prevailing mood of optimism. After Vann's departure from Vietnam, he became one of Rosson's subordinates on the U.S. Army Staff in May 1963. The former advisor had expressed his concerns to several senior U.S. Army officials, and within a month of his arrival received permission to brief the JCS about Ap Bac and his perceptions of the ongoing war in Vietnam. With the date fixed on 8 July, Vann began preparing in earnest, but his timing was unfortunate. General Krulak had just returned from his June visit, and, as discussed earlier, was quite optimistic in his appraisal of the progress against the insurgency. When Krulak received Vann's report on the morning of 8 July, he acted quickly. Within an hour of Krulak's receipt of the briefing text, General Taylor, CJCS, called to remove Vann from the agenda for the afternoon's meeting. Taylor was not known for allowing a subordinate officer to contradict him, particularly when he was only a lieutenant colonel and perceived as a disgruntled one at that. Providing a public forum for a challenge to the Joint Staff's counterinsurgency expert was also the last thing the chairman would permit. Instead of allowing the presentation of a different assessment from Southeast Asia to the assembled JCS, Taylor crushed it to preclude anyone from asking any untoward questions.[104]

After countless visits, reports, and heated meetings, the consensus of senior American officials in early October 1963 was that the policy in Vietnam was generally sound. Ap Bac brought about minor alterations in tactics and procedures among American soldiers, but the larger policies governing their presence and employment did not change. Optimism blinded senior American officials, and brief visits skewed their perceptions, resulting in a failure to address the problems that led to the ARVN defeat on 2 January 1963. Not unlike the Americans and South Vietnamese, the PLAF generally maintained its tactics and policies after the battle as well, changing little as a result of its experiences. The major difference then between the Americans, the South Vietnamese, and the insurgents was simple: The guerrillas had won a major victory with the tactics and policies they employed; the GVN, with its American advisors, had not.

NOTES

1. "Ap Bac Was a Victory—Harkins Rebuffs Reports," *Times of Vietnam* (30 January 1963) (folder 11, box 2, unit 1, Douglas Pike Collection, Vietnam Archive [hereafter DPC]). This quotation provides an interesting contrast to the USASEC's "Lesson Learned Number 9" from the previous year that cautioned its readers that the PLAF, and not terrain, was the primary objective. Memo, H. K. Eggleston, CHUSASEC, to Distribution "B," subject: Lessons Learned Number 9, 27 April 1962 (U.S. Army Military History Institute Digital Library [hereafter USAMHIDL]).

2. U.S. Military Assistance Command, Vietnam, *Ap Bac Battle, 2 January 1963; Translation of VC Document, 20 April 1963*, C0043021, 27 (hereafter *Ap Bac*) (Vietnam Archive); Wilfred Burchett, *Vietnam: Inside Story of the Guerrilla War* (New York: International Publishers, 1965), 88; Senior Advisor, 7th Infantry Division, After Action Report for the Battle of Ap Bac, 9 January 1963, 13 (U.S. Army Center of Military History Historians' Working Files [hereafter AAR and CMH]); Message, CINCUSARPAC to AIG 931 et al., 040240ZJAN63 (frame 187, reel 4, *The John F. Kennedy National Security Files, 1961–1963* [hereafter *JFK*]). As demonstrated here, the tendency to exaggerate the number of casualties inflicted was not solely an American phenomenon. Today, the Socialist Republic of Vietnam officially claims 450 enemy dead, eight helicopters, three APCs, and a warship. Ministry of Information, *"Chien Thang Ap Bac Song Mai Trong Su Nghiep Giu Nuoc"* (Ap Bac Victory Lives Forever in the National Defense), n.p., n.d.

3. *Ap Bac*, 31. Burchett suggests that these villagers were from Ap Bac. Burchett, *Vietnam*, 61.

4. *Ap Bac*, 31.

5. "Article by LPA on the Ap Bac January 2nd Victory Scored by Plain of Reeds People Self Defense Forces," *Liberation Press* (10 February 1963) (folder 8, box 23, Vann-Sheehan Vietnam War Collection, Library of Congress Manuscript Division [hereafter VSVWC]).

6. *Ap Bac*, 32.

7. Ibid., 29.

8. William Prochnau, *Once upon a Distant War* (New York: Times Books, 1995), 234–235; Strategic Studies Institute, *Press Coverage of the Vietnam War: The Third View* by William V. Kennedy, draft (Carlisle Barracks, PA: U.S. Army War College, 1979), B-3; Captain Richard Ziegler, G3 Journal, n.d., 26 (folder 2, box 83, VSVWC). More telling was the ballad that made the rounds in the detachment after the fight. While

factually inaccurate, it captured the Americans' feelings about the operation. See appendix C for its text.

9. Emphasis in the original. AAR, 18.

10. Memo, Senior Advisor, IV Corps, to CHUSASEC, subject: After Action Report—2 Jan 63 Operation DUC THANG 1, 16 January 1963 (folder 11, box 38, VSVWC).

11. "Vietcong Downs Five U.S. Copters, Hits Nine Others," *New York Times* (3 January 1963); Message, JCS to CINCPAC, 021322ZJAN63 (frame 168, reel 4, *JFK*); "Vietnamese Reds Win Major Clash," *New York Times* (4 January 1963).

12. "Vietnamese Reds Win Major Clash," *New York Times* (4 January 1963); "Costly Viet-Nam Battle Angers US Advisers," *The Washington Post* (4 January 1963).

13. Neil Sheehan, *A Bright Shining Lie* (New York: Random House, 1988), 276. In fairness to Harkins, there is some ambiguity surrounding this episode. When Harkins alluded to "a trap," he may have been referring to the southern movement of the 7th Division toward Ap Tay later that afternoon. It is unclear exactly when Harkins received his briefing or when he spoke with Halberstam and Arnett, leaving open the possibility that he was more aware of the situation than others have suggested.

14. Message, Harkins to Dodge, 4 January 1963 (frames 197–198, reel 4, *JFK*).

15. Ibid. (frames 199–200, reel 4, *JFK*).

16. "Vietnam Defeat Shocks US Aides," *New York Times* (7 January 1963).

17. "Vietnamese Ignored U.S. Battle Order," *Washington Post* (7 January 1963).

18. "Copters No Substitute for Men," *New York Times* (5 January 1963).

19. "What's Wrong in Vietnam," *New York Times* (15 January 1963).

20. "Bill Mauldin's Cartoon," *Evening Star* (14 January 1963) (folder 1, box 39, VSVWC).

21. "Kennedy's Foresight of the Events at Ap Bac," *New York Times* (8 January 1963).

22. Although more a commentary than a news report, particularly since Harkins never suggested taking command of the ARVN and Hughes was in Hong Kong, this article was not carried in the editorial section. "U.S. Combat Command Over Vietnamese Urged," *Washington Post* (13 January 1963).

23. "War Without Will," *Wall Street Journal* (10 January 1963). This summation bears a striking resemblance to the comments of an infantry officer writing a year earlier in *Infantry*: "[T]he advisor must relinquish all thoughts of remaking the Allied unit into a comparable US unit." Leonard D. Chafin, "Assignment: MAAG," *Infantry* 52 (January–February 1962): 53.

24. Message, COMUSMACV to JCS, 100830ZJAN63 (frame 203, reel 4, *JFK*); "'Courageous' Vietnamese Praised by Gen Harkins," *New York Herald Tribune* (10 January 1963) (folder 4, box 3, unit 2, DPC); "Harkins Praises Vietnam Troops," *New York Times* (11 January 1963).

25. Message, Harkins to Dodge, 4 January 1963.

26. "Harkins Praises Vietnam Troops," *New York Times* (11 January 1963).

27. Prochnau, *Once upon a Distant War*, 239. Interestingly, Felt wrote in a letter almost 10 years later that Ap Bac was "a bad show on all sides of our house," a characterization of the battle that he chastised the press for using at the time of his visit. Thomas J. Lewis, "Year of the Hare: Bureaucratic Distortion in the U.S. Military View of the Vietnam War in 1963" (M.A. diss., George Washington University, 1972), 19.

28. "Felt Sees Defeat of Vietnam Reds," *New York Times* (12 January 1963); "War on Communists Effective Despite Setbacks Felt Says," United States Information Service, Release FEF6 (16 January 1963) (folder 11, box 2, unit 1, DPC); "Vietnamese Winning

the War against the Reds, Adm. Felt Says," *Pacific Stars and Stripes* (16 January 1963) (folder 11, box 2, unit 1, DPC).

29. Strategic Studies Institute, *Press Coverage of the Vietnam War*, 60–62.

30. Major Jack Macslarrow, My Tho, letter to Major Lam Quang Tho, My Tho, 3 January 1963; AAR, 18–19.

31. AAR, 10.

32. Ibid., 15; *Ap Bac*, 7.

33. *Ap Bac*, 7, 10. When asked about the role of Diem's birthday, Lieutenant General Nguyen Dinh Uoc discounted its importance, giving credit instead to the PLAF spies in and around My Tho. Lieutenant General Nguyen Dinh Uoc, People's Army of Vietnam, interview by author, 16 April 1999, Lubbock, TX.

34. AAR, 19. More telling was Tho's pattern of driving to Saigon, protesting to Diem personally, and successfully getting the president to revoke any mission that Tho did not want to conduct. Lewis, "Year of the Hare," 23.

35. AAR, 18, 20. Interestingly, despite their performances during the battle, both ARVN officers did well after Ap Bac. Tho received a promotion and went to the United States to attend the Command and General Staff Officer's Course at Fort Leavenworth, Kansas. Ba also received a promotion and replaced Tho as the 2nd ACR's commander. Vann worked with Ba again later in the war but put the incident behind him, stating in 1972 that "I've forgiven him for Ap Bac." Lewis, "Year of the Hare," 49.

36. AAR, 18.

37. Major Jack Macslarrow, My Tho, letter to Major Lam Quang Tho, My Tho, 3 January 1963.

38. Memo, Senior Advisor, IV Corps, to CHUSASEC, subject: After Action Report—2 Jan 63 Operation DUC THANG 1, 16 January 1963. Despite the American advisors' and reporters' caustic assessments of the ARVN leadership during Ap Bac, one cannot ignore the glimmers of tactical proficiency demonstrated by certain South Vietnamese officers, particularly the task force commanders, Captain Tri and Lieutenant Thi. Their attempts to maneuver their companies into advantageous positions and Thi's repeated requests to attack into the woodline to envelop the southern PLAF positions clearly demonstrated their tactical awareness and competence. Sadly, there were few officers of their caliber at Ap Bac.

39. Ibid.

40. Le Hong Linh et al., *Ap Bac: Major Victories of the South Vietnamese Patriotic Forces in 1963 and 1964* (Hanoi: Foreign Languages Publishing House, 1965), 16; Sheehan, *A Bright Shining Lie*, 204.

41. Emphasis in the original. *Ap Bac*, 39; Burchett, *Vietnam*, 88; Le Hong Linh et al., *Ap Bac*, 16. In retrospect, this evaluation bordered on the overconfident, particularly as the employment of the rotary wing aircraft increased in lethality through 1963 and 1964. Dr. Nguyen Huu Nguyen, Social Sciences and Humanities Center of Ho Chi Minh City, interview by author, 16 July 2000, Ho Chi Minh City, Vietnam.

42. Minh Tranh, "The South Vietnamese Revolution Must Be Protracted, Arduous, and Complex but Will Be Victorious," trans. unknown, *Hoc Tap* (February 1963): 14 (folder 11, box 2, unit 1, DPC).

43. AAR, 19.

44. Department of the Army, *Mounted Combat in Vietnam* by Donn Starry, Vietnam Studies (Washington, D.C.: U.S. Government Printing Office, 1978), 38, 40.

45. Framing its discussion in terms of the mechanized companies' successes between June and October 1962, the "Lessons Learned" also emphasized the continued reliance on the shock of the APCs to defeat the guerrillas. Describing a technique that seemed to contradict 4/2 ACR's experience at Ap Bac, the memorandum stated that "*TWO OR*

THREE CARRIERS CAPABLE OF IMMEDIATELY RESPONDING TO A DEVELOPING SITUATION SHOULD NORMALLY BE COMMITTED, EVEN IF THE REST OF THE UNIT IS LEFT STUCK IN THE MUD" (emphasis in the original), which was exactly what the lead six APCs of Ba's company did and paid for in heavy casualties. Memo, H. K. Eggleston, CHUSASEC, to Special Distribution, subject: Lessons Learned Number 26, 18 January 1963 (USAMHIDL).

46. Karnow cites Peter Arnett (Associated Press) as the recipient of Felt's barb; Prochnau claims Malcolm Browne (Associated Press). Stanley Karnow, *Vietnam: A History* (New York: Viking Press, 1983), 262; Prochnau, *Once upon a Distant War*, 243–244.

47. Department of the Army, *Public Affairs: The Military and the Media, 1962–1968* by William Hammond, U.S. Army in Vietnam (Washington, D.C.: U.S. Army Center of Military History, 1988), 37–38. Kennedy directly attributes the "breach described by General Westmoreland between the press and the US policymakers in Viet Nam" to Ap Bac. Strategic Studies Institute, *Press Coverage of the Vietnam War*, 22.

48. AAR, 20. Sheehan attributes this passage to Vann's "duplicity" in his attempts to reduce Harkins's outrage with his conduct. Sheehan, *A Bright Shining Lie*, 279–280.

49. John Mecklin, *Mission in Torment: An Intimate Account of the U.S. Role in Vietnam* (Garden City, NY: Doubleday & Company, 1965), 114.

50. Department of State, *Foreign Relations of the United States, 1961–1963*, vol. III, *Vietnam, January–August 1963* (Washington, D.C.: U.S. Government Printing Office, 1991), 88, 117.

51. Memo, H. K. Eggleston, CHUSASEC, to Distribution "B," subject: Lessons Learned Number 4, 11 April 1962; Memo, H. K. Eggleston, CHUSASEC, to Special Distribution, subject: Lessons Learned Number 22, 8 September 1962 (USAMHIDL).

52. AAR, 20; Memo, Senior Advisor, IV Corps, to CHUSASEC, subject: After Action Report—2 Jan 63 Operation DUC THANG 1, 16 January 1963.

53. Message, Harkins to Dodge, 4 January 1963; "Ap Bac Was a Victory—Harkins Rebuffs Reports," *Times of Vietnam* (30 January 1963).

54. Lieutenant General Edward L. Rowny, Washington, D.C., letter to author, West Point, NY, 13 August 1999; U.S. Army Corps of Engineers, *Lieutenant General Edward L. Rowny: Former Ambassador* by Edward L. Rowny, Engineer Memoirs (Alexandria, VA: U.S. Army Corps of Engineers Office of History, 1995), 82. Formally established on 6 November 1962, ACTIV was a Department of the Army asset but was under COMUSMACV's operational control. General Orders Number 66, Headquarters, Department of the Army, subject: Army Concept Team in Vietnam, 21 November 1962 (box 1; organizational history; U.S. Army Concept Team in Vietnam; Headquarters, U.S. Army, Vietnam; Record Group 472; National Archives).

55. Lieutenant General Edward L. Rowny, Washington, D.C., letter to author, West Point, NY, 13 August 1999; Department of the Army, *Field Service Regulations-Operations*, Field Manual 100-5 (Washington, D.C.: U.S. Government Printing Office, 1962), 105–109.

56. Memo, Senior Advisor, 7th Infantry Division, to III Corps et al., subject: Helicopter SOP, 14 July 1962 (folder 13, box 82, VSVWC); AAR, 20; Memo, Senior Advisor, 7th Infantry Division, to 7th Infantry Division et al., subject: 7th Infantry Division Operational Supplement to Helicopter SOP, 12 March 1963 (folder 14, box 82, VSVWC).

57. AAR, 13.

58. Emphasis in the original. Memo, Senior Advisor, 7th Infantry Division and 41st Tactical Zone, to CHUSASEC, subject: Senior Advisor's Final Report, 1 April 1963 (folder 11, box 38, VSVWC).

59. Memo, H. K. Eggleston, CHUSASEC, to Special Distribution, subject: Lessons Learned Number 28, 18 April 1963 (USAMHIDL).

60. Department of the Army, *Advice and Support: The Final Years, 1965–1973* by Jeffrey Clarke, U.S. Army in Vietnam (Washington, D.C.: U.S. Army Center of Military History, 1988), 58–59.

61. Charles Shaugnessy, National Archives, interview by author, 24 July 1997, telephone interview. This inertia should not be a surprise. Of those general officers responding to Douglas Kinnard's post-war survey, only about one-third agreed that the advisory system required "the greatest changes." Douglas Kinnard, *The War Managers: American Generals Reflect on Vietnam*, rev. ed. (New York: DaCapo Press, 1991), 176.

62. Department of State, *Foreign Relations of the United States, 1961–1963*, vol. III, *Vietnam, January–August 1963*, 9–10, 7.

63. Ibid., 63–64, 95, 97. The Wheeler report did address the chain of command issue. In summarizing its conclusions, the team stated that MACV should absorb the MAAG and saw "some virtue in the formal designation of the Assistance Command as a formalized subordinate Unified Command," meaning that Harkins should answer to the JCS and not Felt. The team, however, also tempered its remarks by recommending that COMUSMACV's and CINCPAC's "views in both areas should prevail" since "General Harkins and Admiral Felt are opposed to one or the other of these moves." Ibid., 92.

64. Ibid., 114.

65. Ibid., 196.

66. Memo, Senior Advisor, IV Corps, to Commanding General, U.S. Military Assistance Command, Vietnam, subject: Final Report, 13 February 1963 (U.S. Army Center of Military History Historians' Working Files). American concerns about the ARVN's inability to fire and maneuver did not end with Porter's departure. Just under a year later, the USASEC issued "Lessons Learned Number 36—Fire and Maneuver," a three-page memorandum that observed that "[f]ire and maneuver is not being used by attacking friendly forces in operations against the VC except on infrequent occasions. . . . [A]ll too frequently either improper fire and maneuver techniques are employed or no use whatsoever is made of its application." Memo, D. M. Oden, CHUSASEC, to Special Distribution, subject: Lessons Learned Number 36, 4 February 1964 (box 1; Lessons Learned #1–#60; MACJ3-05; Military Assistance Command, Vietnam; Record Group 472; National Archives).

67. Memo, Senior Advisor, 7th Infantry Division and 41st Tactical Zone, to CHUSASEC, subject: Senior Advisor's Final Report, 1 April 1963.

68. Department of the Army, *Advice and Support*, 81–82; Department of the Army, *The U.S. Adviser* by Cao Van Vien et al., Indochina Monographs (Washington, D.C.: U.S. Army Center of Military History, 1980), 198.

69. Department of the Army, *The U.S. Adviser*, 149–150.

70. Memo, Senior Advisor, IV Corps, to Commanding General, U.S. Military Assistance Command, Vietnam, subject: Final Report, 13 February 1963.

71. *The Pentagon Papers: The Defense Department History of the United States Decisionmaking on Vietnam*, vol. II, the Senator Gravel edition (Boston: Beacon Press, 1971), 717–719. Hilsman clearly outlined what he believed to be the governing strategic concept in Research Memorandum RFE-59, dated 3 December 1962. In it, he described the "two principal features" of the GVN's "basic strategic concept" as "the strategic hamlet program and a closely integrated and coordinated military-political approach directed toward isolating the Viet Cong and regaining control of the countryside on a systematic, area-by-area basis." Despite these two facets' apparent emphasis on counterinsurgency tasks, ARVN combat operations still remained focused upon using conventional tactics against the PLAF. Ibid., vol. II, 700.

72. Office of the Chief of Staff of the Army, "Report of Visit by Joint Chiefs of Staff Team to South Vietnam," 109/63 (folder 11, box 2, unit 1, DPC); Department of State, *Foreign Relations of the United States, 1961–1963*, vol. III, *Vietnam, January–August 1963*, 73–94.

73. Department of State, *Foreign Relations of the United States, 1961–1963*, vol. III, *Vietnam, January–August 1963*, 38, 45.

74. The MACV's original CPSVN was dated 19 January and was the version to which the Wheeler team referred. CINCPAC forwarded this plan to the JCS on 25 January as an enclosure. This optimistic appraisal of the situation led, in part, to Kennedy's 1963 order to withdraw 1,000 Americans from South Vietnam. Ibid., 93, 135–136.

75. *Pentagon Papers*, vol. II, 725.

76. Department of State, *Foreign Relations of the United States, 1961–1963*, vol. III, *Vietnam, January–August 1963*, 265–270. In his CPSVN reassessment memorandum to the JCS, Felt took issue with Harkins' assumption that the insurgency could be controlled by FY 65, arguing instead that the end of calendar year 65 (CY 65) was more realistic, a difference of only six to nine months. Ibid., 292.

77. Ibid., 315; Terence Maitland et al., *Raising the Stakes*, the Vietnam Experience (Boston: Boston Publishing Company, 1982), 56.

78. Department of State, *Foreign Relations of the United States, 1961–1963*, vol. III, *Vietnam, January–August 1963*, 103, 456, 465.

79. Department of State, *Foreign Relations of the United States, 1961–1963*, vol. IV, *Vietnam, September–December 1963* (Washington, D.C.: U.S. Government Printing Office, 1991), 161.

80. Ibid., 144–145, 162–163.

81. Ibid., 165–166; Roger Hilsman, *To Move a Nation: The Politics of Foreign Policy in the Administration of John F. Kennedy*, rev. ed. (Garden City, NY: Doubleday & Company, 1967), 502–505.

82. Memo, Secretary of Defense to Chairman, Joint Chiefs of Staff, subject: Withdrawal of 1,000 US Military from Vietnam, 3 September 1963 (Vietnam, August 1963–October 1963; box 12; records of General Maxwell Taylor; Record Group 218; National Archives [hereafter RG 218]).

83. Memo, Chairman, Joint Chiefs of Staff to Secretary of Defense, subject: Projection of US Military Strength in the Republic of Vietnam (RVN), 11 September 1963 (Vietnam, August 1963–October 1963, RG 218).

84. Department of State, *Foreign Relations of the United States, 1961–1963*, vol. IV, *Vietnam, September–December 1963*, 278–279.

85. Ibid., 337–339, 353; Department of State, "U.S. Policy on Viet-Nam," *Department of State Bulletin* XLIX (21 October 1963): 624. Three days later, Taylor directed Felt to "[e]xecutive [*sic*] the plan to withdraw 1,000 military personnel by the end of 1963. . . . Previous guidance on the public affairs annex is altered to the extent that the action will now be treated in low key." This message followed the president's wishes, as described in National Security Action Memorandum 263: "The President approved the military recommendations . . . but directed that no formal announcement be made of the implementation of plans to withdraw 1,000 U.S. military personnel by the end of 1963." Message, CJCS to CINCPAC, 051824ZOCT63 (Vietnam, November 1963–February 1964, vol. 2, RG 218); *Pentagon Papers*, vol. II, 770.

86. The restrictions placed on aircraft ordnance was a direct result of the 1962 bombing of the presidential palace. Diem, concerned for his safety, did not allow RVNAF aircraft to carry the standard 500- or 1000-pound high explosive bombs. In the few instances when Diem relaxed this restriction, the aircraft did not carry enough fuel to

fly from the departure airfield to Saigon and return. Memo, Office of the Special Assistant for Counterinsurgency and Special Activities to Chief of Staff, U.S. Army, et al., subject: Exchange of Counterinsurgency Lessons Learned, 27 December 1962 (folder 9, box 83, VSVWC).

87. William B. Rosson, "Four Periods of American Involvement in Vietnam: Development and Implementation of Policy, Strategy and Programs, Described and Analyzed on the Basis of Service Experience at Progressively Senior Levels" (Ph.D. diss., Oxford University, 1979), 136.

88. Ibid.

89. Ibid., 175–176, 180; General William B. Rosson, U.S. Army (Retired), interview by Lieutenant Colonel Douglas R. Burgess, 31 July 1975, 295–296. (William B. Rosson Papers, U.S. Army Military History Institute [hereafter USAMHI]).

90. Department of State, *Foreign Relations of the United States, 1961–1963*, vol. II, *Vietnam, 1962* (Washington, D.C.: U.S. Government Printing Office, 1990), 546–548.

91. Ibid., 627.

92. "To Liberate from Oppression," *Time* LXXIX (11 May 1962): 28.

93. "Gen. Harkins Notes Big Strides in Vietnam War," *Pacific Stars and Stripes* (22 December 1962) (folder 10, box 2, unit 1, DPC).

94. Sheehan, *A Bright Shining Lie*, 199.

95. Capitalized in the original. Memo, Senior Advisor, III Corps, to Senior Advisor, 5th Infantry Division, et al., subject: MAAG, III Corps Mission Folder, 1 AUG 63 (folder 6, box 4, Wilbur Wilson Papers, USAMHI).

96. *Pentagon Papers*, vol. II, 95; Rosson, "Four Periods of American Involvement in Vietnam," 179.

97. Bruce Palmer, *The 25-Year War: America's Military Role in Vietnam*, rev. ed. (New York: Touchstone, 1985), 11; Andrew F. Krepinevich, *The Army and Vietnam* (Baltimore: Johns Hopkins University Press, 1986), 64–65; Lewis Sorley, *Honorable Warrior: General Harold K. Johnson and the Ethics of Command* (Lawrence, KS: University of Kansas Press, 1998), 153. Kaiser's recent commentary on Harkins's appointment as COMUSMACV completely discounts Taylor's role in the selection, citing instead the former's knowledge of the Pacific region as CINCUSARPAC as the deciding factor. Moving a CINCUSARPAC to Vietnam was not without precedent; O'Daniel, before becoming the CHMAAG in 1954, held that same position. While Harkins's familiarity with the situation in Southeast Asia most likely played a role in his selection, suggesting that Kennedy and McNamara chose him solely on his merits is unlikely and ignores Taylor's influence on those two leaders. In his recollection of this episode, Hilsman singles Taylor out as the one who suggested Harkins become COMUSMACV. Kaiser, *American Tragedy*, 126; Hilsman, *To Move a Nation*, 426–427.

98. Message, CINCUSARPAC to AIG 931 et al., 040240ZJAN63.

99. Scanlon's remarks squarely contest Harkins's recollection that "I think I visited every village and hamlet in Vietnam. I knew more about Vietnam than most anyone, except Diem, because I had the means to travel and I traveled." General Paul D. Harkins, U.S. Army (Retired), interview by Major Jacob B. Couch, 28 April 1974, 58 (Paul D. Harkins Papers, USAMHI); Sheehan, *A Bright Shining Lie*, 276; Lewis, "Year of the Hare," 43.

100. A prime example of this tendency to dispatch impromptu fact-finding missions was the Krulak-Mendenhall trip. McNamara, after tasking Krulak to visit Vietnam and "get the facts," directed that he leave 90 minutes after the conclusion of their meeting, and it took a personal call from Hilsman to hold the aircraft in order to get Mendenhall aboard. Hilsman, *To Move a Nation*, 328, 501; Mecklin, *Mission in Torment*, 214; Lewis, "Year of the Hare," 113.

101. Hilsman, *To Move a Nation*, 499; One wonders how often COMUSMACV actually experienced his recollection of the briefings he received: "I got the best briefings I could get. Sometimes, the advisor would take me aside, and say, 'This isn't quite as it is, General. He [the ARVN officer] is telling you this because he doesn't want you to go back and report to Diem that he has to be relieved.'" General Paul D. Harkins, U.S. Army (Retired), interview by Major Jacob B. Couch, 28 April 1974, 58–59.

102. Department of State, *Foreign Policy Current Documents, 1963* (Washington, D.C.: U.S. Government Printing Office, 1967), 1.

103. Rosson, "Four Periods of American Involvement in Vietnam," 160.

104. Sheehan, *A Bright Shining Lie*, 336–337, 340–341; Rosson later confirmed that Sheehan's portrayal of the incident was correct but that the incident was less dramatic than as described. General William B. Rosson, U.S. Army (Retired), interview by author, 15 April 1997, Lubbock, TX.

5

Conclusions

Ap Bac was, in my view, a relatively small battle which the
American press blew out of proportion, partly because of Colonel
Vann's statements.[1]

Ambassador Frederick Nolting

Compared to later battles of the Second Indochina War, Ap Bac was rather
small. Less than a regiment's worth of ARVN soldiers, a handful of helicopters
and APCs, and a battalion's worth of PLAF guerrillas participated. The fighting
lasted for only a day and was not part of a larger campaign. Many times, this
fight does not even receive mention in discussions about the war. Despite this,
the Battle of Ap Bac lends itself to certain conclusions about its significance and
effects on later events.

First, the outcome of the battle was a direct reflection of how the U.S. Army
organized, equipped, trained, and motivated the ARVN. Bringing with them the
U.S. Army's experiences of World War II and Korea, American advisors
expected the ARVN to destroy its enemy through the use of maneuver, superior
firepower, and effective leadership. As a result, the MAAG began to transform
the ARVN into a miniature copy of the U.S. Army, from uniforms to weapons
systems, and organizations to bad habits, and in this pursuit the Americans were
eminently successful. What the MAAG was unable to accomplish, however, was
to form the South Vietnamese officers into an apolitical, professional, trained
corps, competent in leadership by example and the management of
technologically advanced weapons systems. More than any other factor, the poor
performance of the ARVN officers allowed the numerically inferior PLAF
battalion at Ap Tan Thoi and Ap Bac to inflict heavy casualties on its opponent
and escape relatively unscathed.

What made Ap Bac particularly upsetting to the junior advisors was the
seemingly sudden reversal in fortunes for the GVN forces and the possibility
that American doctrine and technology could not compensate for the ARVN
leadership's shortcomings. Defeats for the ARVN were certainly not unheard of;
the MAAG had dealt with GVN setbacks before, a prime example being the

battering of the 32nd Regiment near Tran Sup in January 1960. Starting in December 1961 with the arrival of the first American helicopters, however, the South Vietnamese forces slowly began to record victories against an enemy that seemed unable to counter the increasingly technological threat. By the fall of 1962, Ap My Luong aside, the advisors believed the combination of APCs and helicopters near irresistible, particularly after 4/2 ACR caught a PLAF company in the open and decimated it.[2] Within four months of this stunning victory, the same South Vietnamese soldiers, leaders, and weapon systems were, for some reason, unable to dislodge a determined guerrilla enemy. Ap Bac's result was both near inexplicable and galling to the advisors, not to mention embarrassing, particularly since the U.S. Army had been training the South Vietnamese for almost eight years.

The frustration that the American advisors felt as a result of their inability to mold the South Vietnamese officers and soldiers in their image was readily apparent to the press. John P. Vann, despite suggestions to the contrary, did not launch a "mutiny" by using the reporters in Vietnam to destroy American efforts there.[3] For a man who consistently argued that the MAAG or MACV increase the advisors' authority over the South Vietnamese, purposefully undermining his higher command's efforts simply does not make sense. Both Vann's immediate supervisor, Colonel Porter, and his subordinates believed that there was something fundamentally wrong with the advisory effort. Nor was this a solely IV Corps phenomenon. Colonel Wilson, a contemporary of Porter's and the II Corps senior advisor, was also firm in his assessment that the GVN required a "complete transformation" and the CPSVN was "day-dreaming," sentiments closely resembling those held by Vann.[4]

Vann's relationship with American reporters was also perhaps less perfect than portrayed elsewhere. The advisory detachment's after action report contained harsh commentary about the press and recommended "some system of control and/or censorship." While Captain Ziegler, the operations officer, was responsible for putting together the report, it must have certainly been in line with Vann's guidance. It is impossible to determine whose words they are, or for whose benefit, but they clearly do not suggest a strictly harmonious relationship. As for the belief that Vann purposefully leaked reports to the press at Tan Hiep, Porter later wrote that "nothing could be further from the truth." Vann did vent to Halberstam the day after the battle, but he did not express any feelings that other advisors present at Ap Bac did not share. While he maintained a rapport with American reporters and was certainly "outspoken and pull[ed] no punches in briefing his superiors," this did not equate to mutinous activity designed to undermine the U.S. government's efforts.[5]

The strategy of seeking to end the South Vietnamese insurgency through attrition of the enemy's combat forces is traditionally associated with the introduction of tactical American units in 1965, and with good reason. With the onset of "the big unit war," American forces sought to destroy the PLAF in the field by bringing to bear massive firepower and unprecedented tactical mobility—a strategy of attrition that first came to the Second Indochina War when the TRIM assumed the mission of training the VNA in 1955. When

Americans began organizing, training, and equipping the VNA, and later the ARVN, the initial guiding principle was the application of maneuver and overwhelming firepower to defeat a conventional invasion by the DRV. Despite the junior American advisors' discontent with this focus and its later efforts in special warfare, the U.S. military was late in emphasizing true counterinsurgency operations that integrated both military and political action, preferring instead to train the South Vietnamese in conventional infantry and antiguerrilla tactics. The American advisory effort at the time revolved around improving the ARVN's effectiveness in killing insurgents but rarely sought to connect its military efforts to overall political objectives. Vann and his contemporaries may have believed in "discrimination in killing," but their focus was still mainly militarily, and not politically, oriented.

This general belief in the separation between military and political issues ran from the lowest American advisor in Vietnam to the commander in chief, President Kennedy. Throughout the summer of 1963, several senior U.S. government officials returned to Washington and issued summaries that confirmed the soundness of American policy in Vietnam, culminating in the October McNamara-Taylor report that reaffirmed the military program and expected an end to American involvement in Vietnam by the end of 1965. Despite the Buddhist crisis and the ensuing political instability resulting from the Diem regime's repressive measures, these civilians and officers honestly believed that the political situation had little bearing on what was happening in the field. By the time of Secretary McNamara's trip in September, there was an inkling among the senior leadership that domestic Vietnamese politics did play a role in America's policy in Vietnam, but they still had not realized that those factors were, in Hilsman's words, "fundamental and overriding."[6]

Pitted squarely against this rather narrow view of the primacy of the military situation was the PLAF's chosen strategy of *dau tranh*, the double-pronged approach of political and military struggle. While the Americans lulled themselves into thinking that a military solution would correct all Diem's domestic problems and planned for a rapid conclusion to the war, the insurgents saw the conflict in terms of both its political and military dimensions. The guerrillas were under no false illusions that the war would end quickly, nor did they believe that it would follow a set military path. Their previous experiences with the French had taught them patience and a firm belief in protracted warfare, a strategy that a short-sighted American government could not hope to match.

The Americans in 1963 saw military progress in the I, II, and III Corps regions and interpreted this progress as a sign that the ARVN was successful in those areas. What they never considered was that because the PLAF saw greater weakness in the IV Corps area, it increased its military operations there. Lack of activity did not equate to GVN success in the other regions, only an NLF shift to nonviolent political activity. With the doctrine of *dau tranh*, the guerrillas possessed the capability to change seamlessly from or to any level of political or military struggle in any region of Vietnam with little effort. Each region was its own war, and the COSVN, recognizing this fact, treated it as such. A PLAF battalion might conduct a military operation in one hamlet; the next might conduct proselytizing in another. One characteristic did apply to all operations: The PLAF viewed each act of violence in terms of its political gain, and it could just as easily turn military defeats into political victories. By refusing to acknowledge the importance of the political dimensions of its policy in Vietnam, the U.S. drastically reduced its chances of successfully combating *dau tranh* early on.

The Battle of Ap Bac's overall importance is mixed. For the American advisors, the press, and the PLAF, the battle was a significant event. It signaled the PLAF's growing strength and willingness to stand and fight against the numerically and technologically superior ARVN. It also brought to a head the growing conflict between the press in Vietnam and the U.S. government. To the PLAF, it reduced the aura of invincibility of the American helicopters and APCs, and recruiting for the insurgency in some areas increased in the months after the fight. While the DRV still did not openly commit to supporting the southern insurgency, the PLAF's success weighed heavily in the Politburo members' minds. Even today, Ap Bac holds a special place in the hearts of the Vietnamese. While speaking at the Vietnam Center's Third Triennial Symposium in April 1999, PAVN Lieutenant General Nguyen Dinh Uoc cited Ap Bac as proof that "[t]he new application of [American] heli and APC born tactics soon collapsed."[7] Present-day travelers visiting the Socialist Republic of Vietnam can visit a monument on the battlefield, commemorating the fight that took place on 2 January 1963.[8]

The individuals for whom the battle should have meant something, however, took little notice. General Harkins, COMUSMACV, believed it to be just another battle in the process of defeating the insurgency and boldly called it a victory, a declaration supported by Admiral Felt, CINCPAC and Harkins's superior. The ambassador, Frederick Nolting, paid it little heed and later wrote that "Ap Bac was, in my view, a relatively small battle which the American press blew out of proportion."[9] While they acknowledged in their trip report that Ap Bac occurred and was an ARVN setback, Hilsman and Forrestal attached relatively little significance to it, the first of many visitors to Vietnam who reached the same conclusion. Throughout the summer, the Kennedy administration worried far more about how the media portrayed events in Vietnam than why the ARVN suffered such casualties at Ap Bac. Despite all the press ink devoted to the battle, American policymakers did not believe Ap Bac, by itself, was worthy of concern.

Some six years later, U.S. Military Academy cadets read about Ap Bac in terms that the Kennedy administration would have felt appropriate. Given the number of casualties and the withdrawal of the PLAF, the battle was nothing more than "a draw, another of a series of indecisive clashes." For some reason, however, this "draw" grew in stature over the next 20 years, finding its way into the enticingly titled *Vietnam: The Decisive Battles.*[10] Whatever Ap Bac might be, it is not deserving of such an exalted status. To the contrary, it did not determine the outcome of the war, nor did it greatly affect strategy or policy for any of the belligerents. While it may have "assume[d] a significance out of all relation to its true importance" for some observers, the battle certainly did not "precipitate the events leading to the overthrow of the Diem government."[11] American optimism about the military situation in Vietnam ruled through the summer of 1963, and policymakers did not view Ap Bac with anything approaching concern. Arguably, Ap Bac influenced little above the tactical level of war and does not belong in the same category as Napoleon's Austerlitz or General Douglas MacArthur's Inchon landing.

To conclude that Ap Bac possesses little or no historical importance, however, would be of the same type of mistake as to call it decisive or the first step toward Diem's assassination later that year. The Battle of Ap Bac is an interesting historical paradox: Its greatest importance lies in its perceived unimportance by American policymakers. For all their intelligence and drive, senior American government officials missed the warning signs of a flawed policy in Southeast Asia. The Battle of Ap Bac "demonstrated on a grand and dramatic scale all the tiny failings of the system, all the false techniques, evasions and frauds which had marked the war in Vietnam," failings that senior American policymakers, civilian and military alike, missed.[12] Rather than listen to those advisors closest to the action and more attuned to the realities in Vietnam, like Vann, Porter, or countless others, senior American officials drew their own skewed conclusions about what was transpiring in Vietnam in keeping with the administration's greater policy of optimism. It is not surprising then that in the end, "[t]he Americans in Saigon [and Washington] were, in fact, to do everything but learn from it."[13]

NOTES

1. Frederick Nolting, *From Trust to Tragedy: The Political Memoirs of Frederick Nolting, Kennedy's Ambassador to Diem's Vietnam* (New York: Praeger, 1988), 97.

2. Lieutenant Colonel James B. Scanlon, U.S. Army (Retired), interview by Neil Sheehan, 2 March 1977, 1–2.

3. William V. Kennedy, *The Military and the Media: Why the Press Cannot Be Trusted to Cover a War* (Westport, CT: Praeger, 1993), 96.

4. William B. Rosson, "Four Periods of American Involvement in Vietnam: Development and Implementation of Policy, Strategy and Programs, Described and Analyzed on the Basis of Service Experience at Progressively Senior Levels" (Ph.D. diss., Oxford University, 1979), 164. Krepinevich does not single Vann out as a malcontent; to the contrary, he characterizes the American advisors' outrage with MACV's policies as a "revolt from below," suggesting widespread discontent among nearly all advisors. Andrew F. Krepinevich, *The Army and Vietnam* (Baltimore: Johns Hopkins University Press, 1986), 80.

5. Senior Advisor, 7th Infantry Division, After Action Report for the Battle of Ap Bac, 9 January 1963, 20 (U.S. Army Center of Military History Historians' Working Files); Thomas J. Lewis, "Year of the Hare: Bureaucratic Distortion in the U.S. Military View of the Vietnam War in 1963" (M.A. diss., George Washington University, 1972), 48. Kennedy's description of Vann's role is misleading at best. He questions why the reporters present at Tan Hiep did not interview then Captain Andrew O'Meara, "a visible and obvious source." The reasons are simple. Halberstam did not know O'Meara as he did Vann, nor did O'Meara participate in the fighting at Ap Bac on 2 January. As an advisor for a unit in 1st ACR, he and his company did not arrive at Tan Hiep until the morning of 3 January, the day after the battle proper. While he did walk the battlefield,

the captain was not on the ground during the fighting on 2 January. Kennedy, *The Military and the Media*, 96; Strategic Studies Institute, *Press Coverage of the Vietnam War: The Third View* by William V. Kennedy, draft (Carlisle Barracks, PA: U.S. Army War College, 1979), B-1, B-3.

6. Roger Hilsman, *To Move a Nation: The Politics of Foreign Policy in the Administration of John F. Kennedy*, rev. ed. (Garden City, NY: Doubleday & Company, 1967), 510.

7. Speech of Lieutenant General Nguyen Dinh Uoc, delivered at the Vietnam Center's Third Triennial Symposium, Lubbock, TX, 15 April 1999.

8. Located approximately four kilometers north of Highway 1, the monument at Ap Bac sits just to the east of 1/1/11 IN's landing zone and commemorates the three guerrillas who were "sacrificed" during 4/2 ACR's last coordinated attack of the woodline. Also located within the walled enclosure that surrounds the monument are a teahouse where visitors may sign a guest book, a small temple that shelters the three heroes' graves, a UH-1, an M113, and a 105mm howitzer.

9. Nolting, *From Trust to Tragedy*, 97.

10. U.S. Military Academy, *Readings in Current Military History* by Dave R. Palmer (West Point, NY: Department of Military Art and Engineering, 1969), 68; John Pimlott, *Vietnam: The Decisive Battles* (New York: Macmillan, 1990), 24–31.

11. Ellen J. Hammer, *A Death in November: America in Vietnam, 1963* (New York: E. P. Dutton, 1987), 26. Kennedy preceded Hammer in her estimate when he wrote eight years earlier that "[t]he reporting of the Ap Bac affair was a key element in bringing down Diem." Strategic Studies Institute, *Press Coverage of the Vietnam War*, 60.

12. David Halberstam, *The Making of a Quagmire* (New York, Random House, 1965), 147.

13. Ibid.

Appendix A

Brief Chronology of Events

December 1944	PAVN established
September 1950	MAAGI established
December 1950	VNA established
March 1951	Lao Dong established
May 1954	Viet Minh victory at Dien Bien Phu
July 1954	Geneva Accords
November 1954	Hinh incident
February 1955	TRIM established
April 1955	VNA offensive against Binh Xuyen
October 1955	RVN established/VNA becomes ARVN
April 1956	Final elements of FEC depart Vietnam; TERM established
July 1959	PLAF attack on American advisory detachment at Bien Hoa; PLAF agitation against GVN elections
January 1960	PLAF attack against 32nd ARVN Regiment at Tran Sup
December 1960	NLF established
February 1961	PLAF officially established
September 1961	PLAF Kontum offensive
November 1961	Taylor report
December 1961	Honolulu conference
February 1962	MACV established
May 1962	Rosson visit
July 1962	Honolulu conference
October 1962	PLAF ambush of ARVN ranger company at Ap My Luong

January 1963   Forrestal-Hilsman visit; Battle of Ap Bac; Wheeler visit;
                        Rosson visit

April 1963   NIE 53-63

May 1963   Honolulu conference

June 1963   Krulak visit

September 1963   Krulak-Mendenhall visit; McNamara-Taylor visit

October 1963   National Security Action Memorandum 263

Appendix B

Key American Leaders in Vietnam

Organization	Leader	Assumed Duties
U.S. legation	Edmund Gullion	17 February 1950
	Donald Heath	6 July 1950
U.S. embassy	Donald Heath	25 June 1952
	G. Frederick Reinhardt	10 May 1955
	Eldridge Durbrow	20 March 1957
	Frederick Nolting	21 April 1961
	Henry Cabot Lodge, Jr.	14 August 1963
USMAAG, Indochina	BG Francis Brink	10 October 1950
	MG Thomas Trapnell	1 August 1952
USMAAG, Vietnam	LTG John O'Daniel	12 February 1954
	LTG Samuel Williams	24 October 1955
	LTG Lionel McGarr	1 September 1960
	MG Charles Timmes	1 July 1962
USMACV	GEN Paul Harkins	8 February 1962
	GEN William Westmoreland	20 June 1964

Source: Department of the Army, *Command and Control: 1950–1969* by George Eckhardt, Vietnam Studies (Washington, D.C.: U.S. Government Printing Office, 1974), 89.

Appendix C

"The Ballad of Ap Bac"

We were called into Tan Hiep
    On January two
Wc would never have gone there
    If we had only knew

We were supporting the ARVS
    A group without guts
Attacking a village
    Of straw covered huts

A ten copter mission
    A hundred troop load
Three lifts were now over
    A fourth on the road

The VC's started shooting
    They fire a big blast
We off load the ARVNS
    They sit on their ass

One copter is crippled
    Another sits down
Attempting a rescue
    Now there are two on the ground

A Huey returns now
    To give them some aid
The VC's are so accurate
    They shot off a blade

Four pilots are wounded
    Two crewman [sic] are dead
When it's all over
    A good day for the Red

They lay in the paddy
    All covered with slim[e]
A hell of a sunbath
    Eight hours at a time

An armored battalion
    Just stayed in a trance
One captain died trying
    To make them advance

The paratroopers landed
    A magnificent sight
There was hand to hand combat
    But no VC's in sight

When the news was reported
    The ARVNs had won
The VC's are laughing
    Over their captured guns

All pilots take warning
    When treelines are near
Lets [sic] land those damn choppers
    One mile to the rear

Source: Richard Ziegler, G3 Journal, n.d., 26 (folder 2, box 83, Vann-Sheehan Vietnam War Collection, Library of Congress Manuscript Division).

Appendix D

Operational Terms

avenue of approach
"An air or ground route of an attacking force of a given size leading to its objective or to key terrain in its path."[1]

close air support (CAS)
"Air action against hostile targets that are in close proximity to friendly forces and that requires detailed integration of each air mission with the fire and movement of those forces."[2]

combat power
"Combat power is a combination of the physical means available to a commander and the moral strength of his command. It is significant only in relation to the combat power of opposing forces."[3]

concealment
"The protection from observation or surveillance."[4]

cover
"Natural or artificial protection from enemy observation and fire."[5]

doctrine
"[T]he accepted body of ideas concerning war. . . . Doctrine does not, however, alleviate the requirement for sound judgement."[6]

fields of fire
"The area that a weapon or a group of weapons may effectively cover with fire from a given position."[7]

firepower
"It is the amount of fire that may be delivered by a position, unit, or weapon system."[8]

key terrain
"Any locality or area the seizure, retention, or control of which affords a marked advantage to either combatant."[9]

leadership
"The most essential dynamic of combat power. . . . [it] provide[s] purpose, direction, and motivation in combat."[10]

maneuver
"[T]he movement of combat forces to gain positional advantage, usually in order to deliver-or threaten delivery of-direct and indirect fires."[11]

obstacle   "Any natural or man-made obstruction that canalizes, delays, restricts, or diverts movement of a force."[12]

protection   "[C]onserves the fighting potential of a force so that commanders can apply it at the decisive place and time."[13]

strategy   "The way in which a unit commander combines and orchestrates the resources at his disposal to attain a given goal."[14]

tactics   "The planning, training, and control of formations used by military · organizations to bring about successful engagements."[15]

NOTES

1. Department of the Army, *Operational Terms and Symbols*. Field Manual 101-5-1 (Washington, D.C.: U.S. Goverment Printing Office, 1985), 1-8.

2. Ibid., 1-15.

3. Department of the Army, *Field Service Regulations-Operations*, Field Manual 100-5 (Washington, D.C.: U.S. Government Printing Office, 1962), 48.

4. Department of the Army, *Operational Terms and Symbols*, 1-18.

5. Ibid., 1-21.

6. John Alger, *Definitions and Doctrine of the Military Art* (Wayne, NJ: Avery Publishing Group, 1985), 7.

7. Department of the Army, *Operational Terms and Symbols*, 1-31.

8. Department of the Army, *Operations*, Field Manual 100-5 (Washington, D.C.: U.S. Government Printing Office, 1993), 2-19.

9. Department of the Army, *Operational Terms and Symbols*, 1-40.

10. Department of the Army, *Operations*, 2-21.

11. Ibid., 2-19.

12. Department of the Army, *Operational Terms and Symbols*, 1-51.

13. Department of the Army, *Operations*, 2-21.

14. Alger, *Definitions and Doctrine of the Military Art*, 5.

15. Ibid.

Appendix E

ARVN Weapon Systems Characteristics

WEAPON	MODEL	CALIBER	WEIGHT (pounds)	LENGTH (inches)	CYCLIC RATE (rpm)	AMMO TYPE
PISTOL	M1911	.45"	2.5	8.7	N/A	BALL
CARBINE	M1	.30"	5.5	35.6	N/A	BALL TRCR
RIFLE	M1	.30"	9.5	43.6	N/A	BALL TRCR
SUB MACHINE GUN	M1A1	.45"	10.5	32	700	BALL
AUTO RIFLE	M1918	.30"	19.4	47.8	550 hi 350 lo	BALL AP TRCR
MACHINE GUN	M1919	.30"	45 (w/tripod)	41	400	BALL TRCR
MACHINE GUN	M2	.50"	128 (w/tripod)	65	450	BALL AP INCEN TRCR
ROCKET LNCHER	M20	3.5"	13	60.25	N/A	HE AT WP

Source: W. H. B. Smith, *Small Arms of the World,* rev. ed. (Harrisburg: Stackpole Books, 1969); Department of the Army, *3.5-inch Rocket Launchers, M20 and M20B1,* Technical Manual 9-2002 (Washington, D.C.: U.S. Government Printing Office, 1954).

Appendix F

U.S. Army/ARVN Vehicle/ Aircraft Characteristics

VEHICLE/ AIRCRAFT	MODEL	WEIGHT (pounds)	LENGTH	CREW	PAX CAPACITY	SPEED (mph)
ARMORED PERSONNEL CARRIER	M113	20,000 (empty) 24,594 (loaded)	15' 11"	2	10	40 (roads) 22 (off)
AIRPLANE "Bird Dog"	L-19	1,542 (empty) 2,142 (loaded)	25'	1	1	115 (max) 98 (cruise)
HELICOPTER "Shawnee"	H-21	8,900 (empty) 15,000 (loaded)	86' 4"	2	20	127 (max) 101 (cruise)
HELICOPTER "Iroquois"	UH-1A	4,020 (empty) 9,195 (loaded)	52' 10"	2 or 4	6	120 (max) 106 (cruise)
HELICOPTER "Iroquois"	UH-1B	4,502 (empty) 11,206 (loaded)	52' 11"	2 or 4	8	138 (max) 126 (cruise)

Source: Department of the Army, *Airmobility, 1961-1971* by John Tolson, Vietnam Studies (Washington, D.C.: U.S. Government Printing Office, 1973); Barry Gregory, *Vietnam Helicopter Handbook* (San Bernadino: Bargo Press, 1988).

Selected Bibliography

ARCHIVAL SOURCES

National Archives, College Park, Maryland

Record Group 111-PP, Records of the Office of the Chief Signal Officer
Record Group 111-SC, Records of the Office of the Chief Signal Officer
Record Group 218, Records of the U.S. Joint Chiefs of Staff
Record Group 334, Records of Interservice Agencies
Record Group 472, Records of the U.S. Forces in Southeast Asia

National Infantry Museum, Fort Benning, Georgia

U.S. Army Center of Military History, Washington, D.C.

Historians' Working Files

U.S. Army Military History Institute, Carlisle Barracks, Pennsylvania

William P. Brooks Papers
Digital Library
Paul D. Harkins Papers
William B. Rosson Papers
Samuel T. Williams Papers
Wilbur Wilson Papers

U.S. Library of Congress Manuscript Division, Washington, D.C.

Vann-Sheehan Vietnam War Collection

Vietnam Archive, Texas Tech University, Lubbock, Texas

Douglas Pike Collection

MICROFILM COLLECTIONS

The John F. Kennedy National Security Files, 1961–1963; Vietnam, National Security Files, 1961–1963. Frederick, MD: University Publications of America.

U.S. Armed Forces in Vietnam, 1954–1975. Frederick, MD: University Publications of America.

PUBLISHED U.S. GOVERNMENT DOCUMENTS

Congressional Research Service. *U.S. Policy toward Vietnam: A Summary Review of its History* by Ellen Collier et al. Washington, D.C.: Library of Congress, 1972 (folder 3, box 1, unit 2, Douglas Pike Collection).

Department of the Air Force. *The Advisory Years to 1965* by Robert Futrell. U.S Air Force in Southeast Asia. Washington, D.C.: Office of Air Force History, 1981.

Department of the Army. *Advice and Support: The Final Years, 1965–1973* by Jeffrey Clarke. U.S. Army in Vietnam. Washington, D.C.: U.S. Army Center of Military History, 1988.

———. *Airmobility, 1961–1971* by John Tolson. Vietnam Studies. Washington, D.C.: U.S. Government Printing Office, 1973.

———. *Command and Control: 1950-1969* by George Eckhardt. Vietnam Studies. Washington, D.C.: U.S. Government Printing Office, 1974.

———. *The Communist Insurgent Infrastructure in South Vietnam: A Study of Organization and Strategy* by Michael Conley. Pamphlet 550-106. Washington, D.C.: U.S. Government Printing Office, 1967.

———. *Counterguerrilla Operations.* Field Manual 31-16. Washington, D.C.: U.S. Government Printing Office, 1963.

———. *The Development and Training of the South Vietnamese Army* by James Collins. Vietnam Studies. Washington, D.C.: U.S. Government Printing Office, 1975.

———. *Field Service Regulations-Operations.* Field Manual 100-5. rev. ed. Washington, D.C.: U.S. Government Printing Office, 1958.

———. *Field Service Regulations-Operations.* Field Manual 100-5. Washington, D.C.: U.S. Government Printing Office, 1962.

———. *Human Factors Considerations of Undergrounds in Insurgencies* by Andrew Molnar. Pamphlet 550-104. Washington, D.C.: U.S. Government Printing Office, 1966.

———. *Images of a Lengthy War* by Joel D. Meyerson. U.S. Army in Vietnam. Washington, D.C. U.S. Army Center of Military History, 1986.

———. *Leadership* by Cao Van Vien. Indochina Monographs. Washington, D.C.: U.S. Army Center of Military History, 1978 (part 1, reel 4, *U.S. Armed Forces in Vietnam, 1954–1975*).

———. *Mounted Combat in Vietnam* by Donn Starry. Vietnam Studies. Washington, D.C.: U.S. Government Printing Office, 1978.

———. *Operational Terms and Symbols.* Field Manual 101-5-1. Washington, D.C.: U.S. Government Printing Office, 1985.

———. *Operations.* Field Manual 100-5. Washington, D.C.: U.S. Government Printing Office, 1993.

———. *Operations against Irregular Forces.* Field Manual 31-15. Washington, D.C.: U.S. Government Printing Office, 1961.

———. *Pacification* by Tran Dinh Tho. Indochina Monographs. Washington, D.C.: U.S. Army Center of Military History, 1980.

————. *Public Affairs: The Military and the Media, 1962–1968* by William Hammond. U.S. Army in Vietnam. Washington, D.C.: U.S. Army Center of Military History, 1988.

————. *Reflections on the Vietnam War* by Cao Van Vien and Dong Van Khuyen. Indochina Monographs. Washington, D.C.: U.S. Army Center of Military History, 1978 (part 1, reel 2, *U.S. Armed Forces in Vietnam, 1954–1975*).

————. *The RVNAF* by Dong Van Khuyen. Indochina Monographs. Washington, D.C.: U.S. Army Center of Military History, 1978 (part 1, reel 3, *U.S. Armed Forces in Vietnam, 1954–1975*).

————. *RVNAF and U.S. Operational Cooperation and Coordination* by Ngo Quang Troung. Indochina Monographs. Washington, D.C.: U.S. Army Center of Military History, 1980.

————. *Special Warfare U.S. Army*. Washington, D.C.: U.S. Government Printing Office, 1962 (folder 10, box 104, Vann-Sheehan Vietnam War Collection).

————. *Strategy and Tactics* by Hoang Ngoc Lung. Indochina Monographs. Washington, D.C.: U.S. Army Center of Military History, 1980.

————. *Tactical and Materiel Innovations* by John Hay. Vietnam Studies. Washington, D.C.: U.S. Government Printing Office, 1974.

————. *The U.S. Adviser* by Cao Van Vien et al. Indochina Monographs. Washington, D.C.: U.S. Army Center of Military History, 1980.

————. *U.S. Army Area Handbook for Vietnam* by George Harris et al. Pamphlet 550-40. rev. ed. Washington, D.C.: U.S. Government Printing Office, 1964.

————. *U.S. Army Special Forces, 1961–1971* by Francis Kelly. Vietnam Studies. Washington, D.C.: U.S. Government Printing Office, 1973.

Department of the Navy. *From Military Assistance to Combat, 1959–1965* by Edward Marolda and Oscar Fitzgerald. U.S. Navy and the Vietnam Conflict. Washington, D.C.: U.S. Government Printing Office, 1986.

Department of State. "U.S. Policy on Viet-Nam." *Department of State Bulletin* XLIX (21 October 1963): 624.

————. *Foreign Policy Current Documents, 1959*. Washington, D.C.: U.S. Government Printing Office, 1963.

————. *Foreign Policy Current Documents, 1961*. Washington, D.C.: U.S. Government Printing Office, 1965.

————. *Foreign Policy Current Documents, 1962*. Washington, D.C.: U.S. Government Printing Office, 1966.

————. *Foreign Policy Current Documents, 1963*. Washington, D.C.: U.S. Government Printing Office, 1967.

————. *Foreign Relations of the United States, 1950*. Vol. VI, *East Asia and the Pacific*. Washington, D.C.: U.S. Government Printing Office, 1976.

————. *Foreign Relations of the United States, 1951*. Vol. VI, *Asia and the Pacific*. Washington, D.C.: U.S. Government Printing Office, 1977.

————. *Foreign Relations of the United States, 1952–1954*. Vol. XIII, *Indochina*. Washington, D.C.: U.S. Government Printing Office, 1982.

————. *Foreign Relations of the United States, 1955–1957*. Vol. I, *Vietnam*. Washington, D.C.: U.S. Government Printing Office, 1985.

————. *Foreign Relations of the United States, 1958–1960*. Vol. I, *Vietnam*. Washington, D.C.: U.S. Government Printing Office, 1986.

————. *Foreign Relations of the United States, 1961–1963*. Vol. I, *Vietnam, 1961*. Washington, D.C.: U.S. Government Printing Office, 1988.

————. *Foreign Relations of the United States, 1961–1963*. Vol. II, *Vietnam, 1962*. Washington, D.C.: U.S. Government Printing Office, 1990.

————. *Foreign Relations of the United States, 1961–1963.* Vol. III, *Vietnam, January–August 1963.* Washington, D.C.: U.S. Government Printing Office, 1991.

————. *Foreign Relations of the United States, 1961–1963.* Vol. IV, *Vietnam, September–December 1963.* Washington, D.C.: U.S. Government Printing Office, 1991.

Office of the Secretary of Defense. "U.S. Military Advisory Effort." In *United States-Vietnamese Relations, 1945–1967.* Book 3, Part IVB, Section 2 (folder 6, box 1, unit 2, Douglas Pike Collection).

The Pentagon Papers: The Defense Department History of United States Decisionmaking on Vietnam. 4 vols. The Senator Gravel edition. Boston: Beacon Press, 1971.

Strategic Studies Institute. *Press Coverage of the Vietnam War: The Third View* by William V. Kennedy. Draft. Carlisle Barracks, PA: U.S. Army War College, 1979.

29th Engineer Battalion. *Cai Lay* (map). Fort Belvoir, VA: U.S. Army Corps of Engineers Army Map Service, 1955 (sheet 6242III, 1:50,000) (folder 3, box 89, Vann-Sheehan Vietnam War Collection).

U.S. Army Corps of Engineers. *Lieutenant General Edward L. Rowny: Former Ambassador* by Edward L. Rowny. Engineer Memoirs. Alexandria, VA: U.S. Army Corps of Engineers Office of History, 1995.

U.S. Military Academy. *Readings in Current Military History* by Dave R. Palmer. West Point, NY: Department of Military Art and Engineering, 1969.

U.S. Military Assistance Command, Vietnam. *Ap Bac Battle, 2 January 1963; Translation of VC Document, 20 April 1963.* C0043021 (Vietnam Archive).

REPUBLIC OF VIETNAM GOVERNMENT DOCUMENTS

National Geographic Directorate. *My Tho* (map). Saigon: National Geographic Directorate, 1973 (sheet 6229I, 1:50,000) (Vietnam Archive).

————. *Khiem Ich* (map). Saigon: National Geographic Directorate, 1973 (sheet 6229IV, 1:50,000) (Vietnam Archive).

NEWSPAPERS AND PERIODICALS

Evening Star
Infantry
Liberation Press
New York Herald Tribune
New York Times
Pacific Stars and Stripes
Time
Times of Vietnam
Wall Street Journal
Washington Post

INTERVIEWS, PERSONAL CORRESPONDENCE, AND SPEECHES

Bui Tin, Colonel, People's Army of Vietnam. Interview by author, 17 April 1997. Lubbock, TX.

Harkins, Paul D., General, U.S. Army (Retired). Interview by Major Jacob B. Couch, 28 April 1974 (Paul D. Harkins Papers).

Kiem Do, Captain, Vietnamese Navy. Interview by author, 16 April 1999. Lubbock, TX.

Nguyen Dinh Uoc, Lieutenant General, People's Army of Vietnam. Interview by author, 16 April 1999. Lubbock, TX.

————. Speech delivered at the Vietnam Center's Third Triennial Symposium, Lubbock, TX, 15 April 1999.

Nguyen Huu Nguyen, Ph.D., Social Sciences and Humanities Center of Ho Chi Minh City. Interview by author, 16 July 2000. Ho Chi Minh City, Vietnam.

O'Meara, Andrew, Colonel, U.S. Army (Retired), Riyadh, Saudi Arabia, letter to author, West Point, NY, 8 February 1999.

Pham Van Gong, Major, People's Liberation Armed Forces. Interview by author, 17 July 2000. Ap Bac, Vietnam.

Reckner, James R., Ph.D., Lubbock, TX, letters to author, West Point, NY, 26 and 28 August 1999.

Rosson, William B., General, U.S. Army (Retired). Interview by author, 15 April 1997. Lubbock, TX.

————. Interview by Lieutenant Colonel Douglas R. Burgess, 31 July 1975 (William B. Rosson Papers).

————, Salem, VA, letter to author, Lubbock, TX, 16 September 1997.

Rowny, Edward L., Lieutenant General, U.S. Army (Retired), Washington, D.C., letter to author, West Point, NY, 13 August 1999.

Scanlon, James B., Lieutenant Colonel, U.S. Army (Retired). Interview by Neil Sheehan, 2 March 1977 (folder 10, box 76, Vann-Sheehan Vietnam War Collection).

Shaugnessy, Charles, National Archives. Interview by author, 24 July 1997, telephone interview.

Walker, Don, Ph.D., Texas Tech University. Interview by author, 11 September 1997. Lubbock, TX.

BOOKS, JOURNAL ARTICLES, MEMOIRS, PAMPHLETS, PAPERS, AND UNPUBLISHED MANUSCRIPTS

Alger, John. *Definitions and Doctrine of the Military Art.* Wayne, NJ: Avery Publishing Group, 1985.

Andrews, William. *The Village War.* Columbia: University of Missouri Press, 1973.

Association of Graduates. *Register of Graduates and Former Cadets.* rev. ed. West Point, NY: Association of Graduates, 1993.

Brigham, Robert K. *Guerrilla Diplomacy: The NLF's Foreign Relations and the Viet Nam War.* Ithaca, NY: Cornell University Press, 1999.

Burchett, Wilfred G. *Vietnam: Inside Story of the Guerrilla War.* New York: International Publishers, 1965.

Cable, Larry. *Conflict of Myths: The Development of American Counterinsurgency Doctrine and the Vietnam War.* New York: New York University Press, 1986.

Chanoff, David, and Doan Van Toai. *Portrait of the Enemy.* London: I. B. Taurus & Company, 1987.

Clutterbuck, Richard. *The Long, Long War: Counterinsurgency in Malaya and Vietnam.* New York: Praeger, 1966.

Coleman, John. "Advisors to Fighters: America's First Combat Soldiers of the Vietnam War." Paper delivered at The Vietnam Center's Third Triennial Symposium, Lubbock, TX, 1999.

Currey, Cecil B. *Victory at Any Cost: The Genius of Viet Nam's General Vo Nguyen Giap.* Washington, D.C.: Brassey's, 1997.

Denton, Frank H. *Some Effects of Military Operations on Viet Cong Attitudes*. Santa Monica: Rand Corporation, 1966.

Doyle, Edward, et al. *The North*. The Vietnam Experience. Boston: Boston Publishing Company, 1986.

――――. *Passing the Torch*. The Vietnam Experience. Boston: Boston Publishing Company, 1981.

Fall, Bernard. *Vietnam Witness: 1953–66*. New York: Praeger, 1966.

FitzGerald, Frances. *Fire in the Lake: The Vietnamese and the Americans in Vietnam*. Boston: Little, Brown and Company, 1972.

Gregory, Barry. *Vietnam Helicopter Handbook*. San Bernadino: Bargo Press, 1988.

Halberstam, David. *The Making of a Quagmire*. New York: Random House, 1965.

Hammer, Ellen J. *A Death in November: America in Vietnam, 1963*. New York: E. P. Dutton, 1987.

Henderson, William. *Why the Vietcong Fight: A Study of Motivation and Control in a Modern Army in Combat*. Westport, CT: Greenwood Press, 1979.

Herring, George. *America's Longest War: The U.S. and Vietnam, 1950–1975*. rev. ed. New York: McGraw-Hill Inc., 1996.

Herrington, Stuart. *Silence Was a Weapon: The Vietnam War in the Villages*. Novato, CA: Presidio Press, 1982.

Hilsman, Roger. *To Move a Nation: The Politics of Foreign Policy in the Administration of John F. Kennedy*. rev. ed. Garden City, NY: Doubleday & Company, 1967.

Hodgkin, Thomas. *Vietnam: The Revolutionary Path*. New York: St. Martin's Press, 1981.

Kaiser, David. *American Tragedy: Kennedy, Johnson, and the Origins of the Vietnam War*. Cambridge, MA: The Belknap Press of Harvard University Press, 2000.

Karnow, Stanley. *Vietnam: A History*. New York: Viking Press, 1983.

Kennedy, William V. *The Military and the Media: Why the Press Cannot Be Trusted to Cover a War*. Westport, CT: Praeger, 1993.

Kinnard, Douglas. *The War Managers: American Generals Reflect on Vietnam*. rev. ed. New York: DaCapo Press, 1991.

Krepinevich, Andrew. *The Army and Vietnam*. Baltimore: Johns Hopkins University Press, 1986.

Lansdale, Edward G. *In the Midst of Wars: An American's Mission to Southeast Asia*. New York: Harper & Row, 1972.

Le Hong Linh et al. *Ap Bac: Major Victories of the South Vietnamese Patriotic Forces in 1963 and 1964*. Hanoi: Foreign Languages Publishing House, 1965.

Lewis, Thomas J. "Year of the Hare: Bureaucratic Distortion in the U.S. Military View of the Vietnam War in 1963." M.A. diss., George Washington University, 1972.

Lewy, Guenter. *America in Vietnam*. rev. ed. New York: Oxford University Press, 1980.

Lipsman, Samuel, ed. *War in the Shadows*. The Vietnam Experience. Boston: Boston Publishing Company, 1988.

Lockhart, Greg. *Nation in Arms*. Boston: Allen and Unwin, 1989.

Maitland, Terence, et al. *Raising the Stakes*. The Vietnam Experience. Boston: Boston Publishing Company, 1982.

Mao Tse-tung. *On Protracted War*. rev. ed. Beijing: Foreign Languages Press, 1966.

Marr, David. *Vietnamese Traditions on Trial, 1920–1945*. Berkeley, CA: University of California Press, 1984.

Marshall, George, ed. *Infantry in Battle*. rev. ed. Washington, D.C.: *The Infantry Journal*, 1939.

McCoy, James. *Secrets of the Viet Cong*. New York: Hippocrene Books, 1992.

Mecklin, John. *Mission in Torment: An Intimate Account of the U.S. Role in Vietnam*. Garden City, NY: Doubleday & Company, 1965.

Metzner, Edward. *More Than a Soldier's War: Pacification in Vietnam*. College Station: Texas A&M University Press, 1995.

Minh Tranh. "The South Vietnamese Revolution Must Be Protracted, Arduous, and Complex but Will Be Victorious." Trans. unknown. *Hoc Tap* (February 1963): 45–53 (folder 11, box 2, unit 1, Douglas Pike Collection).

Ministry of Information. "*Chien Thang Ap Bac Song Mai Trong Su Nghiep Giu Nuoc* [Ap Bac Victory Lives Forever in the National Defense]." n.p., n.d.

Nolting, Frederick. *From Trust to Tragedy: The Political Memoirs of Frederick Nolting, Kennedy's Ambassador to Diem's Vietnam*. New York: Praeger, 1988.

Palmer, Bruce. *The 25-Year War: America's Military Role in Vietnam*. rev. ed. New York: Touchstone, 1985.

Palmer, Dave R. *Summons of the Trumpet*. rev. ed. New York: Ballantine Books, 1984.

Pike, Douglas. *PAVN: People's Army of Vietnam*. Novato, CA: Presidio Press, 1986.

———. *Viet Cong*. Cambridge: MIT Press, 1966.

———. *War, Peace, and the Viet Cong*. Cambridge: MIT Press, 1969.

Pimlott, John. *Vietnam: The Decisive Battles*. New York: Macmillan, 1990.

Prochnau, William. *Once upon a Distant War*. New York: Times Books, 1995.

Rosson, William B. "Four Periods of American Involvement in Vietnam: Development and Implementation of Policy, Strategy and Programs, Described and Analyzed on the Basis of Service Experience at Progressively Senior Levels." Ph.D. diss., Oxford University, 1979.

Sheehan, Neil. *A Bright Shining Lie*. New York: Random House, 1988.

Smith, W. H. B. *Small Arms of the World*. rev. ed. Harrisburg: Stackpole Books, 1969.

Sorley, Lewis. *Honorable Warrior: General Harold K. Johnson and the Ethics of Command*. Lawrence, KS: University Press of Kansas, 1998.

Spector, Ronald. *Advice and Support: The Early Years of the U.S. Army in Vietnam, 1941–1960*. rev. ed. New York: The Free Press, 1985.

Stanton, Shelby. *Green Berets at War: U.S. Army Special Forces in Southeast Asia, 1956–1975*. Novato, CA: Presidio Press, 1985.

Stilwell, Joseph. *The Stilwell Papers*. Ed. Theodore White. New York: William Sloane Associates, 1948.

Tanham, George. *Communist Revolutionary Warfare: The Vietminh in Indochina*. rev. ed. New York: Praeger, 1961.

Taylor, Maxwell. *Swords and Plowshares: A Memoir*. New York: DaCapo Press, 1972.

Tran Van Don. *Our Endless War*. San Rafael, CA: Presidio Press, 1978.

Tran Van Tra. *Vietnam: History of the Bulwark B2 Theater*. Vol. 5, *Concluding the 30 Years' War*. Berkeley: University of California Indochina Archive, 1995.

Troung Chinh. *Primer for Revolt: The Communist Takeover in Viet-Nam*. rev. ed. New York: Praeger, 1966.

Trullinger, James W. *Village at War: An Account of Revolution in Vietnam*. New York: Longman, 1980.

Truong Nhu Tang et al., *A Vietcong Memoir*. New York: Harcourt, Brace, Jovanovich, 1985.

Tuchman, Barbara. *Stilwell and the American Experience in China, 1911–1945*. rev. ed. New York: Bantam Books, 1985.

Vo Nguyen Giap. *Big Victory, Great Task*. New York: Praeger, 1968.

———. *People's War, People's Army*. New York: Praeger, 1962.

Westmoreland, William. *A Soldier Reports*. rev. ed. New York: Dell Publishing Company, 1980.
Who Was Who in America. Vol. 3, *1951–1960*. Chicago: A.N. Marquis, 1960.

Index

at Ap Bac, 75, 76, 78–81, 83, 84, 86–
  88, 95, 96, 98, 99, 102–104, 111n.
  37, 113n. 81, 124–126
plans at Ap Bac, 71–73, 109n. 20
Buis, Dale, 12
Bui Tin, 11
Bundy, William, 14
Burma, xix, xxi, 29

C-47 "Skytrain," 102
C-123 "Provider," 99
Cai Lay District, 118
Cai Nai, 53
Cambodia, 11, 12
Cao Dai, 5, 8
Central Intelligence Agency, xii, xiii, 33
Chau Thanh District, 56
Chiang Kai-shek, xx
Chin, Captain, 76, 89, 97, 114n. 110
China, xix, xx, 17, 122
Chinh, Lieutenant, 86, 88
Cholon, 8
Chou, Lieutenant, 83, 86, 88, 91, 92, 94,
  112n. 67
Civil Guard, xii, xvi, 11, 40–42, 44, 50, 70,
  118, 141
  at Ap Bac, 68, 72–76, 78–81, 83, 84,
    86, 88, 89, 91, 94, 95, 102, 104,
    123
Collins, J. Lawton, 2, 6, 40, 46
Combat Development and Test Center, 102
command and control, 67, 131, 132
Commander in Chief, Pacific, xvi, 15, 16,
  27, 29, 33–35, 120, 123, 130, 132,
  136, 137, 149n. 63, 150
Comprehensive Plan for South Vietnam,
  136, 137, 140, 150n. 74, 154
counterinsurgency, xii, xxii, 23–26, 36, 38,
  39, 41, 135, 137, 142, 155
  and counterguerrilla training, 27, 33–35
counter mopping-up operations, 53, 68, 70,
  109n. 8, 119, 128
Cramer, Harry, 34
Cunningham, H. Francis, 14

Dakha, 14
Dalat, 1
Da Nang, 34
dau tranh, xiv, 48–51, 55, 63n. 120, 118,
  155, 156
Deal, William, 87, 101

Defense Language Institute, 28
Democratic Republic of Vietnam, 10, 11,
  32, 33, 129, 154, 156
Department of Defense, 2, 3, 5, 6, 9, 10,
  14, 15, 35, 137–139, 141, 142, 144
Department of State, 2, 3, 5, 6, 8–10, 12,
  14–16, 29, 33, 35, 75, 130, 133,
  137–139, 141, 144
Dien Bien Phu, xii, 5, 10
Dill, Harold, 115n. 133
Dillard, Robert, 43
Dinh Tuong Province, xx, 16, 65, 67, 72,
  73
Drummond, James, 104, 109n. 20, 126
Dulles, John, 5, 6, 9
Duong Van Minh, 45
Durbrow, Elbridge, 12, 33, 35, 36, 42, 62
Duyen, 108n. 7; *See also* Hai Hoang

Eisenhower, Dwight, 2, 6
Ely, Paul, 4–6

Feliciano, George, 97, 115n. 122
Felt, Harry, xx, 14, 27, 122, 133, 149n. 63,
  150n. 76
  reactions to Ap Bac, 118, 123, 130,
    146n. 27, 148n. 46, 156
field manuals
  31-15, *Operations against Irregular
    Forces*, 25, 26
  31-16, *Counterguerrilla Operations*,
    26, 27
  100-5, *Operations*, 23-25, 40, 131
First Indochina War, xii, xxi, 4, 10, 11, 23,
  49–51, 53, 54, 63, 70
Forrestal, Michael, 133, 135, 136, 139, 156
French army, 2–4, 7, 9, 10, 18, 39, 40, 46,
  47, 140

Geneva Accords, xii, 5, 7, 9–11, 14, 20n.
  57
Go Cong, 118
Good, Kenneth, 76, 79, 96, 97, 121
Government of Vietnam, 6, 45, 48, 51, 56,
  88, 98, 99, 101, 102, 104, 118, 119,
  121–123, 126, 127, 134
  counterinsurgency and, 33, 37–39, 54,
    55, 75, 135, 149n. 71, 155
  insurgents' activities and, 10–12, 14–
    17, 50, 128
  perceived chances for victory, xx, xxi,

About the Author

DAVID M. TOCZEK is an Assistant Professor of History at the United States Military Academy, West Point, New York.